£1·60

D1743222

Industrial Histories of Britain Series

BRITAIN'S RAILWAYS: AN INDUSTRIAL HISTORY

INDUSTRIAL HISTORIES OF BRITAIN SERIES

General Editor: Professor W. E. Minchinton
Professor of Economic History
University of Exeter

In preparation

HISTORY OF AGRICULTURE

M. A. Havinden
Lecturer in Economic History University of Exeter

NON-FERROUS METAL INDUSTRIES

Roger Burt
Lecturer in Economic History University
of Exeter

Associated volume

THE BRITISH HOSIERY TRADE

Professor F. A. Wells

Industrial Histories of Britain Series

BRITAIN'S RAILWAYS: AN INDUSTRIAL HISTORY

by HAROLD POLLINS

DAVID AND CHARLES : Newton Abbot

To Lena

ISBN 0 7153 5316 0

COPYRIGHT NOTICE

© Harold Pollins 1971

All rights reserved. No part of this
publication may be reproduced, stored
in a retrieval system, or transmitted,
in any form or by any means, electronic,
mechanical, photocopying, recording or
otherwise, without the prior permission
of David & Charles (Publishers) Limited

Set in 11/12pt Plantin
and printed in Great Britain
by Bristol Typesetting Company Limited
for David & Charles (Publishers) Limited
South Devon House Newton Abbot Devon

CONTENTS

LIST OF TABLES, GRAPHS
AND MAPS

7

MAPS

ACKNOWLEDGEMENTS

I should like to thank many people who have assisted, wittingly or not, in the preparation of this book. My first heavy debt is to the successive archivists and their staffs of the British Transport Historical Records for much help over many years. I am grateful to B. R. Mitchell and to D. L. Munby for allowing me to use their unpublished statistical material. I have benefited from discussions with G. R. Hawke and M. C. Reed and I should particularly like to thank colleagues and students at Ruskin College. During the writing of the book they have patiently allowed me to exploit their goodwill and to plunder their expertise as well as the experience of the ex-railwaymen among them. In particular I thank Roy Moore for his statistical advice; W. F. Cooke for his personal knowledge of the railways; V. W. Treadwell for advice on political history and for reading part of the typescript; and Peter Donaldson for the continual deflation of some of my more outlandish statements.

Ruskin College, Oxford.   HAROLD POLLINS
January 1971

PREFACE

There are many ways in which the history of an industry can be written. The emphasis could be on technical change, or on markets, or changing locations; it could be capital investment, or growth of production. More space or less could be given to management and organisation, or to labour relations. Any or all of these approaches is valid, but each of them—in the case of the railways —would take up a large volume. Given the limitations of space I have tackled the history of the railway industry as an exercise in decision-making. In essence this is an examination of the industry's activities in relation to the various pressures and constraints that it faced. For convenience one can distinguish between internal and external constraints:

Internal

a. The needs of shareholders for dividends (qualified by the different classes of shareholders who had different needs);
b. The existence of trade unions and their requirements;
c. The pressures of various kinds of management—technical, commercial, operating.

External

a. The requirements of government and Parliament
    eg (i) safety and other technical matters;
       (ii) fares and charges, controlled to prevent possible monopoly abuse; or to maintain price stability;
b. The state of the capital market;
c. The needs of consumers;
d. Competition
    (i) in the labour and other factor markets;
    (ii) with other forms of transport;
e. Natural factors, eg, geography.

Of course, it does not follow that the industry had to accept all these constraints without question. Governmental intervention was not taken for granted; it was possible to try to influence the state in the policies it was intending to implement. Trade unions might work through parliament to get their policies implemented if this was the only way possible. The important thing, though, is that however these pressures and constraints arose, they were there and had to be taken into account by the management.

This framework is not put forward as a model, to be used rigorously. One could, for example, suggest some form of weighting whereby at one period the influence of A was greater than that of B. But I have used it implicitly in this book and mention it here as a guide to the intention of this study.

It follows from this that while the external world has a massive impact on the affairs of the industry, we are not very much concerned with the contrary effect: the consequences of the railways on the economic and social life of the country. It is of major significance to the development of the British economy that the creation of a railway system may have stimulated the establishment of particular industries. It is not, on the other hand, central to a study of the history of the railways as an industry.

Finally a question of definitions, notably for the statistics. I have interpreted 'railway industry' to mean those activities undertaken by railway companies. These include ancillary businesses —docks, ships, buses—as well as the operation of the railways themselves. This is justifiable on the ground that they were usually extensions of the company's major activity, or were conscious diversifications. A difficulty is that in modern studies—using the Standard Industrial Classification as a basis of definition—these other activities are normally excluded. Another is that under nationalisation there have been numerous changes of organisation, and the control of these non-railway activities has largely been divorced from the railways.

A further question is that of geographical coverage. After some consideration I have included Ireland in the discussion up to the First World War; thereafter only Great Britain is covered. I justify this on two grounds. The first is that the building of the early Irish railways was closely associated with those of the rest of the British Isles, as Joseph Lee has shown in his excellent work. Secondly, some of the series of figures I have used apply to the United Kingdom as a whole and the Irish figures are not separated. The various tables make clear which area is being described.

Part One:

Building and Operating: to 1870

CHAPTER 1

INNOVATION AND PIONEERING

The North East of England has been an area of economic decline for so long in the twentieth century that it takes some effort of imagination to think of it as a centre of innovation. Yet, while due regard must be paid to events and to people in other parts of Britain and in other countries—to Cugnot and Séguin in France, to Trevithick of Cornwall among others—it is right to look to the coal mining areas of the North East as the place where the railways really got under way. If nowadays the opening of the Liverpool & Manchester Railway in 1830 is taken to be the distinctive event which set off the Railway Age, the work of numerous pioneers in the preceding generation or so was the essential prerequisite. It was in the collieries, mainly but not entirely in the North East, that the first railways—the combination of locomotives and specialised track—came into existence to meet the pressing economic needs of the mining industry.

The more general relationship between transport and economic development need not detain us. The growth of output requires some efficient means of supplying undertakings with their materials, and the greater quantity of production has to be sent to more distant markets. Improvements in transport can take the form of a better routeway, or a different kind of traction, either or both resulting in faster speeds and the movement of heavier loads. Before the railways, rivers were improved and canals were built. The roads, too, despite continual criticism, were, in general, better in the early nineteenth century than in the eighteenth as the use of waggons instead of packhorses and the higher speeds of passenger coaches demonstrate.

Yet valuable as these changes were they all suffered from a major limitation. Whatever other deficiencies these transport systems possessed—the varying efficiencies of road authorities (turnpike trusts and parishes), the absence of a standard width of canals which reduced the possibility of through working, and drought or ice which interrupted canal working—their major disadvantage was that imposed by the limitation of using non-mechanical power.

If one meaning of industrialisation is the replacement of human or animal power by mechanical forces, then the significance of the railways is unmistakable. Whereas earlier transport innovations had taken place within the framework of conventional technical knowledge, the railway built on the more recent introduction of steam power. The locomotive was a mobile engine evolved in the early nineteenth century by men whose immediate object was to help solve the transport problems of the coal-mining industry. When combined with a specialised track the essential technical features of the railway industry had been provided.

None of this means that the development of railways was in some sense inevitable. We can see that existing transport methods were not meeting the demands made upon them by an expanding economic system. We can note that to this kind of stimulus the response could be something new, the fruits of technological progress. For the peculiarity of the railways of Britain is that a simple relationship between economic need and railway growth will not do. The disadvantages of canals were not so great, nor the benefits of the railways so enormous, that there was a massive transfer of custom from the old to the new.

The rails came first—wooden ones from the seventeenth century and cast-iron from the later eighteenth—and their importance was that their capital costs were low, and they were particularly suitable for the carriage of heavy goods which would have broken up ordinary road surfaces. Numerous short lines were built, mainly in colliery areas for the transport of coal from the pits to some convenient point, a port or a canal.

Before about 1800 tramroads were often complementary to canals, serving as feeders. But in the early years of the nineteenth century tramroads were seen to possess advantages over them. In 1800, for example, Thomas Telford (1757-1834) the renowned bridge-builder and road engineer, wrote:

> Experience has now convinced us that in countries whose surfaces are rugged, or where it is difficult to obtain water for lockage, where the weight of the articles of produce is great in

comparison with their bulk, and where they are mostly to be
conveyed from a higher to a lower level, that in those cases, iron
rail-ways are in general preferable to a canal navigation.

On a rail-way well constructed, and laid with a declivity of
55ft in a mile, one horse will readily take down waggons con-
taining from 12 to 15 tons, and bring back the same waggons
with four tons in them . . .

This useful contrivance may be varied so as to suit the surface of many different countries at a comparatively modest
expense. It may be constructed in a manner much more ex-
peditious than navigable canals; it may be introduced into many
districts where canals are wholly inapplicable; and in case of
any change in the working of the mines or manufactures, the
rails may be taken up and put down again, in a new situation,
at a moderate expense.[1]

From 1801 public horse-tramroad companies were incorporated
by Act of Parliament. Their significance was not so much the
fact that they were statutory companies possessed of the right
to buy land and to raise money from the public, but rather that
they were open to public use on payment of a toll. Essentially
they were no more than larger versions of private lines but it
was important that they were in public use. One of the essential
features of a railway is this characteristic of being open to the
public; a railway without it would be a subsidiary part of another
industry, not one in its own right.

The growing use of tramroads encouraged a search for better
rails. In 1820 John Birkinshaw patented a method of rolling
wrought-iron rails, an improvement over the more fragile cast-
iron ones used hitherto. His invention came just at the
time when locomotives were being tried, and a stouter track
was required than that previously laid to carry only light
loads.

The history of the translation of the steam engine into the
locomotive is by no means clear or straightforward. As L. T. C.
Rolt says: 'Unless he walks with great circumspection the student
of early locomotive history is likely to become completely lost
in a labyrinth of contradictory facts, conflicting claims and
allegedly original drawings and illustrations which, more often
than not, turn out to be conjectural. Indeed, it is doubtful whether
any other major invention has been the subject of so much
heated argument.'[2]

Nevertheless, at the risk of gross over-simplification one can disentangle some of the major events. Richard Trevithick occupies pride of place, for he demonstrated that high pressure steam could be used and his brief experiment in 1804 on a colliery tram-road at Penydarren, near Merthyr Tydfil, showed that an engine could move on rails. (He, too, of course, was building on the work of others, like Cugnot and Murdock.) Twenty-five years later the multi-tubular boiler was added and the Rainhill Trials of 1829 illustrated the various advances made in the meantime, to produce a machine, which, in its essentials, remained the basis for all subsequent locomotive development.

The first regular use of locomotives had begun in 1812 at Middleton Colliery, near Leeds. It was no accident that the locomotive finds its origin in the coalfields. Within the mining industry there were men with experience of engines, and they were aware of the pressure to seek some new form of motive power. As collieries expanded, the movement of their product assumed a greater importance; often large numbers of horses were used. In 1813 the Whitehaven pits employed 600 people and 1,000 horses.[3] During the Napoleonic Wars the price of fodder rose to heights which impelled the search for some alternative means of communication.

From 1812 different types of locomotives were used on various colliery lines. If one selects for special mention the name of George Stephenson, whose locomotive *Blucher* worked at Killingworth near Newcastle from 1814, this must not be taken to mean that he invented the new machine—it was so obviously the product of many minds—but rather that he was more than an inventor. He combined within himself engineering genius and the vision to foresee the importance of the new invention, as well as the ability to obtain backing for his projects. The first public railway to use locomotives, the Stockton & Darlington, was built in his part of the country. The need to improve the means of transporting coal from the Durham coalfield to the coast had been discussed for two generations. There were surveys for a canal as far back as 1768, and again in the 1790s. But the first practical achievement was the building of a navigable cut on the Tees between 1808 and 1810. This was useful but insufficient, and discussion continued on the need for more direct communication. Two rival groups were in the field, one proposing a

canal, the other a tramroad. The second group, whose chief
spokesman was Edward Pease, won the day and after an unsuccessful attempt obtained parliamentary powers in 1821,
followed by an amending Act in 1823 authorising the use of
locomotives. More than anyone else it was Stephenson who won
over the company to use locomotives. (They also employed horses
and stationary engines.)

The Stockton & Darlington Railway in one sense was only
a colliery line writ large, a bigger version of the several private
tramroads on which coal was transported, but being a public
undertaking involved problems which were new. The required
capital had to be obtained from the public, and the promoters
had to go outside the district for some of the money. In what
was a personal capital market Pease, a woollen merchant and
banker, looked to his Quaker connections, drawing on Friends in
Norwich and London. There was a second difficulty. The Stockton & Darlington suffered, as other railway companies did afterwards, from landowners who objected to the line passing through
their land, and who by their opposition in Parliament caused delay
and expense.

These were not the only problems affecting this and other
early lines. The new engineers such as Stephenson, conflicted with those who had built roads and canals, and when
canal companies and turnpike trusts opposed railways in Parliament they naturally called on their men to give technical
evidence against the railways. Moreover within the engineering
industry there was a singular lack of enthusiasm for building
locomotives; in 1823 the Stockton & Darlington was unable to
place orders, and a company had to be formed—Robert
Stephenson & Co—to do the work.

Railways in the 1820s, in other words, were highly risky
undertakings and a great deal of effort was put into publicising
the new methods. None was more indefatigable in this than
William James, a wealthy man with many interests in collieries
in the Midlands. An enthusiastic advocate of railways, surveying
and promoting them at his own expense, he might well have
been just one of many impractical visionaries, losing a fortune
in pursuit of a dream, for most of his ideas for railways were
not taken up. The only line he had much to do with, the
Stratford & Moreton, did not use locomotives, but his place in

the story is assured because he made the first survey for the Liverpool & Manchester Railway.

Whereas the Stockton & Darlington was promoted in an area lacking good transport, the Liverpool & Manchester was put forward consciously to break the monopoly of the Bridgewater Canal. Inevitably the proposal aroused the keen opposition of this canal and also of the Leeds & Liverpool Canal. By 1824, after Stephenson had made another survey, the railway company was ready to apply to Parliament and in the 1825 session the first major clash took place between railways and their opponents. The Commons Committee sat for thirty-seven days and threw out the Bill. The failure was largely due to the fact that Stephenson's survey was badly done, its deficiencies being gleefully exposed by the opponents of the measure.

The loss of the Bill was a setback to the company; it also brought to an end a premature rash of railway schemes which had appeared during the trade boom of 1824-5. What Tomlinson, the historian of the North Eastern Railway, called 'the first railway mania' should not be exaggerated. It is true that many projects were in the air, but they were a very minor part of the first company promotion boom after the Napoleonic Wars. Lines were put forward to connect most major towns and capital requirements were very large. The Grand Western, a scheme for a line between London and Falmouth, proposed a capital of £3 million. However the fact that some of the routes built later on in railway history were put forward during the mid-1820s is a matter of no moment. For someone to suggest, in that madcap company boom, that it would be a good idea to build a railway between two important towns required no prescience. The wonder is that there was a boom at all, since there was little enough evidence of actual railway working.

But for a few months there was the possibility of many railways being built, so much so that in 1824, at the outset of the promotion boom, a new company, George Stephenson & Son, was created to undertake railway surveys and construction. Although this attempt to monopolise the civil engineering side did not in the long run succeed, one notes again the importance of Stephenson and of the engineers of the North East, some to become famous in their own right, like Joseph Dixon, Thomas Gooch, Thomas Storey and Joseph Locke. Dixon and Storey had worked on the Stockton & Darlington; Gooch and Locke were Stephenson's apprentices. Later they went their own ways but in the conditions of the 1820s the creation of a railway system in which both the civil and mechanical engineering sides were controlled by the Stephensons was a very real possibility.

Most of the schemes disappeared and those that were authorised were short local lines, including the Liverpool & Manchester which obtained its Act in 1826. A few more were incorporated up to 1830, including the Newcastle—Carlisle in 1829, the largest so far. But not even the opening of the Stockton & Darlington in September 1825 (after the boom) could provide the basis for another period of excitement, given the less favourable financial conditions of the late 1820s.

More important than finance, still not enough was known about the locomotive. In the early 1820s the Stratford & Moreton Tramway turned down locomotives for quite legitimate reasons after a careful examination of locomotives in use in the north of England.[4] Even within the Liverpool & Manchester company there were those who were unhappy at the thought of using locomotives. One reason why the directors of the company promoted the Rainhill Trials in 1829 on a section of the uncompleted L & M route was to try to settle the question.

After a generation of publicity and experiments, of polemics and argument, the whole railway world was transformed in 1829-30. In October 1829 the Liverpool & Manchester Railway held the Rainhill Trials; eleven months later the line was opened. The former demonstrated the technical progress made by the locomotive; the latter that a railway could be operated successfully. Within a short period its commercial success was widely known. For most of the 1830s the only useful information available on railway working came from this company. On this basis the railway age at last began. Many main-line companies were promoted and built and by the early 1840s the outlines of the national railway system were in being.

The Liverpool & Manchester, moreover, brought into being a body of railway shareholders from Lancashire, especially Liverpool, who were to play an important part in railway history. They had already been associated with other railways of the 1820s, the Leicester & Swannington and the Canterbury & Whitstable, no doubt because of their close links with George Stephenson who was the engineer to these lines. They are also known to have invested in some of the companies of the 1830s (the dates are those of their Acts of incorporation): the Grand Junction (1833) and the London & Birmingham (1833) which between them made up the trunk route from London to Lancashire were overwhelmingly financed from Lancashire; the Midland Counties (1836); the North Midland (1836); the Manchester & Leeds (1836); the London & Southampton (1834); the Great Western (1835); the Eastern Counties (1836); the Edinburgh & Glasgow (1838).[5]

In the 1830s both railway promoters and investors were working in the dark, but the dividends of the Liverpool & Manchester were never less than 8 per cent and this was an attractive inducement. So much so that as the economy moved into the upswing of the trade cycle numerous companies were promoted, reaching a peak in 1835-6, to the accompaniment of scandals, disgust and demands for some sort of public control.

But it started slowly in the early 1830s. The successful completion of the Liverpool & Manchester Railway set off a rash of schemes for railways, some of them resurrections of the 1824-5 boom. 'The lines projected in this first phase may be considered the direct result of the technical and other advances brought before the public eye by the Liverpool & Manchester.'[6] This needs stressing. Railway investment throughout the nineteenth century was closely associated with the trade cycle. Each time the economy moved upwards, railway schemes were promoted, some companies obtained Acts of Parliament, and construction began as the economy became less buoyant. There were of course particular aspects to each cycle which explain the reasons for these sudden flurries of promotion. One general explanation is that since railway investment was largely undertaken by the issue of capital stock, the state of the capital market was a major consideration for company promoters.

The large companies proposed in the early 1830s however, do not fit into this pattern. With hindsight we can say that they were put forward at an inappropriate time. Neither political nor financial conditions were particularly suitable, and it normally took up to three years between the inception of a scheme and a company incorporation by Act of Parliament. The delay can be accounted for quite readily. One year for consideration of the route, surveys and seeking shareholders willing to pay a deposit on the shares they took, one year for application to Parliament, and a third year for the second application after the failure of the first attempt. It is important that no scheme could be promoted and authorised by Act within the same year. The private Bill procedures of Parliament normally required notices of proposed application to be submitted in the latter part of the year prior to the one in which the company's Bill was to be considered by Parliament. Any relationships which one wishes to discover between the financial conditions encouraging company promotion and the Acts which authorised investment must take this procedural lag into account.

These points need to be made, since without them the wrong conclusions can be drawn from the figures. Thus Matthews argues that 'an Act would not normally be sought or obtained until the plans for the line in question had passed beyond mere aspiration and had reached a fairly advanced stage. Figures relating to these Acts therefore give a fair index of investment *planned* in each year.' If one equates the decision to apply to Parliament with planned investment, then at least one year between the two must be allowed. If a company failed at its first attempt the gap was even greater.

Some examples of the companies' difficulties in the early 1830s will illustrate these points. The Great Western Railway originated in 1832 at Bristol, and obtained the support of the five main corporate bodies in the city. But at the end of 1833 the Bristol committee noted that 'our expectations of support from Bristol have . . . been in great measure disappointed' and deputations of directors visited towns in the Westcountry, South Wales and Ireland to seek financial support.[7] Just as important in holding up action was the opposition of landowners and the owners and operators of existing transport facilities. The most celebrated example was that of the London & Birmingham Railway. Introduced in 1832 its Bill passed the Commons after a long contest with landowners, canal companies and coach proprietors only to fail in the Lords. Since this line was to be part of the main route to Lancashire its success would have severely affected the livelihood of canal companies and coach proprietors. Naturally enough, they opposed it. But the railway company negotiated with the opposition and the Act was obtained in the following year. The Great Western, in its turn, faced opposition from similar bodies, together with Eton College and the London & South-ampton Railway, the first major occasion when railway companies conflicted in Parliament. In 1834 the Bill passed the Commons after a hearing of fifty-seven days during which the Eton op-position forced the company to drop a proposed branch to Windsor. Even so, it failed in the Lords. The Act was passed in 1835 only after the company had made further efforts to con-ciliate the opposition.

In railway literature many of the difficulties of the early rail-ways are attributed to the opposition of vested interests. How important was it? It certainly existed and it could hold up schemes as we have seen. The landowners in particular are singled out for execration. It is argued that they might prevent surveyors entering their land and object to a line going through it, thus causing deviations to be made; they might oppose the Bill in Parliament, thereby adding to the company's preliminary expenses; and that they demanded high prices for their land. There is clear evidence that many railway companies experienced all or some of these difficulties, and there is added piquancy to the stories, for the implication that an obdurate aristocracy was frustrating the new, progressive industrialists (the former using their considerable parliamentary power) fits in neatly with some versions of British social and political history. There is also an implication that in some sense the railways were 'right' and major mistakes must be attributed to others.

A full assessment needs detailed investigations into individual company histories, but as against the allegations one can say that many landowners were not only not opposed to railways, but actively supported them. As J. T. Ward says in his examination of West Riding landowners and the railways, 'Each famous case of opposition can be matched by examples of landowners' support' and he gives many examples of landowning interest in railways. He concludes, 'If the hostility, suspicion, blindness and rapacity of some landowners in the thirties must continue to be mentioned by every railway historian, it is only fitting that the energetic interest of others should also be mentioned.'[8]

Moreover, if rights were to be respected, then there had to be some procedure open to those objecting in any way to railway schemes and some way of providing equitable compensation for the compulsory purchase of land. It may be validly argued that the method of private Bill procedure was not a suitable one; but while landowning peers could use their political influence to defeat a railway Bill or to introduce restrictive clauses, the railway companies soon learned that they could mobilise support in Parliament.

As the economy moved upwards in the mid 1830s the focus of attention was a company promotion boom, with railways taking a major part. By 1835, when the mania began, four main-line companies had managed to obtain their Acts—the Grand Junction, the London & Birmingham, the London & Southampton, and the Great Western. In the three years 1833-5 some 550 miles were authorised. It was evident that companies could be incorporated, that opposition could be overcome (or might be non-existent). Moreover the Liverpool & Manchester was continuing to pay good dividends as was the Stockton & Darlington. And it was very easy to finance a railway mania. Companies normally announced their intention to issue shares of a nominal value of £100, but only a small deposit was required, no greater than 5 per cent. The remainder would be called up as required during construction. A quite small sum could enable a person to be issued with scrip with an apparently higher value. Clearly, too, speculation was that much easier. A person might be willing to increase markedly the amount he paid as a deposit, yet this would only mean a small premium on the full value of the share.

It was a boom of high expectations, in which anticipated dividends were much higher than from alternative forms of investment. They were greater too than any paid by any railway company so far. In November 1836 *Herapath's Railway Journal* published a list of the dividends expected by those companies which had obtained Acts that year. Of the twenty-nine, two were of 20 per cent or more; and eighteen were 10 per cent or more. The highest was that of the Eastern Counties Railway. At the first shareholders' meeting of that company in 1836 one shareholder said: 'If this undertaking fails in producing the dividend of twenty-two per cent, calculated upon in the Report, then I must say, human calculations and expectations can no longer be depended upon.'

With that sort of confidence in the air, company promoters could obviously obtain support for almost any scheme. There was no need for them to go round peddling their shares at public meetings. An advertisement in the newspapers was enough to bring in the applications. In their preliminary stages the companies were less interested in receiving cash than in inducing potential shareholders to sign the Subscription Contract, a document required by Standing Orders to establish that the company had a bona fide shareholding body. Naturally some men of straw were found when the lists were examined, but their numbers were surprisingly few.

Indeed, there is plenty of evidence that much of the mania was a purely surface phenomenon. Most of the companies which obtained their Acts were under the supervision of well-known engineers and were founded on the legitimate needs of their districts. No doubt the parliamentary procedures performed their function of weeding out the unsuitable schemes either by refusing to authorise them, or simply by frightening them off.

TABLE 1

AUTHORISATION and CONSTRUCTION 1825-40 (UK)

Year	(1) No of Acts for new railways	(2) Mileage authorised	(3) Capital Paid up £m	(4) Gross capital formation £m	(5) Mileage opened
1825		14	0.2		27
1826		65	0.2		11
1827		23	0.25		3
1828		34	0.39		4
1829		105	0.38		6
1830		61	0.4		47
1831	5	31	0.59	0.3	43
1832	4	40	0.58	0.4	26
1833	5	218	1.04	0.8	42
1834	5	132	1.32	1.0	90
1835	8	201	2.11	1.6	40
1836	29	956	5.65	3.3	66
1837	15	544	4.40	6.0	137
1838	2	49	9.74	10.6	202
1839	1	55	10.29	11.1	227
1840	–	(-19)	10.62	9.7	528

Sources :   Col 1   BPP (1840) XLV
            Cols 2 & 5   Lewin, H. G. *Early British Railways* (1925), 186, (fractions of ½ mile and over to unit above)
            Col 3   Hawke, G. R. and Reed, M.C. 'Railway capital in the United Kingdom in the Nineteenth Century'. *Econ Hist Rev*, 22 no 2 (1969), 271
            Col 4   Mitchell, B. R. 'The Coming of the Railway and United Kingdom Economic Growth' in M. C. Reed (ed) *Railways in the Victorian Economy* (1969), 30
                           The figures include expenditures on land and ancillary businesses; they include items debited to both capital and revenue accounts.

Note : These figures provide no more than a guide to the general movement of events. Cols 3 and 5 are the most accurate. For a discussion of Mitchell's figures (col 4) and an estimation of the likely error, see : Hawke, G. R. *Railways and Economic Growth in England and Wales 1840-1870* (1970), chapter 8.

A great deal was accomplished and many schemes were successful. In the two sessions 1836 and 1837, when most of the new companies obtained their Acts, some 1,500 miles were authorised. Two-thirds of this came in 1836, which suggests—given the nature of the parliamentary time-table—that many had been in preparation before the mania began. (See Table 1, p 28.)

The promotion boom ended in 1837 with the onset of recession, assisted by the action of Parliament which now intervened to try to regulate matters more closely. New Standing Orders, introduced by the Commons, provided that the various documents required under the Private Bill procedure had in future to be deposited in the March before the session and not, as hitherto, in the latter part of the preceding year. That is, a notice of application for a Bill in the 1838 session now had to be submitted in March 1837. Moreover one-tenth of the amount subscribed had to be deposited at the Bank of England or invested in government securities until the Bill was passed or rejected. These burdens came just at the time when the London & Birmingham, which so far seemed to be having little difficulty with its construction, suddenly announced that it would need almost to double its capital (from £2¼ to £4½ million). A period of recrimination followed the speculation mania; this was no time for new investment plans to be made.

The companies which had obtained their Acts now got down to active construction. It was not the most favourable of times to raise money from shareholders, who faced several years of waiting until the line was built and revenue was earned. Naturally many were slow to pay calls or did not pay them at all. The situation was succinctly described by G. P. Bidder, the engineer of the Northern & Eastern Railway (incorporated 1836). He stated in 1843 that the estimates had been exceeded by costs

by reason of the long credit the Company required, arising from deficiency of funds, owing to non-payment of calls and the small proportion of the capital stock subscribed for.[9]

Perhaps the finest example of the difficulties that could beset a company was the experience of the Eastern Counties Railway. It was the largest so far authorised (126 miles) with expected dividends of over 20 per cent. The Act of July 1836 authorised the company to issue 64,000 shares of £25 each but even as late as March 1838 only about 60,000 had been registered. Yet by the following year, when £16 had been called on 60,231 shares the company had received only £697,000, a deficiency of £$\frac{1}{4}$ million. By 1839 the position had become desperate and work on part of the line was suspended. The board minutes of 1839 are full of reports of attempts to borrow money but very little could be obtained. There was talk of borrowing from the government, in co-operation with other railway companies. In 1840 the board considered issuing shares at a discount of 72 per cent (only £7 of the £25 nominal value would be called but each share would receive a dividend on the full nominal value). An alternative scheme was put forward by the company's Liverpool share-holders: an issue of debentures of £8 6s 8d (£8.33) each, payable in instalments, to be transferred into shares at the end of three years. This proposal was adopted.[10] By 1843 less than half the line was built, and the remainder was abandoned.

Not all companies had this experience, but most had difficulties in raising money and various devices to obtain funds were resorted to. It was obviously useful to offer shareholders some return while the line was being built or some guarantee of a return when open. Companies resorted to paying interest on dividends (until this was outlawed in 1847); they issued preference shares (so much less risky for shareholders). Irregular devices such as loan notes (which were no more than IOUs) were used until prohibited by Parliament in 1844.[11]

Bidder wrote of the financial causes of the rise in costs but there were other factors. That the eventual cost of major public works is often greater than the estimate would nowadays occasion little surprise. What is astonishing is that in the early railway age the various engineers were not more inaccurate than they were. It was said at the time that some estimates were purposely kept low in order to attract investors. But a more reasonable general explanation of the excess of costs over estimates is quite simply that in the 1830s the experience of undertaking these great engineering works was very small. The example of the London & Birmingham illustrates this. Its original estimate was for £2$\frac{1}{2}$ million; by the end of 1838, soon after the line was opened, actual expenditure was £4$\frac{3}{4}$ million.[12]

The company's Act was obtained in 1833 and the work began well. During the first three years the company's *Reports* gave figures showing that the contracts had been taken up within the engineer's estimates, although expenditure on land was higher than expected partly because of the extra acreage required. But in 1837 the tone changed and the estimates were dramatically increased to £4½ million. Part of this was caused by additions to the original plans and by the use of heavier and more expensive rails. Outweighing all of these were the difficulties of the work on various parts of the route, of which the extraordinary situation at Kilsby, where the company had to take over the contract directly, was only one example. In August 1838 the *Report* noted that the stations would cost some £630,000 more than the estimate. This increased cost could not be blamed on any individual: 'they had no experience to guide them in forming a proper estimate'. In 1846 the *Edinburgh Review* took up this point:

> The very limited number of engineers who, having already been employed in the coal districts of the northern counties were presumed to have had some experience in railway work, were soon engrossed to the full extent of their time and powers. Great enterprises, consequently, fell under the superintendence of persons having neither the peculiar knowledge nor experience which they required.

These sentiments were perhaps a natural reaction to a decade during which engineers had been over praised. A better case could be made for arguing that the contractors were much less used to this kind of work. The main lines of the 1830s were normally let in short sections, the work being done by men in a small way of business. Only later did the great contractors emerge, able to undertake the construction of a whole route.

It was not only that estimates were often exceeded, for reasons sometimes outside the control of the companies. The railways of Britain were generally more expensive to construct than those of other countries. In the literature great emphasis is placed on the cost of obtaining Acts and on the cost of land. In practice these expenditures were not very high proportionately. They certainly cannot account for the great difference between the cost of construction in Britain and elsewhere. Part of the explanation we have already touched on; it was the price paid for being a pioneer, the cost of making mistakes or of an apprenticeship. In the 1830s, when locomotive power was weak, many engineers took it for

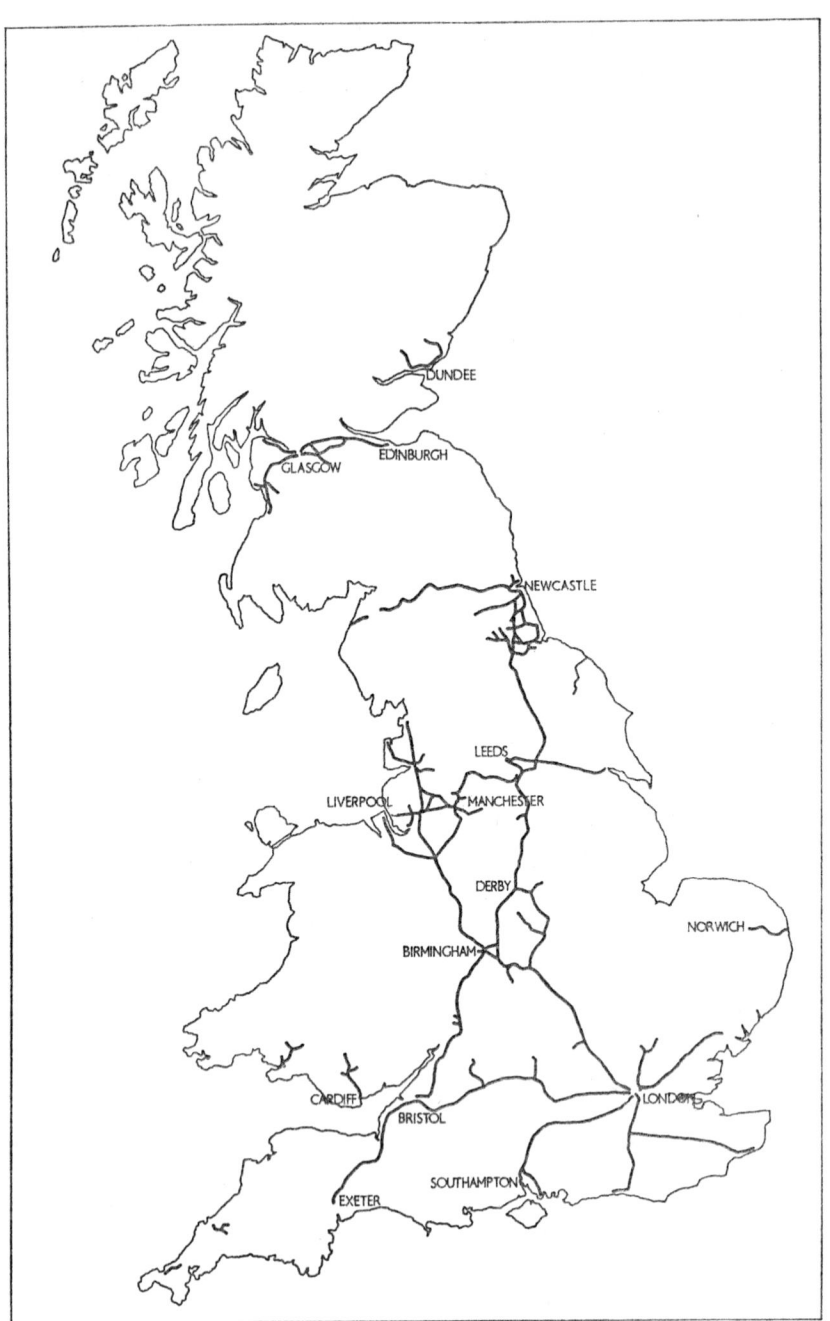

Railway network in 1840

granted that gradients should be easy and this requirement naturally meant the construction of massive earthworks, of embankments, cuttings and tunnels where the land was hilly. These were expensive.

Two further features of the 1830s need emphasising. Railway technology developed empirically. The locomotive had emerged from the practical efforts of engineers, from native wisdom and genius rather than from the application of theory or of scientific method. It was the same with the gauges which were adopted. What became the standard gauge, 4ft 8½in, was taken over from the traditional width between the wheels of coal wagons of the North East, was used on the Stockton & Darlington and subsequently on most lines. In fact the width was well-suited to the low centre of gravity of the early locomotives, but it was adopted by chance, rather than by an understanding of the technical problems involved. Naturally other engineers advocated different widths, and there was a variety of gauges, mostly between 4ft 8in and 5ft 3in (which were fairly quickly altered to the standard width except in Ireland). Only one company went for a completely different gauge, the Great Western, whose engineer, Isambard Kingdom Brunel, talked his board into adopting the broad gauge, 7ft ¼in. An important motive was the desire to create a territorial monopoly. Given the wish of all companies to expand their spheres of influence, and to protect them from the incursions of other companies, this difference of gauge was bound to cause trouble, and the break of gauge meant that through running of trains was impossible. In the 1840s the railway world divided into two schools, the broad gauge Great Western and its narrow gauge rivals, both promoting competitive schemes in Parliament. The matter was settled by the Gauge Act of 1846 which established the narrow gauge as the standard for Britain. During the course of the second half of the century the Great Western had to convert its lines to the standard gauge.

The second feature was the beginning of the long debate about the desirability and form of public regulation of the railway companies. The mania itself had given rise to anxiety and Parliament had discussed such matters as the control of rates and charges. A more immediate need was for some sort of executive control over the companies. Parliament gave the companies certain powers in their Acts of incorporation, but did not then ensure that the

C

law was obeyed. The first effort in this field was the establishment in 1840 of the Railway Department of the Board of Trade. Its main functions were initially to do with safety—notably the inspection of newly constructed lines before they were opened. It was set up just in time to inspect the railways which were finishing their construction; many of the companies which had been authorised in the mid-1830s were opened in the early 1840s.

Thus the 1830s were crucial for the development of the railway system. Within little more than a decade after the opening of the Liverpool & Manchester in 1830 the basic outlines of the network were in existence. There had been a rapid change, a development from small, local lines to major routes of 100 miles or more. Lines radiated from London to the south, the west, north-west and the east, and elsewhere the nucleus was in being on which major companies were to be founded—for example, the Manchester & Leeds which eventually became the Lancashire & Yorkshire, and several which were to become the Midland Railway. Most of the capital investment took place in the three years 1838-40, and the income and employment thus created must have tempered slightly the downward movement in the economy. What is particularly important is the fact that despite the gloom of those years the money was forthcoming, in one form or another, and that the bulk of the authorisations were built.

Notes to this chapter are on p 207.

CHAPTER 2

INVESTMENT:
MANIAS AND CONTRACTORS

Railway construction in the 1830s was a magnificent achievement
in the sense that almost all the mileage authorised was built,
despite the long series of financial difficulties which had beset the
companies. But they were opened at the wrong time. In the early
1840s trade was poor and dividends were low. While the problems
of operating now engaged the attention of the companies and of
the journals, many companies set up committees of inquiry to try
to establish what had gone wrong. Why had they cost so much?
Why were dividends so low? In an atmosphere of gloom some
commentators called for a halt to further construction. Sir John
Clapham refers to those 'who were thinking that the railway
system was not very far from complete'.[1] Almost immediately
afterwards the country was engulfed in the greatest railway promotion boom ever.

On the face of it the pessimists should have won the day.
Dividends were much lower than the bright expectations of the
mid-1830s: only a handful of companies paid more than 4 per
cent. The Eastern Counties was paying 1 per cent. Yet low as
these figures were, they were usually higher than the rate of
return on government stock, after interest rates fell in 1842.
Railway share prices began to improve in 1841, and as the
economy started to move upwards, railway traffic grew and
dividends rose (even though there was considerable doubt as to
their legitimacy, whether or not they really derived from profits).
Railways, therefore, now looked relatively attractive to investors.

On the eve of the mania, in August 1844, *The Economist*
wrote: 'Of all the great channels of public investment during the
last fifty years, no one has maintained throughout so uniform a
reputation and success as railways.'[2] It was enough to give com-

fort to those with spare cash and to encourage them to put their money in the next batch of schemes.

Parliament too took a hand. In 1842 the Commons' Standing Orders were changed, making the procedures easier than in the years since 1837. Plans could now be deposited in the November preceding the session and the 10 per cent deposit was reduced to 5 per cent (but it was quickly increased again in 1845 when the mania was at its height). Inadvertently, too, Gladstone's Act of 1844 helped to foster the mania. Following on the deliberation of a Select Committee this Act was intended, as its preamble stated, to subject new lines of railway 'to such conditions as are hereinafter contained for the benefit of the public'. The Act laid down that the Treasury had the right, after twenty-one years, to revise the charges of any company if for three years the 'clear annual profit divisible upon the subscribed and paid-up capital stock of the said railway' were 10 per cent or more. Moreover the Act gave the Treasury the option of purchasing the new railways after twenty-one years, the compensation being twenty-five years purchase of the profits. If the average rate of profit were less than 10 per cent, and the company thought the twenty-five years purchased insufficient, there was a procedure for negotiating for more. Thus the figure of 10 per cent return, enshrined in an Act of Parliament, became a symbol of the government's view that railway property would appreciate to that amount. Government policy to contain railways produced instead an explosion.

There was a small trickle of new promotions in the slump period, slowly building up in the early 1840s but suddenly blossoming out in 1844. Whereas in 1843 just under 100 miles were authorised, in 1844 the figure was over 800. Most of this had been promoted by existing lines, or by new companies assisted by the old ones. Already the major companies were talking of the need to create territorial monopolies. The chairman of the London & Birmingham, the banker George Carr Glyn, told the 1844 Select Committee that he considered competition undesirable since it led to reduced fares and to inferior working stock; in any case it was self-defeating because it led eventually to combination and to higher fares. Any further extensions should be built by the main-line companies.

The Select Committee did recommend that the Board of Trade should examine new projects and report to Parliament to help it in its decisions. The Railway Department had already examined Bills and made suggestions for clauses to be incorporated but now their actions were greatly augmented. From 1844, renamed the Railway Board, it 'began to prepare a most ambitious series of reports. Their purpose was to guide Parliament through the whole of the railway Bills of the coming session, and to recommend for each scheme whether it should be passed, postponed or rejected.'[3] This attempt to regulate the growth of the railway system did not work in the way that Glyn wanted. Indeed the publication of its views merely added to the speculation since the public assumed that a favourable report might lead to success in Parliament and the scheme's shares would thus be valuable. Moreover the board had gone by the end of 1845 when plans for over 700 schemes were deposited, due to be heard in the 1846 session.

At the end of 1845 W. F. Spackman produced a list of over 1,000 railway schemes with a total capital of over £700 million. It was not very accurate, but it does give an indication of the size of the mania. Since many of these were competing lines only a proportion would have obtained Acts in any case, but this did not prevent the schemes coming forward. Unlike the 1830s, when new promotions were based on very primitive arithmetic of costs and returns, by the mid-1840s there was much more evidence, however shoddy in some cases. There was better knowledge of costs of construction and of operating expenses and revenues. Some companies were now paying fairly good dividends. And those promoting schemes could argue that they did not want their town or district to be left out, to decay for want of railway accommodation.

Naturally, in such a period of intense excitement, when the mere placing of an advertisement in the papers brought in masses of applications, there must have been sharks and rogues. But it was not all like that. There was a kind of crazy logic in these company promotions. Whether or not a particular scheme succeeded in Parliament seemed to be very much a matter of luck depending upon the views of the various Private Bill Committees. Existing companies reacted to the appearance of new schemes by promoting their own or by taking over the new projects. Thus in 1850 the directors of the Lancashire & Yorkshire explained recent events to their shareholders:

. . . the chief additions to the original undertaking are Lines *not projected* by your Directors, but originating with independent Companies . . . Lines for the most part effecting objects in accordance with the general design of the Manchester & Leeds Company and occupying positions more or less injurious or otherwise to the permanent interests of the Company, according as they might become combined with one or other of the numerous systems of Railways occupying the great Manufacturing district.[4]

In general there is little if any evidence that companies possessed a backlog of schemes, intended to create a rational network ready to be submitted to Parliament when the money market was ripe. At the same time, some companies were not averse to promoting schemes purely to ditch competitors.

One can therefore see the various motives on the demand side of the capital market. The satirists had an equally rewarding time when they contemplated the supply side, the mad speculative fever. Compared with other types of investment the railways were highly suitable for potential shareholders. Government stock paid low returns. Manufacturing industry still managed to finance itself. The railways had limited liability. Overseas investment was known to be highly risky, as the disasters of the previous two decades had shown. Moreover, as before, only a small amount of money was required to purchase title to a security. To get in on it was the thing. Not only scrip but letters of allotment changed hands rapidly, and the prices of existing companies' shares rocketed. The reduction in their yield was offset by rising dividends, partly a reflection of the increasing receipts due to booming trade, partly due to accounting devices such as reducing depreciation allowances.

The mania was primarily devoted to the promotion of new lines but it was more than that; it was the era of amalgamations. Mergers between railway companies were not new but the creation in 1844 of the Midland Railway out of three companies centring on Derby was a major innovation. The Midland Railway was created to end price competition between two companies, the Birmingham & Derby Junction and the Midland Counties, which offered alternative routes between Derby and Rugby, 'a very important stretch of line, for almost the whole of the traffic from north-eastern England to London passed over the

North Midland through Derby, and the London & Birmingham provided the sole route from Rugby onwards'.[5]

This step was followed during the mania by other amalgamations. The London & North Western was formed from a combination of the Grand Junction (itself incorporating the Liverpool & Manchester), the London & Birmingham, and the Manchester & Birmingham; the Manchester, Sheffield & Lincolnshire by companies between Manchester and Grimsby; the Lancashire & Yorkshire whose nucleus was the Manchester & Leeds; and the London, Brighton & South Coast.

Amalgamations could be justified in many ways; 'end-on' mergers made operating and administrative sense. But the man who created the Midland—George Hudson—went beyond this. His purpose was to create some sort of system out of the patchwork of lines and during the mania period he put this into operation. By various methods he came into control by 1846 of some 1,000 miles, just when a new promotion, the Great Northern, was under consideration by Parliament. This was for a line from York to London and would be a major competitor to Hudson's network. The contest in Parliament was bitter and expensive; the GNR won, but Hudson was left with some bad bargains. He had taken over the Great North of England Railway during the fight, at a guaranteed 10 per cent dividend. It was a poor line, paying low dividends but it had to be taken over for political reasons. It was not a decision based on a calculation of what the line would add to the net revenues of his empire.

The mania was at its height in 1844-5, share prices reaching their peak in the summer of 1845 but still remaining high throughout 1846. Most of the projects would have disappeared any way, but a series of events outside the railway world brought the mania to an abrupt end. The Irish potato famine coupled with Peel's repeal of the Corn Laws meant heavy imports of food; and in the autumn of 1847 wheat prices fell drastically, producing failures of corn dealers. Moreover, at the same time the price of cotton rose sharply because of the shortage of supply from America. The increased cost of these imports placed a heavy strain on bullion reserves. As the Bank of England's reserves fell, there was a fear that further advances and discounts would have to be refused; the panic ended abruptly when the Bank Charter Act was suspended which authorised the bank to provide further loans. By the beginning of 1848 the situation was satisfactory: the panic was over, but it had meant the end of the railway promotion mania.

TABLE 2

AUTHORISATION and CONSTRUCTION 1841-54 (UK)

Year	(1) New mileage authorised	(2) Miles abandoned by statute	(3) Miles opened each year	(4) Capital Paid up £m	(5) Gross capital formation £m
1841	15		277	7.16	6.5
1842	55		164	7.13	5.3
1843	91		105	5.1	4.7
1844	811		192	6.34	4.9
1845	2816		288	13.86	13.0
1846	4541		634	38.19	30.2
1847	1295		712	39.03	43.9
1848	373	35	1253	33.99	33.1
1849	17	20	812	29.83	24.9
1850	7	18	621	10.63	13.1
1851	126	132	256	7.87	9.9
1852	231	180	493	15.94	9.7
1853	940	n.a.	350	9.08	10.2
1854	482	n.a.	368	12.81	12.7

Sources: Cols 1, 2 & 3   Lewin, H. G. *Early British Railways*, 186; *The Railway*
(a) 1841-1852   *Mania and its aftermath* (1936, reprinted 1968),
                        505ff

(b) 1853 & 1854   Board of Trade Report, BPP XXVII (1859)
      Col 4   Hawke and Reed, 'Railway Capital . . .' (1969), 271
      Col 5   Mitchell, 'The Coming of the Railway . . .' (1969) 30-1.
                          These figures include expenditure on land purchase
                          and ancillary businesses.

See also Note to Table 1, p 28

The results of the mania can be seen in the statistics of authorisations (Table 2 above). The peak was in 1846, but there was still a considerable authorisation in the next two years. Altogether in the four years 1845-8 9,000 miles were sanctioned. Actual construction began fairly quickly and investment expenditure showed the familiar lag. Between the beginning of 1846 to the end of 1849 about £130 million were spent, the peak year being 1847 when over £40 million were spent, and a quarter of a million men were employed on construction. These sums of money seem small beer by today's standards. Some idea of their significance can be obtained if one compares them with such figures as there are of national income at the period. Gross National Income was in the region of £400 to £500 million in the 1840s; and domestic fixed capital formation was around £40 million. Thus at its peak in 1847 railway capital formation amounted to between 8 and 10 per cent of national income, and the whole of the country's capital investment.

It is important to stress the magnitude of this achievement. Much of the literature, in the tradition of historical pathology, emphasises the darker side of railway investment. Contemporaries satirised the mad rush into railway securities by all manner of people; they noted the scandals—notably those associated with George Hudson—and the general carelessness over railway company accounting. There was a proposed government audit of railway accounts; an Act was passed in 1850 to facilitate the abandonment of authorised lines; of the 9,000 miles sanctioned in 1845-8 only 5,000 had been built by 1858 (the date of Galton's last report to the Board of Trade). About 1,500 miles had been abandoned by statute and on more than 2,000 miles the powers for compulsory purchase of land and completion of the works had expired.

TABLE 3

RAILWAY SHARE PRICES 1827-50
June 1840 = 100

1827	45.9	1839	79.9
1828	54.5	1840	86.4
1829	54.3	1841	83.8
1830	61.7	1842	89.4
1831	65.2	1843	98.2
1832	68.0	1844	121.3
1833	69.3	1845	149.0
1834	67.8	1846	139.4
1835	71.1	1847	117.1
1836	111.1	1848	95.5
1837	81.4	1849	77.1
1838	91.1	1850	70.4

Source: Gayer, A. D., Rostow, W. W., Schwartz, A. J. *The Growth and Fluctuation of the British Economy 1790-1850* (1953), I, 437. These are average annual figures. Detailed monthly figures are given in Table 17, p 375. Part II, chapter I, pp 358-367 is an account of the methods used.

Yet in the latter part of the 1840s the work of construction went on. Money was raised by the companies from shareholders, by loans and in other ways (such as paying creditors in railway stock). The money came in at the worst possible time for everybody. Share prices more than halved between 1845 and 1850 when they fell to 70 (See Table 3 above). Dividends fell equally dramatically. Naturally enough the mania of the 1840s has attracted most attention in the history of British railways. Apart from anything else its details provide good copy for those seeking evidence of the moral degradation of the Victorians. Yet while in the next generation the route mileage doubled and there was to be another mania in the 1860s, which superficially repeated the excitement of the 1830s and 1840s, in the immediate aftermath

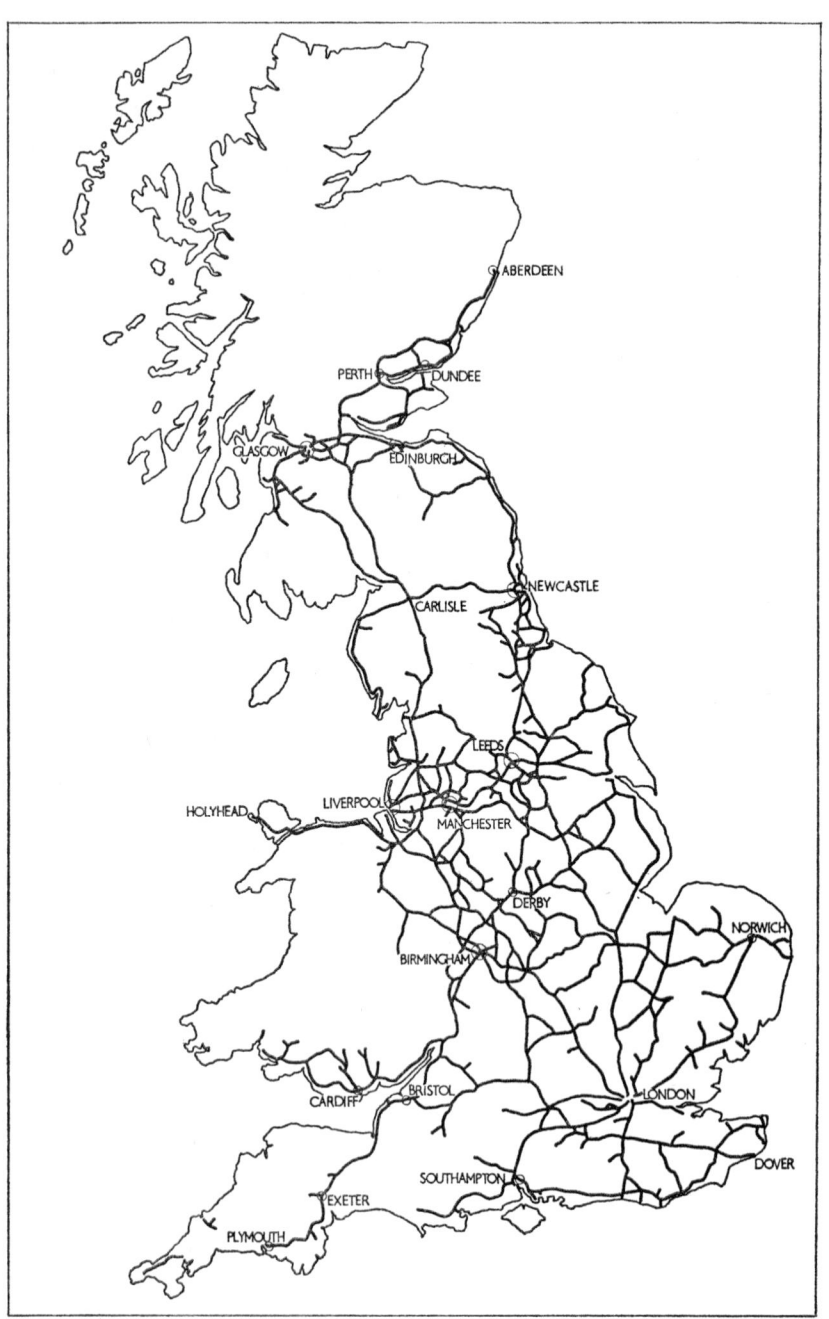

Railway network in 1852

of the Hudson era the tone was one of disillusion and dismay.

Share prices were down; dividends were down; and as against the enthusiastic adoption of commitments in 1845 and 1846, the railway companies began to retreat from expansion. As early as 1848 the London, Brighton & South Coast Railway Board reported proudly that: 'there is no large Railway Company which has so small an extent of works in progress or in prospect.' The chairman of the London & North Western said in 1851: 'my opinion is, that no large undertaking is firmly based and placed in a proper position until the capital account is closed.' This was a sentiment which most companies supported. Shareholders, who had vociferously supported the campaigns of the mid-1840s, now asserted themselves and called a halt. At company meetings limits were set to capital expenditure in an attempt to close or at any rate to contain the growth of capital accounts; any expediture had to be specially authorised by the shareholders. Directors were no longer trusted and care was taken in the election of auditors. For example, in 1851 the LNWR, a company which on the whole came through the 1840s without an aura of scandal, established a Shareholders' Audit Committee whose function was to recommend to the shareholders the names of those people they considered suitable for election as auditors.[6]

But the policy of closing capital accounts could not work. Traffic was expanding and facilities had to be improved to accommodate it, and the attempt by some companies to finance the necessary capital expenditure out of revenue was short-lived. Moreover, the established companies were overtaken—a familiar feature of railway history—by new company promotions, which forced them to take action to defend their territory. In the 1850s their actions were largely defensive. In that decade share prices remained below par, dividends grew only slowly, and the Crimean War and the financial crisis of 1857 were not encouraging years for companies to pursue active policies of expansion.

The pamphleteers were busy too. Some, like Herbert Spencer in his *Railway Morals and Railway Policy*, deplored the depths to which society had fallen, as the speculative mania and the scandals had revealed. Others were soberly examining the financial accounts, trying to establish the reason for low dividends.

Chattaway, in his *Railways, Their Capital and Dividends*, put the blame for low dividends squarely on heavy capital expenditure, including the costs of parliamentary procedures, and the high cost of land. He added: 'extravagant outlay in construction; ruinous guarantees, leases and purchases of other undertakings; and the formation of branch lines throughout barren and profitless districts.'

With varying degrees of emphasis, this analysis was accepted and repeated by other commentators and by committees of railway shareholders. There was little the shareholders could do in the short run to put things right—the lines were built—but they would not be caught again. It has been argued that one important effect of the speculative mania of the 1840s was that it vastly widened the field of shareholding and encouraged many people to think of putting their money into commercial enterprise and not to concentrate on government securities. This has an element of truth in it. Yet in the early 1850s the campaign for an extension of limited liability to industry was just as much occasioned by disillusionment with the railways. It was not the success of the railways but rather their failure which gave momentum to the campaign.

Nevertheless the appetite for railways was not satiated. Towns in districts which had been by-passed began to demand railway facilities, whether they paid or not, they were obviously useful, and the fall in interest rates made railway securities relatively attractive in spite of their low dividends. In 1852 and 1853 there was a brief promotion boom, resulting in the authorisation of over 1,400 miles in 1853 and 1854.

Generally, these new promotions were not put forward by the existing companies. They were still tidying up, and were more interested in questions of operating and management. It made more sense to them to improve their administration by amalgamations. In the 1850s Parliament was generally opposed to mergers and the companies found themselves in that decade trying to operate a system, created in haste, in which one company's lines joined another's. In practice this often led to conflicts when one company tried to run its trains over another company's metals. There are many stories, part of the folklore of the industry, about the physical confrontations at junctions, of company A's trains being detained, and not allowed to proceed. (The interests of the consumers seem seldom to have been considered.)

In that kind of situation we should expect companies to decide to have their own route to avoid these ridiculous farces. For example, the Midland Railway, anxious to improve its running to London, but having no rails of its own south of Rugby, tried to amalgamate with the LNWR. When this did not get through Parliament it took over the Leicester & Hitchin Line which joined the Great Northern nearer London. This new arrangement also produced many conflicts and difficulties, and the MR made further plans to build its own line into London.

In the 1850s, though, expansion by the existing companies was largely defensive. Following an attack on it by its Manchester shareholders the board of the LNWR explained in 1863 that the company had spent over £24 million since the late 1840s as a safeguard in case Parliament sanctioned competing schemes. The general sentiment of the 1850s was summarised by David Salomons of the East Kent Railway (incorporated 1853 and in 1859 renamed the London, Chatham & Dover Railway). In 1854 he said: 'the old proprietors of railways, who, in former times, were foremost in promoting new schemes . . . abstained of late from subscribing to new undertakings.' In the unfavourable conditions of the 1850s the small companies found it difficult to raise money. And with the existing companies reluctant to spend, the total of railway investment was low, only about £9-10 million per year. (Tables 2 and 5, pp 40 and 48.)

There was no shortage of schemes. The fall in bank rate in the early 1850s caused railway securities to become relatively attractive and there was a brief promotion boom. Some construction began just as the Crimean War placed demands on the economy, producing further difficulties. The Midland Railway, for example, building its Leicester & Hitchin extension, experienced a shortage of cash and an increase in the cost of labour and materials. 'In order to conserve both labour and capital, arrangements were made for the major cuttings to be reduced in depth.'[7] (While this economy reduced capital expenditure it created severe gradients, producing long-term problems of operation.) The first authorisation of what was to be become London's underground was in 1853, when the North Metropolitan Railway obtained its Act. An amending Act the following year provided for changes in the route and an increase of capital. But despite the financial support of the Great Western Railway and of railway contractors, no work was done because of the Crimean War and the financial crisis of

TABLE 4

MILEAGE OPENED 1844-58 ACCORDING TO YEAR OF AUTHORISATION (UK)

Year authorised	Opened in 1844	1845	1846	1847	1848	1849	1850	1851	1852	1853	1854	1855	1856	1857	1858
Before Dec 1843	204	131	16	2	1	3	4								
1844	-	159	366	142	118	311	213								
1845		6	224	573	604	501	379								
1846				84	403	45	26	65	106		50				-
1847				2	56	7	-	122	288	122	121	26	45	44	5
1848						2	1	71	10	179	29	22	66	44	14
1849							2	7	16	15	11	22	16	11	-
1850								-	-	-	-	-	7	16	-
1851								4	15	-	1	-	-	-	-
1852									11	23	15	24	-	19	22
1853										11	106	21	39	5	137
1854											35	88	161	121	50
1855												23	35	68	103
1856													41	48	85
1857														14	7
1858															3
Total	204	296	606	803	1182	869	625	269	446	350	368	226	410	390	426

Source: Capt Galton's Report to the Board of Trade, 1858 (BPP 1859, XXVII)

Note: The annual totals of mileage opened for 1844 to 1852 are different from those in Table 2. Table 2, based on Lewin, is more accurate, but he did not provide figures broken down in the way presented here.

1857. A Bill was prepared for the winding up of the company, to be introduced in the 1858 session, but matters improved soon after. The Corporation of London subscribed one-fifth of the capital and enough money then came forward for work to begin, six years after the original Act had been obtained.

The end of the Crimean War had raised hopes and nearly 700 miles were authorised in the following session. But the financial crisis of 1857, when bank rate reached 10 per cent, severely affected companies. Applications to Parliament fell and only some 300 miles were authorised, while existing companies found it difficult to raise money for construction or for the redemption of their terminable debentures. The Great Western Railway in particular was in trouble. It had to pay such high rates to renew its loans that there was little left for its other shareholders.

It was a short-lived crisis. From 1858 the company expanded rapidly, until the onset of the 'Great Depression' in the early 1870s. In that period national income almost doubled and it rose each year except for the three years 1867-9.

Railway promotion followed the expected pattern. During each of the eight sessions 1859-66 over 1,000 miles were applied for, totalling in all some 20,000 miles. Of this, one-half was in the three sessions 1864-6. The financial crisis of 1866 reduced promotions to very low figures, the lowest year for applications being 1868 when only 80 miles were applied for. They picked up again fairly quickly; in the three sessions 1872-4 about 5,000 miles were applied for. Capital expenditures followed, with a time-lag, rising from 1859, and reaching a peak in 1865, falling to a low level in 1869 and 1870 and then rising to another peak in the mid-1870s. (See Table 5, p 48.)

Why was there this substantial expenditure in the 1860s? There are the obvious explanations of a booming economy, of increasing traffic especially freight and of revenue rising faster in the 1850s than the growth of the system. Gross receipts per mile thus soon recovered from the depths of the early 1850s. But if the upward movement of the trade cycle exerted the same influence as before, there were other factors which were particularly significant for the railways. One general point is that once a line was built and opened it encouraged the promotion of lines to join it. Or the completion of a line might set off other promotions in the same district. Thus the opening of the first part of the

TABLE 5

PROMOTION AND CONSTRUCTION 1855-70 (UK)

Year	(1) Mileage applied for	(2) Mileage authorised	(3) Mileage opened in year	(4) Paid up capital £m	(5) Gross capital formation £m
1855	655	383	226	11.49	11.3
1856	676	322	410	10.01	9.0
1857	1470	663	390	7.67	9.6
1858	698	328	426	10.22	9.3
1859	1129		460	9.94	9.9
1860	1406		431	13.69	11.0
1861	3017		432	14.19	14.4
1862	1800		686	23.12	16.2
1863	1993		771	18.98	20.0
1864	3099		467	21.08	23.0
1865	4270		500	30.02	28.2
1866	3575		565	26.38	25.6
1867	364		393	20.33	17.5
1868	80		381	9.38	13.2
1869	280		n.a	7.11	11.7
1870	240		n.a	11.24	12.3

Sources: Col 1   Annual Reports on Railway and Canal Bills. These begin
                         in 1855, and were published in BPP.
          Cols 2 & 3 1855-8   Capt Galton's Report. BPP (1859) XXVII
          Col 3 1859-70   *Railway Returns*
          Col 4   Hawke and Reed, 'Railway Capital . . .' (1969), 271
          Col 5   Mitchell, 'The Coming of the Railway . . .' (1969), 31
See also Note to Table 1, p 28

London underground in 1863 was followed by a boom in the promotion of railways in the London area. There might, too, be special economic reasons for individual promotions. As Michael Robbins has demonstrated, the impending exhaustion of local ores in South Wales resulted in the promotion of schemes for the building of lines to carry iron ore from the Midlands to South Wales. And the main-line companies faced with a multitude of possibly competing lines fought to maintain their territory.

Moreover, Parliament again took a hand. By now the advantages of railways were self-evident but in less populated districts the funds were not likely to be forthcoming nor might the line pay. (There were a number of publications about the possibility of building horse-powered railways, less costly to construct and to operate; in practice these were adopted in urban areas and light railways did not enter the scene until the end of the century.) The House of Lords set up a Select Committee on the charging of entailed estates for railways, which reported in 1863. The Committee's function was to inquire whether the power given to landowners to charge their estates with terminable annuities in order to raise money for improvements, should be extended to enable them to raise money on similar terms 'for the purpose of taking shares in railways'. The report noted the great difficulty in raising money to build a railway intended to benefit an agricultural district unless at least some of the shares were taken by the owners of the land to be benefited. Landowners in some cases had become large shareholders in railways passing through their district, and might have contributed more but for legal obstacles. The committee argued the desirability of landowners raising money for taking shares in companies which were intended to improve their property.

The attitude of Parliament was reflected in two Acts of 1864, the Railway Construction Facilities Act and the Railway Companies' Powers Act. Both authorised the Board of Trade on certain conditions, to issue a certificate giving railway companies various powers without having to go through the Private Bill procedures. The first Act applied to the promotion of new lines: the second allowed existing companies to alter their statutory powers. Not much use was made of these Acts but promoters were encouraged by the fact that Parliament was ready to ease their legislative and administrative burdens.

In the early 1860s the chairman of the London & North Western Railway, Richard Moon, said:

> You will find that capital is going out to India, and all over the world seeking for employment in railways. What is the state of things in England? There is not one of the great companies in this country who can raise sixpence without preference or guaranteed shares.

The figures of paid-up capital for the period 1850-70 bear this out (Table 6 below).

TABLE 6

RAILWAY CAPITAL, 1850-70 (UK)

	Shares			
Year	Ordinary £m	Preference £m	Loans £m	Total £m
1850	150	37	52	239
1870	230	159	142	530
Increase				
Amount	80	121	90	291
Per cent change	53	327	173	122

Source: *Railway Returns.*

D

While paid-up capital rose by a factor of one and a quarter, equity capital rose by only one half. The increase in debt was more than average and in preference shares by more than three times. Thus, of the increase of nearly £300 million, equities accounted for less than a quarter while preference shares provided about two-fifths.

Richard Moon's speech continued: 'There are no proprietors willing to come forward to make a railway. They are made by contractors, engineers, and speculators, who live on the fears of the companies'. In the 1830s and 1840s there had been complaints of lawyers' and engineers' lines. To these were now added contractors, making a third sinister group. Whatever the truth about the former, the evidence about contractors is abundant and clear.

But the older companies also took part in railway promotion and investment in the 1860s. To some extent this was done reluctantly, as Richard Moon's statement implies, in order to safeguard territory. But in some cases they were consciously expansionary. The Midland Railway's Leicester & Hitchin extension was opened in 1857 but the arrangement whereby traffic travelled via the Great Northern Railway to King's Cross proved unsatisfactory. The one pair of tracks could not cope with increasing traffic; there was intense rivalry between the staffs of the two companies in which the Midland's trains came off second best; and facilities at the London terminal were inadequate. As early as 1859 the Midland was negotiating the purchase of land for its own goods station and in 1862 decided to build its own line to a new station at St Pancras. This was authorised in 1863. Three years later it obtained powers for a line in the northern part of its system, between Settle and Carlisle. Hitherto, its Scottish traffic had been carried from Ingleton northwards on LNWR rails and the purpose of this new line was to bypass that company's metals.

In southern England there were conflicts between the three companies in the south and south-east of London. The LBSC obtained Acts for shorter lines to Eastbourne and Hastings. 'Both these schemes' says Robbins, 'were undertaken less on their own merits than as moves in the complicated manoeuvres of the long battle for the railway control of East Sussex'.[8] These schemes came to nothing, but of more importance was the feud between the LCD and the SER, which lasted until the end of the century.

The South Eastern had built a line in the 1830s to Dover, via Redhill; the Chatham company's line to Dover further north was a product of the 1850s, and was opened in 1861. The SER retaliated by building a short-cut from St John's to Tonbridge and both companies built lines mainly in areas of small populations, primarily to obtain shorter routes to the coast.

While the established companies pursued their expansions and their conflicts, it was the newcomers who did most of the promoting. In the two sessions of 1864 and 1865, out of 7,369 miles applied for, 4,942 (over two-thirds) were by new companies. It was not unusual for new companies to be promoted during manias. What was new and significant was the extraordinary part played by contractors. In the 1860s the railway contractors widened their activities beyond civil engineering and embraced functions more appropriate to others by extending their influence into the financial side of construction.[9]

In essence a contractor would agree to build the line in return for taking payment in the company's securities. In earlier days it had not been uncommon for railway companies, when hard pressed, to pay some of its creditors in shares, but as early as the 1850s some companies looked to contractors to take some of their shares. The East Kent Railway, for example, obtained the agreement of Sir Charles Fox that he and his friends should take about one-half of the company's shares.

During the 1860s this method of financing became widespread. Contractors were involved during the preliminary discussions, sometimes providing the money for the parliamentary deposit and agreeing to build the line, often at a higher price. John Fowler, the engineer, told a Lords Committee in 1866:

> In most cases where the contractors find the greater part of the capital and takes (sic) payment in shares, the contract price will be higher than if the company would go into the open market, and pay for the works in cash.

(But part of the increase may have been to cover other expenditures, on land for example, which the company in any case would have had to incur.)

The contractors in their turn needed funds. They could sell some of the shares, but more normally they obtained finance from the credit and finance companies whose growth mushroomed in the company boom of the 1860s. The first of them was launched in 1863. W. T. C. King, the historian of the discount market, has described them as professing 'functions so vague or so embracing as to defy description, but most closely resembling those of a modern "finance" company and mortgage bank rolled into one.' They helped to make possible the general company boom of the mid-1860s when 2,500 joint stock companies were registered in the three years of 1863-5, the first company boom after the introduction of limited liability. On the other hand the magnitude of their contribution cannot be calculated. Speaking of railways Lord Redesdale told the Lords in 1866 that 'last year all the schemes which were brought before Parliament looked to the finance companies for assistance.' But in that session one-third of the mileage applied for came from existing companies, which did not normally use contractors as financiers or finance houses.

Another method of financing construction was by the issue of Lloyd's Bonds. A railway company which had incurred a debt would give the creditor one of these bonds which guaranteed payment of principal and interest at a future date. The barrister with whom they originated, John Horatio Lloyd, explained their nature and function to a Lords Committee in 1864. The bonds were particularly useful to a railway company which had exhausted its funds. The contractor would be able to continue his work if he were given these bonds on which he could obtain an advance. The rate of interest was usually higher than on debentures and the bonds were eventually discharged by a capital issue or paid out of revenue. From the contractor's point of view their advantage was that he could obtain money at a rate better than on his own security. He could undertake works to a greater extent than otherwise. The railway company had no need to find the money for construction until the line was open and profits were available. There is now no way of knowing how widespread was the use of Lloyd's bonds. J. H. Lloyd thought there were several millions of them in circulation; Samuel Morton Peto, one of the greatest contractors, claimed to have helped the LCDR to liquidate over £1¼ million issued by that company alone.

These various financial devices might have worked but small contractors, thus enabled to expand their work, were tempted to over-reach themselves. Throughout the 1860s there were reports of contractors becoming bankrupt, and it all ended dramatically in May 1866 when Overend, Gurney & Co crashed. It was ironical that this company, with which Thomas Richardson (who had helped to finance the Stockton & Darlington company) had been connected, should now, having changed its character, be instrumental in bringing despair to the railway world. The essential point was that this finance company's funds were locked up in long-term paper, such as railway securities, and now they could not meet the needs of their depositors. The crash was spectacular. Overend, Gurney had been a pillar of the City. The subsequent panic led to a 50 per cent fall in the Bank of England's reserves and bank rate rose to 10 per cent.

The collapse brought down Samuel Morton Peto who was closely associated with the LCD. Even Thomas Brassey is said to have lost £1 million. Only some eighteen months earlier, *The Economist* in its celebrated article on 'the advantages that would accrue from an ownership of the railways by the state' had argued that a firm such as Peto, Brassey & Co could well undertake the management of the railways. Now, in the aftermath of the crisis, railway construction fell away, applications to Parliament for new mileage were low and many lines were abandoned. As in 1857 the high rate of interest at which terminable debentures were renewed (if they could be renewed at all) drastically reduced the amount available for equity dividends, the GWR again being the main sufferer. But other main line companies had over-reached themselves by building extensions and branch lines. There was the inevitable outcry from shareholders and a number of committees of enquiry made reports. One important consequence of the crisis was the realisation that terminable debentures could be inconvenient and the companies rapidly replaced them by issuing debenture stock.

Thus in the three decades from the early 1840s, over 13,000 route miles were built and railway capital rose from £60 million to £530 million. There had been two major periods of construction, in the 1840s and the 1860s, but it is right to concentrate attention on the former. During the 1840s despite financial problems much had been accomplished and out of it emerged the industry's long-term organisation. The creation of a small number of major companies mainly by amalgamation began in the 1840s to be continued in 1854 with the establishment of the North

Eastern Railway and in 1863 of the Great Eastern. However the role played by new companies after 1850 must not be neglected, and their capital requirements introduced a new mode of financing into the story at a time when investors were relatively shy of railways.

Notes to this chapter are on pp 207–8.

CHAPTER 3

OPERATING THE NEW SYSTEM

The railways were successful. Their function was to move people and goods, and this they did in increasing numbers. There was plenty of criticism of the way they did it, but fairly soon railways came to be taken for granted, as the natural form of inland transport. Yet the figures show that the growth was uneven. In the 1840s receipts from passenger trains were greater than from freight. This needs explaining, for much of the argument about the need for railways centred on the requirements of freight traffic —the backwardness of the canals, for example. It can be explained: people flocked to the railways because a new demand was being created, something which for most people was previously unavailable. It was a new 'commodity'. Freight traffic however was not something new, it already flowed in established channels.

> [The railways] provided a better and cheaper service in most cases, or at least compelled existing forms of transport to do so in self defence, and the benefits of this no doubt affected many industries and ultimately led to the establishment of new enterprises; but they did not to any significant extent make possible what had been previously impossible.[1]

In many ways the operating activities of the 1830s and 1840s look chaotic, and one has an impression that not much thought had been given to the question of working the lines. Perhaps promoters had not considered the implications fully, although they by no means ignored their future operating activities. The first engineers were conscious, for example, of the need to relate the permanent way to the power which locomotives then possessed. The companies moreover had to make some sort of estimates of incomes and costs. Three sets of figures were bandied about, all interrelated: capital cost; expected revenue; expected operating

TABLE 7
OPERATING, 1843-70 (UK)

Year	Millions of passengers carried (a)	Million tons of freight carried	Receipts Passenger train £m	Freight train £m	Miscellaneous (rents, tolls, steamboats etc) £m	Total £m	Operating expenses £m	Net revenue £m	Operating ratio (proportion of expenses to receipts) per cent
1843 (b)	23.8	n.a.	3.2	1.4	n.a.	4.6	n.a.	n.a.	n.a.
1845 (b)	33.8	n.a.	4.0	2.2	n.a.	6.2	n.a.	n.a.	n.a.
1850	72.9	n.a.	6.8	6.4	n.a.	13.2	(5.9)	(7.3) (c)	45
1855	118.6	64.7 (d)	10.7	10.8	n.a.	21.5	10.3	11.2	48
1860	163.4	89.9	13.1	14.7	n.a.	27.8	13.2	14.6	47
1865	251.9	114.6	16.6	19.3	n.a.	35.9	17.1	18.8	48
1870	336.5	169.4 (e)	19.3	24.1	1.7	45.1	21.7	21.7 (f)	50 (g)

Source: *Railway Returns*

Notes:
Most of the series do not begin until 1843
(a) Excluding season ticket holders
(b) Year ending 30 June. All other entries: year ending 31 December
(c) Estimate by B. R. Mitchell. *The Coming of the Railway*. Given total receipts the figure for operating expenses has thus been deduced.
(d) 1856
(e) 1871
(f) Excluding £1.7m miscellaneous receipts, thus maintaining consistency with the other years for which no figures are available
(g) The percentage given in the *Railway Returns* is 48, presumably reduced by including £1.7m miscellaneous receipts.

n.a.=not available
Passenger Train receipts include receipts from 'season tickets, carriages, horses, etc., and Post Office Mails'.

cost. The anticipated net revenue would determine the level of return which investors could look forward to. They had to be shown that the particular enterprise was profitable and the figures were a necessary part of the information supplied to Private Bill Committees. Equally evident was the nebulous basis on which these figures were put forward. There was experience, it is true, of civil engineering projects for the capital side. But the companies promoted in the 1830s, including the main lines, relied on the operating statistics of the Liverpool & Manchester, even though that railway had been open for only a short time and its conditions were not likely to be closely paralleled elsewhere.

Trying to assess the traffic potential was much more hazardous. The companies often employed professional traffic-takers, especially as witnesses before parliamentary committees. They could get quite reasonable figures of existing freight traffic flows if there was a canal along the route, owned by an enterprise which published accounts. But existing passenger traffic, normally using the roads, could not so readily be established. The number of vehicles passing points along the road could be counted, and some guess made about the numbers being carried. These figures then had to be increased to allow for the greater traffic expected to arise because of the cheapness, speed and reliability of the proposed line.

Forecasting trends is a chancy business, and the railways probably did the best they could with the limited information available. In addition to the very real problem of assessing future traffic was the fact that there were important changes of policy about the legal basis of railway working. The first Acts establishing railway companies had been based on canal legislation. It was assumed that a railway company was an undertaking which provided the routeway but did not necessarily itself act as a carrier.

It was the avowed purpose in the construction of the railway lines, that they should be open for public use, on the payment of tolls. This was enacted to prevent monopoly, that is, to prevent the railway companies from getting exclusive control over the conveyance of passengers and goods along their respective lines; and even railway proprietors said that they wanted no monopoly: that they were merely toll-takers, and that it was neither their wish nor their interest to undertake the work of a public carrier upon their own lines. It was expected that merchants and others would put their own carriages on the line, and either furnish their own horse or steam-power, or pay the railway company for the use of their power.[2]

With the horse tramways such a method was feasible, but the advent of steam required a different approach. Various practices were adopted. Some passengers arrived with their own carriages to be placed on the train. Some companies did all their own carrying. Others delegated their freight business to the established haulage companies like Pickford's and Chaplin & Horne. The trend of opinion was soon in favour of the railway companies becoming carriers and by the late 1840s and early 1850s most companies had done so. This was a necessary prerequisite to the growth of freight traffic. In the confusion of the different methods of operating there had been too many unresolved problems, as we shall see; these undoubtedly hindered the development of that side of railway working.

The immediate impact of the railways of the 1830s was on passenger travel. The opening of a railway with lower fares, more frequent services, faster speeds and—despite the mass of evidence about travelling conditions—greater comfort than stage coaches, led to a rapid transfer of custom from the roads. But as well as taking over the existing traffic the railways increased the total amount of travelling. The *Annual Register* of 1832 expressed a commonly felt emotion of awe and excitement when it reported on the early experience of the Liverpool & Manchester Railway. Before the opening of the line the maximum capacity of the road vehicles was 688 persons per day. The railway carried an average of 1,070. The fares had been 10s (50p) inside and 5s (25p) outside; the railways charged 5s and 3s 6d ($17\frac{1}{2}$p) respectively. The time by coach was four hours, whereas the railway journey took one and three-quarter hours.

All the coaches but one have ceased running, and that chiefly for the conveyance of parcels. The mails all travel by railway, at a saving to government of two-thirds of the expense. The railway coaches are more commodious than others. The travelling is cheaper, safer and easier.

Later, Lardner wrote that 'the brilliant and unexpected results of the business in passenger traffic have not unnaturally dazzled the public, and engrossed the attention of proprietors, directors and managers.'³ His views need qualifying. Firstly the statistics of passenger receipts include revenue from carrying mails and other goods, and really refer to the income of the passenger department. Some downward adjustment is therefore necessary. Secondly the early companies only reluctantly accepted the need to provide reasonable facilities for their customers. There were un-lit carriages, and third-class passengers might find their open trucks only available when attached to goods trains. Nor were the arrangements for the interchange of traffic at points where the lines of different companies met well organised. There was not much integration of services in the sense of convenient train connections. In the early 1840s the Board of Trade put pressure on the companies to improve their coaching stock and the Regula-tion of Railways Act of 1844 compelled them to provide cheap fares—one 'Parliamentary' train to travel the length of the line, each way, stopping at every station, charging one penny per mile. It was, the companies soon found, the lower-fare-paying passengers whose numbers increased so rapidly.

The long-distance road-passenger industry disappeared quite quickly once the railways were established, although short-dis-tance services increased to supply feeder services. When one considers the controversies on the 1920s and 1930s it is an interesting irony that one factor in the competition between the railways and the roads was the higher level of taxes and other costs on road transport. A stage coach in regular use would have to pay turnpike tolls; a £5 licence duty; a tax of £1 5s each on the coachman and guard; a duty based on the carrying capacity of the vehicle (not on the numbers actually carried; and a tax on horses. There was also payable a mileage duty on the number of miles travelled. In the late 1830s some reductions were made but there remained an undoubted inequality of treatment. The railways had only to pay a passenger duty, at first one halfpenny per mile for every four passengers. This was changed in 1842 to 5 per cent of the gross receipts from passengers. (In both cases the charge was on the numbers carried, not on carrying capacity.)

Nevertheless such disparities were not really a major factor in the success of the railways. In the late 1830s the fares on passenger coaches rose. 'This general increase occurred when proprietors realised that in view of the development of the railways, they had little time in which to make further profits, after which they would have to dispose of their premises, horses and vehicles for the best price, which was likely to be a low one.[4] The advantages of the railway were obvious, at least as far as passengers were concerned.

With freight it was different. In the early 1840s goods accounted for only about 35 per cent of total railway receipts. But it would be wrong to infer from this that the railway companies neglected this kind of traffic. To put the position in perspective one has to make clear that the overwhelming importance of passenger receipts refers to the initial opening of most of the main lines (some of the individual companies, of course, were heavily dependent on freight, especially coal). It was in the 1840s that things changed. Between 1843 and 1852 (in which year freight receipts surpassed those from passengers) the increase of passenger receipts was about 140 per cent; from £3.2 million to £7.7 million; for freight it was about 470 per cent from £1.4 million to £7.9 million.

The companies certainly made efforts to attract this kind of custom. In 1845 the LSWR reduced its freight charges and the tonnage carried in the second half of the year rose by 40 per cent above the quantity carried in the comparable period of 1844. But receipts rose by only 4 per cent.[5] The low price elasticity of demand for railway freight services is to be found in a number of factors peculiar to the 1830s and 1840s.

The railways had to break into and capture existing traffic flows rather than cater for and promote a new demand. At first their attempts to compete with canals were not very successful. The railways had the advantage of speed and their charges were lower. Yet the canals were able to retaliate and retain traffic by lowering their charges, for, as the Select Committee on Railways of 1844 suggested: 'the saving of time [on the railways] does not give such a decided superiority over the old modes of conveyance'. And the railways stirred the canals from their lethargy. Indeed, the possibility of railways being built had caused some canal companies to improve their equipment and services. The Grand Junction Canal (operating between the Midlands and London) introduced a number of changes between 1828 and 1838, ie during the decade before the opening of the London & Birmingham Railway. It rationalised its complicated system of tolls, reduced certain rates, experimented with steam-powered vessels, and extended reservoirs and doubled a flight of locks in order to reduce congestion. Once the railway was opened competition was severe, and lasted for two decades until an agreement was reached between the two enterprises.

Average receipts per ton fell partly because freight was conveyed over shorter distances, but more especially because rates were reduced. Thus total income and dividends fell; but there is no evidence here of the kind of collapse experienced by the road passenger industry. Twenty years of competitive rate-cutting ended in 1857 when agreement was reached with the GWR and the LNWR. Apart from an increase in 1859 the charges remained steady for the next thirty years.[6] Rates agreements of this kind were one method of reducing competition between canals and railways. Another, especially in the 1840s, was the purchase by railways of canal undertakings.

TABLE 8

GRAND JUNCTION CANAL TRAFFIC AND DIVIDENDS 1838-58

	1838	1858
Toll receipts	£152,657	£67,634
Tonnage carried	948,481	1,142,450
Average receipts per ton	3.2s	0.93s
Dividend	10%	3½%

Freight traffic also developed slowly because of the nature of that traffic, and the individualistic attitude of the separate railway companies. With passengers the problems of traffic management were not difficult and could be learned quickly. There was a limited number of passenger classes, the passengers presented themselves at stations and a regular time-table of services could be provided. The organisation of freight traffic, however, required specialised knowledge and different techniques. It was necessary to be acquainted with the trades in the district and with their traffic needs—the pattern of arrival of goods at depots and stations and their diverse destinations. The established undertakings had this kind of experience and had built up a network of agencies and offices. Thus:

Pickfords offered a fairly comprehensive distribution service by land and water, chiefly between London and Lancashire; they employed a large staff who were well versed in the complexities of through and cross-country traffic, and in the collection and delivery, invoicing, loading and despatching of all forms of merchandise.[7]

The early railway companies had neither this expertise nor the network of contacts, and they were much too autonomous to appreciate the necessity for working with each other in order to provide through services. Amalgamation of companies in the 1840s provided one answer when the organisation of services came under one administration. But when wagons and trains travelled over 'foreign' lines numerous problems emerged such as the detention of wagons and the variety of classifications of goods and rates. There was a mass of other items likely to cause conflict between companies.

> When goods travelled over the lines of more than one company should the terminal charges, i.e. the costs incidental to loading and unloading the goods, be included in the total receipts to be divided between the companies, or should they be deducted before the remainder of the receipts was divided? Should sheets and ropes covering goods waggons be 'sent through' and, if so, what should be the basis of compensation to the company that owned them? How could the different companies' ropes be identified? How should compensation be paid for goods damaged in transit? What arrangements should be made for payment for the repair of damaged waggons?[8]

To settle such questions the Railway Clearing House was established in 1842. Its initial function was to settle accounts between companies on the model of bank clearing but its work expanded into other fields. From 1847 railway goods managers' conferences were held under its auspices which very quickly ironed out many of these problems including a classification of goods. Agreement was reached on many items; the method of dividing receipts (based on mileage); the deduction of terminal expenses before the division of receipts; a demurrage charge on sheets and ropes; arrangements for settling claims for loss and damages. But it could not be reached in all cases, notably that of coal. One major reason was that the private owners of coal wagons proved to be too independent.

> The consequence of the absence of Clearing House controls and the diversification of railway waggon ownership were the multiplication of coal traffic agreements negotiated on a company to

company basis. With the inevitable variations of charges thus negotiated it proved more difficult to fix freight rates for the carriage of coal which were competitive with the freights charged for coastwise traffic.[9]

The operating figures from the early 1840s to 1870 provide the outline of the industry's activities. The outstanding feature was the virtually continuous growth in traffic and gross receipts. Only in one year, in 1858, did receipts fall below the level of the previous year. But the growth rate was by no means constant. In the 1840s it was very high, naturally enough for a new industry, followed by a general fall in the rate. During the period the receipts from passengers and freight moved differently. Both rose, but during the 1840s freight receipts rose very fast indeed and in 1852 overtook passenger receipts. By the mid-1850s the proportions had reached 55:45. This relationship subsequently remained more or less constant. (In Ireland, however, receipts from passenger trains were always greater than from freight trains.)

Traffic continued to rise because of the growth of the economy; the expansion of the railway system; the capture of traffic from the remaining canals; and the decline in railway charges. The railways were becoming more efficient in terms of unit costs, as they brought their capital equipment into full use. Their greater efficiency did not arise from technical change. There were no major technical innovations between the 1840s and the late 1860s, when steel rails began to be introduced, although the change from coke to coal in the 1850s did result in considerable economies in fuel used per train-mile.[10]

At first sight is may seem odd that rates should have been reduced to match the fall in costs, especially as there was a substantial decline in competition between the companies. There were various arrangements by which the participating companies pooled receipts, and shared them out in an agreed way. There were rates conferences by which charges were agreed and rates wars avoided. Rates fell, partly because, as we shall see, there was some competition beween the railways and other forms of transport; and partly because the companies pursued a variety of objectives including the obvious one of attracting traffic, sometimes irrespective of cost considerations.

The industry expanded rapidly but it was not particularly

profitable. On average net profits were in the region of 4–4½ per cent of paid-up capital. This comparatively low margin meant that any increases in operating costs or reductions in revenue could cause serious difficulties, especially in view of the industry's highly-geared capital ratios. The large proportion of stock which attracted prior payments out of profits meant that high rates of interest were disastrous.

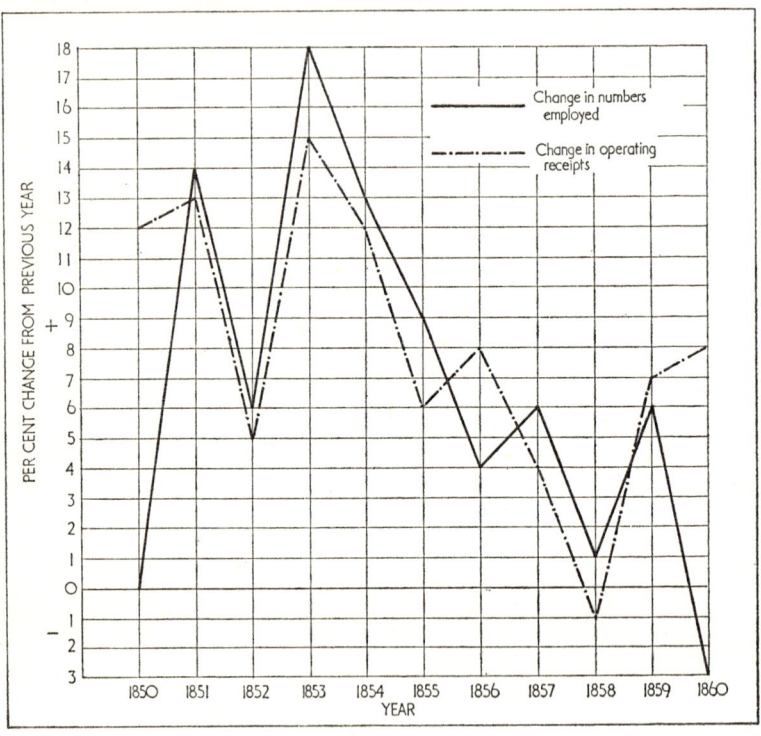

1 Railway employment and operating receipts, 1849–60

In times of difficulty, when profits were low, the possibility of making economies was not great. They could not economise on fuel except by cutting services; the price of coal was normally outside their control. They might have economised on repairs and renewals but the available evidence suggests that, in general, this expenditure usually moved upwards and did not fluctuate. Hawke explains this by the requirements of safety which limited the degree to which maintenance and replacement could be postponed. In addition he singles out the high status of the professional engineers employed by the companies. Their prestige and the mystery of their technical expertise ensured that their ideas held sway.

The main input in which cuts could be made was labour. Changes could be made in wages or in conditions. More normally it was by varying the numbers employed. The available figures of railway employment (annual for 1847-60 and occasional thereafter), while showing a general upward trend, do reveal a markedly close relationship with revenue. The railways' labour policy was presumably to treat labour as the major variable, recruiting or not and even dismissing according to the demands of traffic as measured by receipts. Labour was really the only factor over which the companies had much control. (See Table 9 below, and Graph I, p 64.)

TABLE 9

RAILWAY EMPLOYMENT AND OPERATING RECEIPTS 1849-60 (UK)

Year	Number employed 000s	Per cent change over previous year	Operating receipts £m	Per cent change over previous year
1849	56	—	11.8	—
1850	56	0	13.2	12
1851	64	14	14.9	13
1852	68	6	15.7	5
1853	80	18	18.0	15
1854	90	13	20.2	12
1855	98	9	21.5	6
1856	102	4	23.2	8
1857	110	6	24.2	4
1858	109	1	24.0	−1
1859	116	6	25.7	7
1860	112	−3	27.8	8

Source : *Railway Returns*
See also, Hawke, *Railways and Economic Growth*, chapter 10 for a fuller discussion.

Note : The employment figures relate to one day in each year.
Receipts are for the twelve months ending 31 December.

Organisation

The railways had begun as small units but the rapid expansion of the system, together with the amalgamation of companies soon produced large-scale enterprises. In the late 1840s the LNWR employed 10,000 people and the company's capital was of the order of £20 million. Outside of government departments and the armed forces the deployment of such large numbers of people and financial assets was unknown.

E

The peculiar managerial and organisation problems of the railways—not unique to the early period—have been well described by J. T. Dunlop:

> . . . the train operating divisions use small crews working together and in movement far from close and immediate supervision; complex and expensive equipment is utilised with a high ratio of capital to worker; the technology has produced steadily increasing speeds and longer trains; a very high degree of responsibility (and considerable skill) is required of the major operating positions; the costs of accidents can be consequential; the hours of operation for equipment may be around the clock, and they do not conform to normal factory schedules, although repair shops and many clerical operations conform to conventional work-weeks; the transportation services are regarded as vital to many other industries and to the community generally; there is a high degree of continuity of operations in many departments, and the public-utility status of the railroads requires the maintenance of published service; there is intimate contact with the public in the train service and in the selling of tickets and at corresponding points with freight customers.[11]

The early railway managers soon had to come to terms with this new kind of organisation, especially with the problems of control of activities over a wide geographical area. This applied not only to the unit of 'production'—the train—but also to the numerous points at which money was received. How to avoid misappropriation was a constant matter for discussion.

Various answers were given to these questions. The early boards had little knowledge or experience and tended to maintain centralised control, dealing with all manner of minor matters. Functional committees were soon established, normally serviced by a senior official who was in charge of a department. Very early on—although the companies varied in their practice—one officer, usually the general manager, was appointed with overall responsibility.

As the work became more complex, delegation had to be introduced. In general British railway companies adopted a departmental organisation, usefully summarised by M. R. Bonavia.

> The departmental system meant that there was a continuous chain of responsibility from the local official to the heads of

departments. Each officer was only responsible to his departmental superiors, and thus in the event of a dispute co-ordination between departments could only be enforced by headquarters, and ultimately by the one non-departmental official, the General Manager.[12]

There was not a divisional organisation in which authority for all aspects of railway operating was delegated to one official. This kind of organisation necessarily implies centralisation of decision-making and cannot but have added to the reputation of the railways as being slow and bedevilled by red tape.

The title did not always mean very much. In one important company the general manager did not perform these co-ordinating functions. The GWR's general manager (the title was first introduced in 1863) was essentially a traffic manager, and the various chief officers had direct access to the board. The general manager had no authority over them and no way of supervising their proposals. It was not until 1920, under Felix Pole, that changes were made.[13]

A major initial problem facing the companies was to find suitable senior staff. It was not too difficult to find some with the relevant financial and administrative experience from commerce. Three important early secretaries were Henry Booth of the Liverpool & Manchester; Richard Creed of the London & Birmingham; and C. A. Saunders of the Great Western. Their transfer to the railways was a straightforward operation. So was that of officers from the armed services, especially from the navy which was being run-down in the 1830s. A number of surplus captains found employment with the new railways (but the best-known of all, Capt Mark Huish, had been in the East India Company's employ). Their experience of handling men and of secretarial and financial matters was of considerable use to the railways.

But none of these had experience of traffic operation. The specialist knowledge required could only be obtained from the road coaching industry. Mr Turnbull has explained how that industry was raided by the railways. One of the Liverpool & Manchester's two chief agents came from Pickford's at double the salary. Perhaps the greatest capture was by the London & Birmingham who secured the services of Joseph Baxendale, a co-partner in Pickford's. He quickly moved from the management

of the railway's carrying department to become general superintendent, responsible for 'the out-of-door arrangements and
basic running of the railway'.

These staff difficulties were peculiar to the early years. Within
a fairly short period the companies were able to draw upon their
own resources and to appoint men who had grown up within the
system, often transferring to other companies. It does not follow
that this pattern was desirable. The railways, it might be argued,
suffered from in-breeding and such movement as occurred was
from the railways to other industries rather than inwards. It is
important that such limited appraisals as there have been of
managerial efficiency at this period rate it rather low. The major
emphasis of railway management was on the organisation of
large bodies of men and the administration of extensive financial
assets. One notes the continuing history of financial defalcations;
the need for Parliament to legislate to improve accounting
methods (eg by the Regulation of Railways Act of 1868); and
the general lack of statistical information on which managerial
decisions could be made. This generalisation needs qualification;
when Mark Huish was general manager of the LNWR he produced
most elaborate reports for his board which combined detailed
statistical breakdowns with rational examination of the facts.[14]

Nevertheless, one looks in vain for examples of forward planning or for the use of accounts as aids to management decisions,
rather than as reports of past activities.

Pricing Policy[15]

The railway companies were not free agents in their rate-
setting. Their individual Acts laid down maximum charges and
when the companies became carriers they found a body of
existing common law enjoining them to act as common carriers,
ie to carry for anyone offering goods, to charge reasonably, to
carry with care and to bear full liability. The basis of the
law was the protection of the consumer; it was in no sense an
attempt to prescribe some optimum policy in economic terms.
However, in the Acts goods were divided into classes and the
maxima were based on their nature and value. This combined
two types of criteria; charging according to cost of carriage and
to value of the goods.

Under the Railway Clauses Consolidation Act of 1845 rates were to be charged equally under like circumstances. Since circumstances were seldom alike this clause was non-operative, but the purpose behind it—to prevent discrimination by the companies—was made clearer in a clause in the Railway & Canal Traffic Act of 1854, which prohibited the companies from charging any rates in which there was 'undue preference'.

The railways laboured under other obligations. They had to carry mail (at rates to be mutually agreed or to be settled by arbitration); they had to carry military and police forces at fixed rates; they had to run a Parliamentary train at 1d a mile; and some companies had to provide cheap fares for workmen. These duties were placed on the companies for a variety of reasons. No doubt it was right and proper that the companies should compensate for the social costs incurred when working class housing was destroyed, by providing cheap fares. But it is questionable whether they should have been the agencies for social policies, as redistributors of the national income.

However, the legal constraints were not too restrictive. Companies could change their rates, provided they were below the maxima, without needing the approval of a tribunal or a government department. And they could adopt discriminatory pricing policies provided there was no undue preference. A unique exception was in South Wales, where the Taff Vale and Rhymney companies had to charge equal ton-mile rates. These companies could not introduce discriminatory charges, and goods, largely coal, were carried at a fixed rate per ton-mile.

The companies, these exceptions apart, followed their own policies; in practice they tended to be similar, and by the early 1850s a general pattern had been established. The following examples show the way the railway world was developing.

The Stockton & Darlington began in 1825 with fixed rates per ton-mile for each class of goods traffic. Very quickly the company charged a lower rate for coal intended for export. This probably unprofitable practice was justified on the ground that it would stimulate the long-term development of the traffic. Later, rates on coal sent to certain depots were reduced because of competition from other transport undertakings. In 1846 the board of the LNWR was recommended to insert in its amalgamation Bill a proposal for lower maximum charges 'in order to meet the expectations of the Public that some economy in rates and charges should be experienced when Goods were conveyed over long distances'. It was recommended that when the distance exceeded 60 miles there should be a reduction in the ton-mileage rate.[16]

Similar considerations applied to passenger traffic. In 1850 a long report was presented to the Road and Traffic Committee of the LNWR. It was a detailed attempt to explore the reasons for the decline in passenger traffic receipts and included this statement:

That Railway experience affords as yet no satisfactory test, by which, in all cases, it can be positively determined by what means, and at what rates of charge, the largest amount of net Revenue from Passengers is to be obtained; that if, in some instances, a comparatively high charge has led to an increase of receipts, the same result has, in other instances, followed a greatly reduced scale of fares; and the inference from such facts appears to be conclusive, that the adoption of one uniform rate throughout, without reference to circumstances, cannot be the successful mode of meeting the requirements, habits and means of the population of every district comprised within the limits of a line of such extent, varied character and relations, as that of the London and North Western Company.[17]

Thus passenger fares had to be adjusted according to circumstances, one of which might be the desire to encourage people to live along the line and so use a railway. This was the purpose of extraordinary fare concessions which some London lines proposed in the 1850s.

The net result of all this was that by the 1860s the rate structure was exceedingly complex. The Royal Commission on Railways (1865-7) was told of the millions of local rates, for both passengers and goods on the major lines. It is impossible to explain the rationale of all of them—some may have been conventional, for example, and perhaps no one thought of justifying them. But it is possible, as Hawke has demonstrated, to disentangle the various motives the companies had in mind, and the various objectives they were pursuing.

The railway companies, despite the various duties placed upon them by the state, were commercial undertakings, aiming to make a profit; their Acts formally authorised them to distribute any surplus. But this was by no means their main objective, and it is unrealistic to speak of their purpose being to maximise profits. For example, companies wanted to encourage the economic development of the region they served which meant making rate reductions for those enterprises located at some distance from their markets. The purpose was to enable them to compete on equal terms with those undertakings nearer the market. Thus tinplates from various parts of South Wales were carried to Liverpool at the same rate despite the fact that the distance varied from 160 to 206 miles. James Allport, general manager of the Midland, told the Royal Commission: 'I think it is the duty of managers of railways to develop the resources of their districts to the utmost possible extent', and this could be done, as others explained to the Commission, by lower rates, either to enable the goods they carried to compete with those of other districts, or for the raw materials imported into their own areas. These 'regional policies' were self-imposed. Others were introduced and made essential by the existence of competition. Where two railways served the same points the shorter route naturally determined the rate; and the railways' monopoly power was limited by the possibility of sea transport and even by local horse transport.

Although the companies measured their policies against the yardstick of profit, it is evident that while they could easily find out their gross revenues, their knowledge of costs was primitive. As early as the 1820s Thomas Storey of the Stockton & Darlington kept records of the cost of locomotive power, but his aim was to compare the cost of locomotives and stationary engines. Such figures as there were seem to have been kept irregularly. Mark Huish, general manager of the LNWR, told his board in a report in 1855 that it was impossible to trace the comparative profits of passengers and goods on the various lines now amalgamated into the company. 'Occasional estimates were made,' he wrote, and added:

It is not really a matter of great moment whether one description can be worked at a cheaper rate per centage than another. It may evidently be more for the benefit of a Railway to have a large traffic worked at even 70 or 80 per cent, than a very restricted one costing only 30 or 40 per cent on the receipt. The real question is, of course, how the largest aggregate balance of profit can be obtained.[18]

The figures he gave, from the Liverpool & Manchester, the London & Birmingham and the LNWR were passenger and goods receipts per mile, compared with the expenses per mile of locomotive power.

The companies, that is to say, could well have a rough notion of their working costs; but one sees no evidence of understanding the problem of allocating fixed and joint costs. In any case, in the determination of pricing policy it was other factors, such as competition and the desire to encourage regional trade, that had a major importance.

There was certainly competition between the companies. It happened in construction, as we have seen, and it was present in operating. It went on, in one way or another, until the compulsory merging of the 1920s and even beyond that to some extent. Its existence is well documented in that railway literature which consists largely of the relations between companies, of how one company outdid another.

Yet parallel to these stories is the whole series of attempts to reduce competition. Amalgamation was one way; the Clearing House was another; a third was pooling arrangements; and there were agreements on rates themselves. As might be expected, attempts to reduce competition were in part a reaction to bad times. In the late 1840s and early 1850s when share prices had fallen and dividends were low, as well as searching for scapegoats, the companies sought remedies. One method of reducing competition was the pooling of receipts. In essence a pooling agreement was a system whereby the total receipts were divided among the companies over whose lines the relevant traffic was carried. The Octuple Agreement of 1851 concerned the eight companies involved in the main line traffic between England and Scotland. The receipts were equally divided between the western route and the eastern. Each of the companies in each route was to obtain a proportion of receipts divided on the basis of the distance tables prepared by the Railway Clearing House. Part of the arrangement was that rates and fares between the same points were to be the same, whatever the route that passengers or goods travelled.

Another method rested on the fixing of rates rather than the division of receipts. There were individual arrangements between companies, and subsequently rates conferences were held whose function was to fix the rates for the areas they covered. They were voluntary but were long-lived and successful in their objectives. A parliamentary inquiry in 1872 concluded that 'there is now no active competition between different railways in the matter of rates and fares'. Such competition as there was was in non-monetary matters, in facilities and accommodation. It is this kind of competition in the 1860s that helps to account, as Kellett has shown, for the massive promotion of terminal stations in major cities. You could not compete by price; you competed by providing better services.

The railways were the product of private enterprise yet there is a twentieth-century ring about their early years. Within the industry, price competition was reduced, and at the same time the companies got used to the idea of some kind of government intervention, whether over safety or over charges. At the same time the companies' freedom of action was restricted by the limited freedom of action they had over the factors of production they required. With so many prior commitments profit margins were narrow and sudden changes in costs and revenues—and the industry certainly experienced these—could result in severe fluctuations in the net receipts position. Fortunately for the industry, in this period operating expenses were normally below 50 per cent of total receipts; it was when this figure went higher, later in the century, that the situation became serious.

Notes to this chapter are on pp 208–9.

CHAPTER 4

CREATING A LABOUR FORCE

It was the scale of railway activity that was so impressive. There was the vastness of the civil engineering works; there was the massive accumulation of capital. The industry was highly capital intensive: the ratio of capital to labour up to the 1860s was of the order of £3,500-£4,000 to every man employed. Yet at the same time the railways employed large numbers of men. In 1847 (the first year for which comprehensive figures are available) the permanent staff comprised 47,000 men; by 1860 the number had risen to 112,000; and in 1873 the total was 275,000. Despite this rapid growth the companies seem to have found it surprisingly easy to get staff in such numbers. No doubt some who had been employed as navvies stayed on in the railway service. Some clerical and administrative staff had been required during the constructional phase and these would have remained with the companies. Railway police, it seems, were often recruited from the armed services.[1]

One recruit, John Pearman, came 'from a line of small farmers in South Oxfordshire', and he began work in his thirteenth year (he was born in 1819) as a sawyer. In 1840 he thought it:

> . . . time to give up such hard work, which brought little more than a living to myself, but much for my employers. The railway started,* and I was employed as a guard, and remained at it for two years; but not liking London, I was far from being settled, although we made good wages and were not worked too hard. But I felt I should like to travel and see other countries.
>
> Well one day I had a tiff with the superintendent, and my temper being very hasty, we nearly got to blows. So I made up my mind to be a soldier.[2]

* The Great Western Railway. Brunel's great line extended at this time only as far as Swindon.

Pearman was only one of thousands of railwaymen and may

74

not have been at all representative. However, his rural background, the apparent lack of training for the job and the rapidity of his exit from the railway world are all characteristic of the period. The main source of railway labour was the comparatively unskilled market, notably agriculture and general labouring. There was no training and the turnover of labour was quite high. Moreover, this labour, while available in quantity, was unused to the discipline of industry, and not at all used to trade unionism or to the possibility of influencing collectively the terms and conditions of work.

In the period 1830 to 1870 there were no more than ten strikes; but in addition some thirty petitions and memorials were sent by railwaymen to the boards of their companies.[3] Thus in four decades railwaymen are known to have attempted only on about fifty occasions to make some collective impact on their employers. Most of these efforts failed and it was not until the 1860s that any major success was achieved when enginemen had their hours reduced to ten a day. In general railway managements had little need to concern themselves with interruptions of operation caused by labour disputes. There were to all intents and purposes no trade unions and the companies' personnel policies could be decided unilaterally, without the necessity of consulting or bargaining with their employees.

Management worked on the assumption that it was their right to determine terms and conditions of employment. Recruitment and dismissal, promotion, wage determination, discipline were all their prerogatives. It was taken for granted that collective action by employees was unacceptable. Any man dissatisfied with his conditions should make his own representation to the management. But discipline was military in quality and the fear of dismissal undoubtedly inhibited many from pursuing this course of action. Moreover, the companies had behind them the force of law.

The Select Committee on Communication by railway reported in 1839 in these terms:

> It is essential to the safety of the Public and to the maintenance of regular intercourse by Railroads that the Companies should have a more perfect control over their servants . . . where the lives of many persons depend on the good conduct and ready obedience of subordinate officers, and where the smallest irregu-

larity may be attended with fatal consequences, a system of exact discipline should be encouraged, and powers should be given to the directors for the purpose of upholding their authority.

This recommendation was acted upon in the following year. Individual railway company Acts had already included clauses giving them power to impose fines on their employees, eg for drunkenness. The Regulation of Railways Act of 1840 was a general Act, applying to all railway companies, and its provisions were more severe. As amended in 1842, the relevant clause stated that any employee of a railway company who was found drunk 'while so employed upon the said railway' or 'who shall commit any offence against any of the bye-laws, rules, or regulations of the said company, or who shall wilfully, maliciously, or negligently, do or omit to do any act whereby the life and limb of any person passing along or being upon such railway or the works thereof respectively shall be or might be injured or endangered, or whereby the passage of any of the engines, carriages or trains shall be or might be obstructed or impeded' could be charged before a Justice of the Peace, the maximum penalty being two months hard labour or a £10 fine.

A major motive of the state was safety in operation: the 1840 Act had established the Railway Department of the Board of Trade with certain safety duties which imposed restrictions on the railway management's freedom of action. The law similarly intervened to regulate the actions of railway staff. In any case there was little that was unique or unusual in this Act; it was very much in line with the general body of labour law of the period. Perhaps the phrase 'whereby the passage of any of the engines . . . might be obstructed or impeded' was unusual, because it went beyond the normal references to industrial indiscipline to include the possible legal prohibitions of strikes or other collective action (presumably refusing to drive a train could be interpreted as impeding the passage of a train).[4]

The needs of safety, though, could work in favour of the staff. In the early 1840s, when many companies were trying to reduce costs, the North Midland Railway dismissed some footplate staff and reduced the wages of the remainder.[5] They resigned and new crews were taken on. After an accident in 1843 the Railway Department investigated and 'told the company it should not require the men to drive 146 miles a day, seven days a week, with the exception of alternate Sundays'. It also referred to 'the inexpediency of sudden and sweeping reductions affecting the Class of Servants upon whose skill and good conduct the safety of the Passengers depends'. The board's reply illuminatingly summarises some of the ideas on which its policies were based. The men 'refused to submit to a reasonable and proper reduction and left [the directors] no alternative but to take the course they adopted, or to make the Engine Drivers masters of the Line, thus compromising the safety of the Public by the absence of discipline and subordination.'

The North Midland board further sent the Railway Department a table of hours worked 'from which it will appear that the Statement in your Letter must be taken with some restrictions'. But added 'The Directors however being desirous of meeting the views of the Lords of the Privy Council for Trade will take immediate steps for allowing additional intervals for rest to the Engine Men driving Passenger Trains'.

In general the Board of Trade's continuing inquiries into accidents and the action taken to avoid their repetition, while primarily undertaken for the safety of the public, necessarily had the effect of improving railwaymen's working conditions, if the changes which were made rendered their work less dangerous. But that is a different matter from a direct interposition by the state between employees and employers and this North Midland example is notable for its uniqueness. There was for the railways no equivalent of the Factory Acts.

The railway boards had pretty complete control over their employees internally, but there was one major constraint, the situation in the labour market. In the early years, as railway employment grew rapidly both in this country and overseas, it was possible for those with some specific skills such as footplate staff to find alternative jobs fairly easily. There was an acute shortage of men experienced in operating locomotives in the early 1840s, when many lines were being opened. Despite a great deal of talk about companies not recruiting men dismissed by other companies, the shortage prevented this system working. Thus, to revert to the North Midland example of 1842-3: the report into the accident of 1842 noted that 'of 18 men who had replaced those who had resigned, the company had discharged 10 "after a few days trial, on account of incompetence or misconduct, after having in several cases occasioned accidents. So far from having produced unexceptionable characters, at least six of the new men were discharged servants from other companies".' [6]

But in general the railway labour market was not normally so tight since there was usually no shortage of recruits from agriculture. There was a high labour turnover, companies were not afraid to dismiss men; and it might be argued that conflict on the railways in this period took the form of individual action. Those employees who were acutely dissatisfied with their working conditions did not try to change them; rather they left their employment for something more suitable. The most interesting question for discussion is why the industry's labour force was so peaceful. Not only were there so few attempts at collective action; there were very few attempts to create trade unions. Some of the conditions for trade unionism certainly existed. The enterprises for which they worked were large and bureaucratic; the quantity of capital per employee was high and the divorce between capital and labour was complete since no railwayman could ever hope to become his own master.

Recent research into twentieth-century strike statistics has shown that railwaymen in most countries are not particularly strike-prone. The reasons are found in the nature of the work and in the nature of railwaymen's communities. They are in general not isolated as are strike-prone miners and dockers.[7] But valuable as are such general statements they do not satisfy the historian who has to explain the peculiar circumstances of particular historical periods.

Thus the absence of trade unions in the early railway age may be accounted for in many ways. One is that in that period unskilled labour was not normally organised in unions; and the bulk of railway labour was unskilled. The skilled men, the footplate crews, were in general well looked after by the companies and had little in common with other railways employees. Indeed it is here—in the attitudes of the companies—that one most usefully finds convincing explanations for the lack of unions and for the absence of collective bargaining.

Conditions varied from company to company and from time to time but it is possible to sketch a generalised picture of the companies' labour policies. They can be summarised as discipline, grading, loyalty and paternalism. The first two were basically repressive, but the second two can be described as being more positive ways of regulating labour.

Discipline, it can be said straight away, was strict. The basis of it was the judicial process whereby railwaymen charged with offences within industry could be arraigned before a JP. There is plenty of evidence that the companies did not hesitate to use the Acts and that railwaymen were charged and punished especially of course if their negligence was said to have contributed to an accident.

> In general, the wide powers of legal punishment, including as they did any breach of railway regulations, not only enhanced the authority of such regulations but also diminished the likelihood of any objection to the companies' punishments which, however heavy, were at least less severe than the legal ones.[8]

Fining, for example, was normal and continued right up to the end of the century. Drivers could be fined for unpunctuality and for exceeding the speed limit. Other breaches of regulations, including absence from duty; insubordination; misconduct, asleep on duty, applied to all staff and were quite normally subject to steep fines. In the early 1840s, on the GWR the average fine for 'breach of regulation' was 33s (£1.65) for drunkenness £1, for absence 12s (60p) and for theft 10s (50p). At that date the wages of porters was less than £1 per week, and the highest paid drivers were getting 7s 6d (37½p) per day.

A second method of maintaining discipline was by the threat of dismissal. In the early 1840s about 11 per cent of the GWR staff were dismissed in a period of twelve months; about 12 per cent of that of the LBSC in 18 months. The major reasons were absence from duty (often only for an hour or two) and drunkenness.

Part of the explanation for the severity of the discipline was therefore the familiar problem of transforming men, often from agriculture, into industrial workers, changing their rhythms, their pace of work and their attitudes to the needs of a mechanised environment. On the railways the element of danger, when breaches of the rules might cause accidents and fatalities to the public, added to the insistence of the management in inculcating a proper attitude to the rules. This view is supported by the fact that dismissals for breaches of the rules (as a proportion of the labour force) tended in time, to fall presumably because the railway labour force became more acclimatised to industrial requirements.

Discipline was further facilitated by the existence of grades of employment. The numerous grades reflected the nature of the work. In our context the important thing was the development of sectionalism, the tendency of men in a particular occupation to set themselves apart from others. The companies made use of this. The locomotive superintendent of the LSWR agreed with a question put to him at a select committee of 1858 that 'there is no love lost between the engine drivers and the signalmen'. And he continued: 'I think it would be a pity that there should be any; it would not be so good.' In other words, the signalmen were expected to 'supervise' the drivers by reporting any breaches of the rules. Such a policy can be regarded as a Machiavellian divide and rule approach. No doubt it was. From the management's point of view it can be argued that some form of supervision of staff who could not possibly be under constant surveillance was necessary. Signalmen were stationed along the line and could see what the management could not.

The third string to the railway companies' personnel policies was a sense of loyalty, which was very closely associated with the fourth, paternalism. For much of the period, appointments to all positions in the company were in the gift of directors. 'Men thus favoured naturally felt under a more direct obligation than did workmen in other occupations. Many men must have felt that to demand higher wages or better conditions in such circumstances was like biting the hand that fed them.'[9] Bonuses or increments of pay depended on good behaviour. Loyalty was thus used by the companies as a method of regulating their staff. But, despite the heavy labour turnover of the early years, the loyalty was there to be used. In what other trade union history would one find sympathetic and affectionate accounts of the machines the men worked with, such as Norman McKillop provides in his history of ASLEF? 'Alienation' is not a word that quickly springs to mind. Like the armed forces the railways combined strict discipline with feelings of pride and loyalty.

The companies did provide benefits for their staff, even though this paternalism may legitimately be regarded as another way of controlling them. The companies established friendly societies

which provided benefits for sickness and accidents and sometimes pensions on retirement. Schools were established in railway
towns, and others, used by railwaymen's children, were financially
supported by the companies. A circular of 1847, issued by the
LNWR, expresses the motives behind this policy:

> The Directors consider the proper education of young persons
> a matter of such vital importance that they cannot but look with
> distrust at the man whose negligence condemns a child to
> ignorance. They regard the performance of this duty as an ad-
> ditional proof of his trustworthiness and good character.[10]

Similarly the encouragement of facilities for religious worship—
some churches were built, a few more were given grants—may be
regarded as, in this context, a desire to obtain a body of well-
behaved employees.

Some of these policies of labour control were facilitated by the
growth of railway towns. At a place like Crewe, where virtually all
employment was dependent on one company, the regulation of
employees' lives was extensive.

It followed from all of this that trade unionism was almost
entirely absent from the railways in this period although conditions
were theoretically right for it. The most important reason for its
absence was very obviously the attitude of the companies, the
right to run their own business. Trade unions, which necessarily
have the objective of reducing that unilateral right, had no place
at all. A circular issued by the LBSCR in 1852 illustrates this:

> The directors are in principle opposed to 'combination' of any
> description for the purpose of interfering with the natural course
> of trade. They think that masters and men should be left in
> every establishment to settle their own terms and arrange their
> own differences without foreign interference or dictation.[11]

These various general explanations for the absence of trade
unions and for the peacefulness of labour relations are persuasive.
But one has to take note of the fact that the few outbursts of
collective action—strikes and petitions—did tend to cluster in
two main periods: the late 1840s and the mid-1860s. Both were
periods of general labour unrest but the earlier period contains
no very definite evidence of railway trade unionism—indeed in
the 1840s railwaymen tended to oppose Chartism. However there
was a Locomotive Steam Enginemen and Firemen's Friendly

F

Society dating from 1839 and this may have had some trade union functions. And there may have been some form of rudimentary organisation in 1848 when the LNW enginemen went on strike. Representatives from eight other companies attended meetings, and in *The Times* and elsewhere there were references to clubs and unions.

More significant than all of this and of the occasional hint of collective action in the 1850s and early 1860s was the upsurge of activity in the mid 1860s.[12] Railwaymen were not likely to be unaware of or to be unaffected by the ferment in the labour world. For these were the years of the demand for the repeal of the Master & Servant law; when the legal position of trade unions had become uncertain and the train of events had set in culminating in the establishment of a Royal Commission into trade unions. There was the agitation for the reform of the franchise. For railwaymen in particular there was the public alarm at accidents, to which their long hours of work were said to be contributory causes. The financial condition of some railway companies after the crisis of 1866 caused managements to economise in ways such as longer unpaid overtime and a slowing down in the pace of promotion. Perhaps too the rise in prices was a factor, as may have been the fact that, in general, there had been no major changes in pay since the early days of the railways.

Surprisingly the first body to be formed was a Railway Clerks Association formed in October 1865. Support was limited to London, and it was completely unsuccessful. In the following January a Railway Guards, Signalmen and Switchmen's Society for the United Kingdom was set up. Demands for reduction of hours and increases of pay were sent to the traffic managers of the main line companies but no negotiations took place. But some increases of pay for signalmen and guards followed soon afterwards: it is not known if they can be attributed to the union's activities. The third was the Engine Drivers and Firemen's United Society, set up in London in April 1866. Though it only lasted a year it claimed to have 15,000 members (which is unlikely). It had its own journal, *The Train*, and it had a national programme, although negotiation was to be on a company basis. The proposals included a ten hour day, payment for overtime, higher pay for Sunday work, a maximum daily mileage, and increases of pay.

This society was the most successful of the lot. Five major companies—the Midland, GNR, LSWR, GWR and LNWR—decided to agree to the men's demands, but on two others there were strikes. Both of these companies, the NER and LBSCR, were in financial difficulties because their recent heavy capital expenditures and high rates of interest left fewer funds available for distribution to equity shareholders. The Brighton company accepted the idea of overtime and Sunday payments but not other demands. Instead of a ten-hour day they proposed a sixty-hour week. But this was unacceptable to the men on the reasonable grounds that there was no guarantee that the hours worked in any one day might not be excessively long. The board would not negotiate on this matter and notices were handed in. The actual strike was short-lived, lasting less than two days. The company could not break the strike by getting drivers from other companies, although they managed to run a skeleton service. Instead they offered re-instatement to all the strikers together with a promise of an annual review of pay for footplate staff.

The NER strike was a much more serious affair. Footplatemen normally worked a twelve-hour day, on top of which there was frequent unpaid overtime. In 1867 a deputation asked for a ten-hour day but this was refused. A month later over 1,000 men handed in their notices and the board negotiated further, promising the ten-hour day. This did not prevent the strike taking place, due to resentment that NER men had gained less than elsewhere and to a lack of trust in the word of the directors—there was some confusion over the interpretation of the directors' promises.

The strike began on 11 April, and the company made determined efforts to beat it. Drivers were recruited from other companies, and strike leaders were sued for breach of contract. These cases were dropped because the strike was a failure; the company found it possible to fill the places of the 1,000 men on strike. These new men were offered permanent employment and the strike collapsed. The union's funds were exhausted and it completely disappeared.

The record of this period illustrates two important facets of railway labour history. Firstly, railwaymen thought first of their own grade, and this may have been one of the causes of their failure. Secondly, where possible the companies would break a strike rather than negotiate or concede demands. Nowhere is this seen more clearly than in Scotland where there was no strike activity because of the stand taken by the three major companies: North British, Caledonian and the Glasgow & South Western. In September 1866 the three general managers issued this stern statement:

> . . . while they, with their several officers, are most desirous of meeting the legitimate demands of their employees, they will most firmly withstand all dictation by the men; and they give notice that any attempt at combination by the respective employees will be met by the directors in such a manner as they think fit. The directors take this opportunity of cautioning the men in their employ against combination, or joining any union, for the avowed purpose of dictating to their employers.

These sentiments might well have been published by the railways at any time up to World War I.

Notes to this chapter are on p 209.

Part Two:

The Golden Years: from the 1870s to World War I

CHAPTER 5

EXPANSION UNDER DIFFICULTIES

For convenience we examine the capital and revenue sides of the railway industry in separate chapters even though the two were closely related. Up to the 1860s and 1870s it is right and proper to give priority to construction. Thereafter it makes more sense to discuss operating first.

In the period from 1870 to 1914 the railways became essential to the fabric of the economy and of society. Increasingly they came to affect almost everybody in a direct and personal way. To many they possessed characteristics far beyond those appropriate to a provider of transport services. 'In south Lancashire people associated the London & North Western with the Church and the Conservatives; the Midland with Chapel and the Liberals'.[1] Doubtless the majority merely regarded them as bodies which ran trains: to be cursed, praised or taken for granted.

In this period the demand for transport grew rapidly. The great army of people who used to walk to work in London now began to travel in larger numbers. Though buses and trams were important in towns, the railways remained nevertheless the major segment of the transport sector.

The published figures of passengers carried and the tonnage conveyed by the railways show a trebling between the 1870s and 1912. Whatever else the 'Great Depression' (1873-96) may have meant in terms of unemployment and adjustment we do know that —because of the fall in prices—real incomes rose. At the same time imports rose, as farmers and home manufacturers were not slow to point out. Exports too increased, but at a slower rate, given the favourable terms of trade. In any case the goods had to be carried to and from ports. This was the job of the railways.

The growth of real incomes was important, too, in the demand for passenger services. While total population was growing at a slower rate than earlier in the nineteenth century, more people could afford to travel. As towns expanded people were encouraged to live in districts away from their work and to travel daily. Visits to the seaside and the countryside became more popular. Even such lines as the mineral railways of South Wales, so obviously geared to the carrying of coal, had quite extensive passenger services.

Much of this general expansion of demand for transport necessarily came to the railways, for they provided the bulk of transport services. Only in certain parts of the country and for certain commodities could canals continue to operate profitably; the carriage of coal by coastal shipping grew, and in towns short-distance passengers could choose between trains, trams, buses and cabs. After 1900 the electric tramway and the motor vehicle brought an element of competition. Some commuter lines were affected, often quite severely, but the new methods could not seriously interfere with long-distance traffic. Freight traffic hardly suffered from competition from road vehicles until after World War I.

These general statements are derived from the figures published in the *Railway Returns*. In 1870 the companies' gross annual receipts were £45 million. By 1912 they had more than trebled, reaching nearly £130 million. Both passenger and goods receipts increased in the same kind of proportion, although the revenue from goods traffic was rather less buoyant. The greatest rate of increase was what the *Railway Returns* called 'Miscellaneous', viz the earnings from docks and steamboats, which rose fivefold in the period, but the absolute figures were comparatively small (see Table 10, p 89).

These are gross figures and only tell part of the story. The railways were doing more work; in almost all years (there were some exceptions) the figures were higher than in the previous one. The remainder of the story is less rosy. Obviously some companies did worse than others. This we can take for granted. The important general fact is that profits rose at a much slower rate. While profits rose at about 2 per cent per annum, income rose by about 3 per cent. The cause is quite clear: operating expenses were rising. Between 1870 and 1912 gross receipts increased nearly threefold. Working expenses went up nearly four times.

The fact that the railways were not doing too well financially, contrasts very sharply with other kinds of evidence. This was the period of great new locomotives, of the railway races and a greater

TABLE 10

OPERATING, 1870-1912 (UK)

Year	Millions of passengers carried (a)	Million tons of freight carried	Receipts Passenger train (b) £m	Receipts Freight train £m	Receipts Miscellaneous £m	Total £m	Operating expenses £m	Net revenue (c) £m	Paid up capital (d) £m	Net receipts as proportion of paid up capital Per cent
1870	336.5	169.4 (e)	19.3	24.1	1.7	45.1	21.7	23.4	530	4.4
1880	603.9	235.3	27.2	35.8	2.5	65.5	33.6	31.9	728	4.4
1890	817.7	303.1	34.3	42.2	3.4	79.9	43.2	36.8	887	4.1
1900	1,142.3	425.0	45.4	53.5	5.9	104.8	64.7	40.1	1,160	3.5
1910	1,306.7	514.4	52.8	61.5	9.7	123.9	76.6	47.4	1,301	3.6
1912	1,294.4	520.3	54.3	64.0	10.2	128.6	81.2	47.3	1,318	3.6

Source: *Railway Returns* (except for (d) below)

Notes:
(a) Excluding season ticket holders
(b) Including receipts from 'season tickets, carriages, horses, etc., and Post Office mails'
(c) Including miscellaneous receipts
(d) Figures from Hawke and Reed, 'Railway Capital in the United Kingdom . . .' (1969)
(e) 1871
The form of accounts was altered in 1913

popular interest in the doings of the railways—the *Railway Magazine*, a journal for enthusiasts, was first published in the 1890s. There were also important changes in management and the beginning of systematic courses of instruction for railway staff.

Yet there were also anxious contemporary discussions about the way in which British railways were falling behind other countries' railways and at their lack of enterprise and initiative. An important task is to make sense of these contrasting images and impressions.

Despite a significant degree of close working, the industry was still composed of separate and autonomous companies. In such a diverse set of enterprises there were examples of good management and profitability alongside struggling companies seldom paying dividends of any respectability. It is very easy to understand why the NER was doing well—the coalmining industry was booming and the company had a virtual monopoly of its territory; whereas the GER had two types of traffic which were not particularly profitable. It was an agricultural line and it was a commuter line, running intensive services with numerous below standard fares, especially for workmen.

One can similarly identify for other companies the individual reasons for their financial condition. Yet there remains the nagging fact that the aggregate statistics tell such a clear story, and one is entitled to look for general explanations.

Recently Derek Aldcroft has essayed an examination of this period. He summarises the reasons for the decline in profitability in these terms:

> . . . the extension of the railway network into relatively unprofitable areas and the provision of less economic services, the increasing number of cheap fares and rates accorded to customers and the rise in construction and running costs, particularly at the end of the nineteenth century. Moreover, because of increasing parliamentary control over pricing policy, the railways were finding it difficult to raise their charges at a time when costs were rising.[2]

The worst kind of situation would be where companies had built lines at high cost—perhaps forced to do so through fear of possible competition from other lines—on which services had to be run at low charges, and where costs of operation were rising. Unfortunately the detailed evidence is not always available, and what there is is contradictory. The example of London can be used. 'Suburban traffic on the Great Northern grew so rapidly that it soon became an embarrassment to that company, for it started to interfere with the main-line goods traffic, the Great Northern's most profitable source of income.' The track was doubled and trebled, entailing tunnelling as well as widening, obviously expensive works, and the fares which were charged were low. The GER similarly provided for a rapid growth in commuter traffic, much of it being at cheap workmen's fare rates. The company constantly complained that its activities were unprofitable, yet it went out of its way to encourage this traffic. 'By creating a large suburban traffic the railway managed not only to perform a useful public service but also, it would seem, to reap a modest financial reward.'[3]

Railway company statistics were notoriously poor. They did not bother with useful series, like ton-mile statistics, and they did not keep separate records of their various lines. They could not know whether one line was more profitable than another. But it is possible, using the available aggregate figures, to obtain some understanding of what was going on. The first clue is provided by the operating ratio, the proportion of operating expenses to gross receipts (see Table 11, p 92).

The ratio was more or less constant in the 1870s and 1880s. It rose in the 1890s, particularly rapidly around the turn of the century. Then it was static up to World War I. Thus the period can be divided into two parts, the 1890s marking the division.

The operating ratio is merely an expression of a relationship. If one looks more closely at costs and revenues, calculating them per train-mile, the two periods become much more distinct. In general, both fell in the first period and rose in the latter. These movements might be simply a reflection of the general index of prices in the economy, which fell in the 'Great Depression' and rose thereafter. But they might also be explained by changes in efficiency. (See Table 12, p 93.)

William Acworth suggested that something like 50 per cent of railway operating expenditure was fixed. If revenue fell the companies could not reduce expenditure very much, and profits would fall. Subsequently Josiah Stamp (in 1918) and C. D. Campbell (in the late 1920s) examined the same phenomena. For the period 1880 to 1912 Stamp demonstrated there was no significant correlation between gross receipts and profits—the very opposite of Acworth's findings: the cause of fluctuations in profits was to be found in changes in costs. Campbell's findings confirmed Stamp's analysis; in rather more detail he showed that a major factor on the cost side was the price of coal. In his examination of the trade cycle he found that high gross revenues might be accompanied by lower profits if the price of coal had risen.[4]

TABLE 11

OPERATING RATIO, 1870-1912

Year	Per cent	Year	Per cent
1870	48	1891	55
1871	47	1892	56
1872	49	1893	57
1873	53	1894	56
1874	55	1895	56
1875	54	1896	56
1876	54	1897	57
1877	54	1898	58
1878	53	1899	59
1879	52	1900	62
1880	51	1901	63
1881	52	1902	62
1882	52	1903	62
1883	53	1904	62
1884	53	1905	62
1885	53	1906	62
1886	52	1907	63
1887	52	1908	64
1888	52	1909	62
1889	52	1910	62
1890	54	1911	62
		1912	63

Source: *Railway Returns*

This casts light on the changing fortunes of the railways. The great boom of the early 1870s was extraordinarily expensive for the railways. Train-mile costs in 1870 were 31d (13p); in 1874, at their peak, they reached 39d (16p).

The rise in operating expenses during that boom has been vividly described by Tomlinson as it affected the NER. From 1854, when the company was formed, to 1871 costs had been about 45 per cent of gross receipts, but the company's published accounts for the first half of 1872 showed that they had risen by 13½ per cent 'chiefly due to the general advance in the rate of wages and the "unprecedented rise in the price of fuel".' In July the major companies collectively resolved to raise charges, and the NER fell into line when it found that the lowest tender for coal showed a

200 per cent increase over the prices of twelve months before. In the second half of 1872 gross receipts rose by £207,000. If operating expenses had remained at the recent proportion of 45 per cent, they would have risen by about £93,000. In fact, the increase was £239,000. The higher price of coal and coke accounted for £87,000 of this.[5]

Much of this price rise was temporary and costs per train-mile fell from 39d (16p) in 1874 to 32d (13½p) in 1888, a fairly continuous fall, parallel to the general index of wholesale prices. From 1889 costs rose, slowly at first, but regularly each year up to World War I.

TABLE 12

OPERATING RECEIPTS AND EXPENDITURE PER TRAIN-MILE
1870-1912 (UK)
Selected years

Year	Total operating expenditure		Total operating receipts		Passenger train receipts		Freight train receipts	
	d	(p)	d	(p)	d	(p)	d	(p)
1870	31	(13)	62	(26)	54	(22½)	70	(29)
1873	37	(15½)	68	(28½)	60	(25)	77	(32)
1874	39	(16)	68	(28½)	61	(25½)	77	(32)
1888	32	(13½)	58	(24)	48	(20)	70	(29)
1900	39	(16)	59	(24½)	49	(20½)	71	(29½)
1910	43	(18)	64	(26½)	48	(20)	96	(40)

Source: Calculated from Mitchell, B.R. *Abstract of British Historical Statistics*, 225-9. The original source is the *Railway Returns*.

Note: Pence to nearest 1d; decimal equivalent to nearest ½p.

Total receipts per train-mile followed a similar pattern. The peak was in 1874, at 68d (28½p) followed by a continuous fall until a low figure of 58d (24p) in 1888. But in the 1890s they remained fairly constant, hardly varying by more than 1d (½p) from the low figure of the late 1880s. In 1901 they reached 60d (25p), and thereafter moved upwards each year.

Receipts from passenger trains (which included parcels) showed the same trend—a peak in 1874 (61d; 25½p) followed by a decline to 1888 (48d; 20p), then a decade of stability. But there was no improvement in passenger receipts after 1900, and receipts per train-mile remained in the range 46d to 50d (19p to 21p). The peak of receipts from freight train operation was in 1873 (77d; 32p) falling to 70d (29p) in 1888; again followed by stability in the 1890s. But after 1900 receipts per train mile rose very rapidly even surpassing the high returns of the early 1870s.

Thus between 1873 and 1890 costs and revenues both fell, and the operating ratio remained the same. During the 1890s they diverged, revenues were stagnant but costs rose. In particular costs rose in the second half of the decade. During 1893-6 costs per train-mile had hardly varied from 34d (14p), but beween 1897 and 1901 they rose to 41d (17p) and thereafter remained at or above that figure.

In other words the railways' difficulties which excited so many commentators in the early twentieth century, were mainly the problems of the late 1890s. Of the reasons for the extra cost per train-mile, the most important were the price of coal and of labour.[6] This was the period when the economy was picking up and the Boer War was adding to costs. The price of coal certainly rose but the evidence about labour costs is not so clear. On the basis of inferior figures it has been suggested that between 1886 and 1913 railwaymen's earnings rose by about 8 per cent, part of this being due to the higher cost of overtime. Normal weekly hours fell from 72 in the 1880s to 60 just before the first World War I.[7] And the legislation of the 1890s which attempted to impose restrictions on railwaymen's hours of work may also have had some effect.

It is surprising, in view of the evidence of contemporaries displayed by Aldcroft, that costs should have been falling in the 1870s and 1880s. He draws attention to the effects of competition in facilities, especially on the freight side.

> Traders were wooed feverishly by the companies who granted many services—for instance the use of their wagons for storage —free or at nominal charge. To satisfy traders' wishes, British railways developed to a fine art the practice of collecting numerous small consignments from a multiplicity of depots and stations and dispatching them immediately. The practice of dealing in small lots in this manner meant that the railways sacrificed their main advantages of rapid and economic movement of freight in through-trains. The wagon rather than the train became the unit of movement and many of the wagons, especially those carrying general merchandise, were filled to less than half capacity. Moreover the wagons in use were extremely small, the average being eight to ten tons capacity, since the type of consignments carried and the opposition of most traders provided little incentive to adopt larger, more economical wagons.

He refers also to the lavish quantities of rolling stock on British railways. The number of locomotives, passenger and freight vehicles per length of line was much greater in this country than in other industrial countries. In general, railway managements were inefficient and did not adopt new techniques of operating.[8]

Yet, costs per train-mile did not rise all the time; and some of these deficiencies could still be detected on British Rail in the 1960s. What was the explanation for the falling costs in the 1870s and 1880s?

If coal and labour costs were those which had the greatest influence around 1900 then perhaps they were important earlier on. Coal prices certainly fell from a peak in 1873 to low points in the late 1880s. The price of 'Best coal in London' was 32s (£1.60) per ton in 1873 and 16s (80p) in 1886 and 1887. A rough estimate of coal consumption by railways in 1887 is given by Mitchell as 6.2 million tons. In that year the train-mileage run by railways in the UK was just under 180 million. Thus each train-mile consumed about one-thirtieth of a ton of coal. If the price of coal used by the railways fell between 1873 and 1887 by 16s (80p) per ton then the saving per train-mile would have been one-thirtieth of that amount ie about 6d ($2\frac{1}{2}$p). This is almost precisely the actual fall in operating expenses between those dates. If the price of coal used by the railways had fallen by less than this amount, it would still have accounted for a substantial proportion of the reduction in the cost per train-mile.

There is virtually no information about labour costs, but while it does not seem that wages were drastically cut, they were more likely to fall than to rise. Thus there is no mystery about the fall in operating costs in the Great Depression. The railways benefited from falling prices. There is certainly no evidence that falling unit costs can be attributed to more efficient operating methods. Indeed, it is probably true that operating costs were rising, but that they were concealed by falling prices of inputs. From the 1870s trains were becoming heavier and therefore more costly to run. The standard third-class carriage of the 1870s weighed about ten tons and had seating capacity for fifty passengers; about 4cwt of wood and iron for each passenger. By the late 1880s the longer bogie carriages weighed about 18 tons and carried seventy people, about 5cwt per passenger. At the same time speeds were increasing. Between the early 1870s and the late 1880s the time taken between London and Edinburgh (using the same route) fell from 11 hours to $8\frac{1}{2}$. And there are many other examples of quite impressive reductions in travel-time by both passenger and goods trains.

Ross was sceptical of the value of these higher speeds. As well as higher capital costs for stronger permanent way and bridges, and for locomotives, there was greater wear and tear and the larger locomotives needed more fuel, water and oil. Moreover, the elimination of intermediate stops probably increased the train-mileage, for new train services had to be put on to serve the places now passed by the through trains. (Nor did he think that much new traffic was created. Higher speeds merely reallocated the available pool of passengers between the competing companies.)

He added too that when a few trains went at very high speeds the operating consequences were extremely awkward. They required a clear path ahead and this reduced the line's capacity. This he said, 'is greatest when every train on it runs at the same speed, and the greater the departures from the mean, either in way of excess or defect, the more is its carrying power impaired.'[9]

The slower rate of building locomotives in the 1870s and 1880s may also have raised costs since maintenance expenditure would necessarily increase. But one should add that some costs fell. Steel rails needed less frequent replacement than did iron; and the greater speeds of some trains may have been accomplished at lower operating cost per mile than that of slow, stopping trains.

In the 1870s and 1880s, then, operating costs fell mainly because the cost of their inputs fell. At the same time receipts per train-mile were falling. The consequence of providing mass transport was that the average fare paid tended to fall. The expansion of passenger traffic was primarily that of low-fare-paying people: third-class and workmen's fares. Partly this was the result of Government policy; partly the railways themselves went out of their way to obtain traffic.

The whole railway world had been shocked by the sudden decision of the Midland Railway, in the early 1870s, to encourage passenger traffic.

> The present era of railway travelling dates from 1872, when the Midland Railway inaugurated the policy of treating third-class passengers as a source of revenue worthy of consideration and

encouragement. Up to that time the railways had united in regarding them as little more than a necessary evil that must be kept down to the smallest possible dimensions . . . What the Midland did in 1872 was to admit third-class passengers into all its trains, and in so doing it was necessarily imitated more or less promptly by the other railways of the country. Three years later it carried its innovations a step further, and, deciding to abolish second-class compartments altogether, improved its third-class accommodation to the level of the old second.[10]

Not all companies followed this second course; indeed there were attempts to hinder the Midland in carrying out its policy. The details need not worry us. The important thing is that the railways were now pursuing passenger traffic for which low fares were charged.

Government intervention came in 1883 with the Cheap Trains Act. There had been some workmen's fares before this date, but this was a general Act, applying to all companies. The new Act introduced two major innovations. First, it repealed the 1844 provision which had compelled companies to run a train each day at 1d a mile. Instead they had to provide, to the satisfaction of the Board of Trade, a 'due and sufficient proportion' of accommodation at fares not exceeding one penny a mile. Secondly, they had to run 'proper and sufficient' trains for workmen, between 6pm and 8am at times and at fares to the satisfaction of the Board of Trade. This legislation could only have affected the later part of the Great Depression. Similar other government intervention, into freight charges, although introduced earlier, in 1873, was probably even less important. But it was a most significant piece of legislation for it provided the first mechanism for the regulation of these charges.

The background to the Railway & Canal Traffic Act of 1873 was the revival of merger activity by major railway companies. Amidst the promotion boom of the early 1870s there were ten proposals of amalgamations, and many more—seventy-one in all —advocating working agreements. Of these the proposal to merge the LNWR with the L & Y caused great heartsearching. In terms of size alone it was a frightening proposition. This initiative produced the other amalgamation proposals. The resultant agitation led to the establishment of a Joint Select Committee to examine the whole situation.

G

Quite usefully the Committee looked into the various possibilities of regulating monopolies, and recommended, *inter alia*, the establishment of a commission. This body was set up under the 1873 Act, but only for five years. Essentially its main function was to carry out the provisions of the 1854 Act; to hear complaints and to make awards regarding undue preference and the provision of reasonable facilities.

Its life was prolonged annually after the first five years, but the consensus of opinion is that it did not accomplish very much. The railway companies were able to defy the commission, and the expenses involved prevented railway customers from taking much advantage of its existence. Nevertheless, the Commission was the first of a series of independent bodies whose function was to regulate railway charges, primarily from the point of view of fairness to the public.

The first decade of its life coincided with the Great Depression. Industry was faced with lower profit margins and an obvious target for complaint was the railways. Accusations of malpractice against the companies grew and further select committees inquired in 1881 and 1882. It was not merely that traders accused the railways of unfairness, they also tried to get charges reduced. The only immediate result of the select committees was the Cheap Trains Act of 1883. Further legislation did not come until 1888, delayed partly because of the political crisis over Irish Home Rule, though equally important was the opposition of the railway companies. Whereas they had not been greatly agitated by the 1873 Act, this time the various proposals to strengthen the work of the Commission angered them. When, in 1884, Joseph Chamberlain, the President of the Board of Trade, introduced a Bill to this end, the companies formed the Railway Companies' Association to fight it.

The 1888 Act was perhaps the most important piece of railway legislation in the nineteenth century. It established the Railway & Canal Commission on a permanent basis and gave it judicial powers to deal with complaints about facilities and rates. The Act also empowered the Board of Trade to establish a uniform classification of merchandise and to fix maximum rates for each class.

The first of these was the easier, for the Railway Clearing House classification was there to hand. The second proved almost impossible to carry out. The companies were required to lodge their proposed classifications and schedules with the Board of Trade within six months of the passing of the Act but there were thousands of objections and it was not until January 1893 that the new scheme could come into force.

Essentially new maximum rates were to be fixed, divided into two parts: a charge for conveyance and a charge for terminals. Tapering rates were also part of the scheme, lower rates per mile the longer the distance the goods were carried. It took a lot of argument in 1889 and 1890 to hammer out some figures for each class of goods. But the actual job of translating these into the rate books of every station in the country was so immense that it was impossible, in the time allowed, to negotiate the thousands of special rates. On the appointed day for the scheme, 1 January 1893, the companies were able to publish only the new maximum rates. Inevitably many traders found they were paying more than they had been used to; the years of complaint and legislation had worked against them. The subsequent uproar led to yet another select committee, which in turn was followed by the Railway and Canal Traffic Act of 1894. This Act remained the basis of railway charging for some thirty years.

The Act made it quite clear that where a railway company had raised (or in the future would raise) its charges above those in operation before 1 January 1893, and a complaint had been made that the charge was unreasonable, it was the duty of the company to prove that the increase was reasonable. And, very important, it was not sufficient for the company to show that the proposed rate was within the maxima fixed by Parliament.

This meant that the companies were bound to set new maxima below those already fixed. It meant that future increases of charges were virtually impossible, except, as laid down by the Act, to compensate for certain increases in prices and wages. For the next twenty years of peacetime operation charges could go down but they could not rise.

But—and this is where Aldcroft's analysis needs modification—receipts per train-mile on the freight side rose after 1900, and reached new heights, greater even than in the boom of the 1870s. Given no increase in charges the only explanation for this must be that there was some improvement in efficiency. In their pioneer work *The History and Economics of Transport*, Kirkaldy and Evans argued that 'in the future increased profit balances could only come from greater economy of working rather than from increased charges'.

Obviously the larger locomotives and higher capacity wagons must have made some impact on costs. Then there were important improvements in signalling. Four companies, the L & Y, the NER, GCR, and GWR changed some of their signal boxes to electrical and pneumatic methods, which saved manpower. Presumably the larger locomotives, with their higher speeds, meant that fewer engines were required, with the result that the demand for foot-platemen was lower.

An idea of the improvements in efficiency can be gained from some officially published figures for the years 1901-10 (see Table 13, p 101). They give the numbers employed on the railways in the first week of December in each year. The figures are not complete. They refer to twenty-seven companies employing over 90 per cent of all railway employees and do not include white collar workers. But if we assume that the census each year was taken on a comparable basis, then we can compare these figures with the train mileage to give us a figure of the number of men employed per train mile. In the first decade the number of train miles per man employed rose from an average of 889 in the first five years to 911 in the second five years. This is less than a 2½ per cent change but does at least suggest that labour was being utilised more efficiently. One possible explanation of this development is that the companies, after the establishment of a new pattern of industrial relations in 1907, tried to side-step its effects.

'Efficiency' can be measured and in some senses it can be experienced. But it is a word liable to mean too much. From Sir Felix Pole's autobiography, the decade or so before the war on the GWR can be interpreted as a period of great improvement, or alternatively of muddle. In his chapter 'Management' when he writes of Sir James Inglis, general manager from 1903 to 1911, he displays loyalty and enthusiasm. Under Inglis there were numerous improvements: 'Fast trains, long distance runs, introduction of road and rail motor services, improved advertising, the construction of cut-off lines, whereby the Great Western system was transformed, and many other outstanding changes were due to him.' Receipts went up by over 20 per cent in his eight years. But the operating ratio went up, rather more rapidly, from 61.49

to 62.9 per cent. Pole had to prepare statistical information for Inglis. 'I am confident' he writes 'that he did not know the true cause of what appeared to be the disproportionate growth of expenditure, and I very much doubt whether the Chairman and Directors did either.'

TABLE 13

RAILWAY EMPLOYMENT AND TRAIN MILEAGE, 1901-10 (UK)

Period (first week in December)	(1) Number employed (000s)	(2) Train mileage (million miles)	(3) Col 2 ÷ Col 1
1901	441	395.2	893
1902	448	399.8	892
1903	448	394.1	877
1904	445	397.0	892
1905	449	400.9	893
1906	458	414.3	904
1907	479	418.3	873
1908	459	423.2	922
1909	459	419.2	913
1910	463	423.2	935
1901-5			889
1906-10			911

Sources :

Col 1. Board of Trade, *Report on Changes in Rates and Wages and Hours of Labour in the United Kingdom in 1910.* Quoted Pratt, *History of Inland Transport,* 435

Col 2. *Railway Returns*

Pole writes that the explanation lay in the way the accounts were prepared. The 1868 Act made no reference to reserves or to depreciation. 'Therefore, as the railway accounts in use at that time had the single heading "Maintenance of Locomotives", any provision in excess of actual expenditure had to be shown in the accounts as having been actually spent.' The GWR chief accountant wanted some provision for renewals and the result was this:

When preparing the accounts he would enquire of the Chief Mechanical Engineer whether the number of locomotives that had been renewed was adequate, based on estimated life. Naturally, the Chief Mechanical Engineer was prepared to work on a high theoretical basis and readily agreed that he should have renewed a larger number. Upon this, the accountant charged in the accounts the estimated cost of renewing, say, 150 locomotives, whereas the actual number renewed was, say, 130. The same procedure was adopted in the case of rolling stock, and the difference between the actual and theoretical expenditure was held in suspense and appeared as a liability in the general balance sheet under 'Sundry Outstanding Accounts'. This figure which had for years shown very little variation, increased between the years 1903 and 1911 from £1,118,688 to £2,699,534. In addition, from various sources, the Superannuation and Provident Funds were increased from £247,351 in 1907 to £1,390,883 in 1911.

Pole's devastating conclusion is that the chief accountant was determined that Inglis should have no credit for the progressive policy being put into operation. The accounts were therefore prepared so that no increased dividend could be made. 'In fact, the dividend was decided first and the surplus earnings were disposed of in such ways as the foregoing.'

Moreover, on the GWR, the general manager was not in practice the chief executive officer. The heads of departments had direct access to the directors. Thus vast programmes of expenditure might be approved without the knowledge of the general manager. And 'the architectural features of buildings were decided solely by the Chief Engineer': not even the board had the drawings submitted to them.

For Pole, writing as a general manager, such a situation was intolerable, and when he took over the position in 1921 he got it changed. But it does not follow, of course, that the low status of the general manager before the war necessarily proved inhibiting to new ideas and new policies. Perhaps it even encouraged them, by enabling the Board, where it had control, to push ideas forward, when a chief executive might have held them up.

Inglis had tried to make changes in organisational structure but was not strong enough to get them accepted. Elsewhere there were important developments, particularly on the NER, associated with the name of George Stegmann Gibb. He became general manager of the company in 1891 and remained there until 1906 when he went to the Metropolitan District.

According to H. G. Lewin, who worked under Gibb, the general manager wanted to improve on the 'rule-of-thumb methods hitherto prevailing on most of the British railways', particularly in view of the problems associated with the growth of traffic.

He therefore decided to train a few young men of better education and wider outlook than those who had hitherto risen to high office from the ranks, bearing in mind that they must be prepared to learn the work of the lower grades themselves, and also as a *sine qua non* that they must work amicably with the existing staff.

Subsequently, after visiting America, he managed to change the structure of the company in 1902, when the commercial and the operating sides of the traffic department were separated. A major result was that operating expenses of the NER fell, at a time when on other companies they were generally rising.[11]

This structural change does not sound particularly exciting or important (or novel: the North Staffordshire Railway had done it in the 1880s). But it was a significant change particularly on the major lines. On the small lines the general manager was in fact the chief officer, responsible to the board for everything. On the larger lines, while nominally so responsible, he tended to concentrate on traffic matters. Under him there would be two officials, whose functions reflected the two major features of railway traffic: passengers and goods. Respectively these were the superintendent of the line and the chief goods manager. (On some lines there might be a mineral manager, if coal traffic was heavy.) They were responsible for canvassing for traffic; arranging charges; and making up the trains (and loading and unloading duties in the case of freight). In addition the superintendent of the line had the task of supervising the movement of all traffic and the actual running of all trains. (The engine power was supplied by the locomotive superintendent.)

The NER reorganisation involved the superintendent of the line becoming general superintendent of the operating branch. A new department, the commercial branch under a chief passenger agent, was formed to take over the former commercial duties of the superintendent. The purpose of this was to relieve him of many office duties to enable him to concentrate on working the traffic. The chief goods manager's functions also changed; he was relieved of the task of working the traffic (now in the hands of the superintendent) and he was left with commercial duties.

Thus the general superintendent's department performed the tasks of supervising the running of trains; loading and unloading; controlling the supply of engines, carriages and wagons; preparing timetables together with certain personnel functions; dealing with claims under the Workmen's Compensation Act, and enforcing the observance of the company's rules and regulations.

The two departments under the chief goods manager and the chief passenger agent had the responsibility of securing and charging for their respective traffics: the fixing of fares and charges; despatching invoices; preparing public timetables, and so on.

These were important changes but this company, while continuing the general policy of a line of command downwards, with some degree of delegation of authority, did not—as its successor the LNER did later—establish officials in geographical areas with general supervisory powers (equivalent to those of a general manager at top level). Thus on the NER there were three divisional superintendents, five district goods managers, and two district passenger agents. Each was responsible to his chief officer, not to any local official.

A further innovation introduced during Gibb's regime was the improvement of the company's statistical services. There had for long been a great deal of criticism of the kind of statistics used by the railways. America was the country with which comparisons were made—Gibb's structural changes merely brought the NER into line with American practice, and since that country's railways used ton-mile statistics they were advocated in Britain too. Most companies would have nothing to do with them—they were expensive to collect anyway—but Gibb built up a statistical department, using figures of ton-miles and passenger miles, thus providing the NER management with much better information on which to base decisions.

This history of the NER's managerial changes is special to that company (although others adopted some of its practices). Nor can we be sure that those developments were stimulated by the inflexibility of freight charges. The personality of Gibb himself may well have been the deciding factor, although bits of evidence suggest that other companies were seriously examining their organisation and operating. One consequence of the legislation of 1888-94 was to force the companies, by joint action, to seek economies: the tightening up of dealing with claims for goods damaged in transit; the reduction in time allowed for the detention of wagons; and for free warehousing. The upsurge in amalgamation proposals, in working agreements and in pooling traffic can be attributed to the same cause.

None of these was new, but there were certainly more of them or extensions of old ones just before World War I. Perhaps Parliament's authorisation in 1899 of the closer working of the old rivals, the SER and the LCDR, may have been an important factor in encouraging others to do the same. Thus the old pooling arrangements between the L & Y and the LNWR, dating from the 1870s, was extended in stages after 1906, culminating in the Midland joining in.

A final point is this. In the decade or two before World War I the railways put a great deal of effort into the education and training of their staff. For some years they had assisted the work of mechanics institutes and similar bodies, in which railwaymen could participate in classes in engineering and similar subjects as well as a wide range of social activities. Now they began to expand these in various ways and in new directions. Thus the GWR began a school of signalling at Paddington in 1903, providing courses which offered company employees a knowledge of railway operating and management. Classes were held in accounts and in shorthand for clerks. These were normally followed by examinations and the award of certificates, useful for aspiring workers keen on promotion. Other companies had similar methods of encouraging staff to obtain qualifications. The Great Central inaugurated a scheme in 1908 intended to recruit men with higher educational qualifications than those possessed by the typical junior clerk entrant. Every year six positions were offered to existing staff, under the age of twenty-five, who did best in an examination. They were promoted, given higher pay and undertook higher grade training. It was an impressive kind of management training. There was a four years' course, in which the trainee obtained both practical and theoretical training in all aspects of railway work.

Not all such courses and training were provided by the companies themselves. In the mid-1890s William Acworth gave courses of lectures at the new London School of Economics on railway economics, which were attended by GWR and GER employees, the companies paying the fees. From 1904 seven major companies provided a guarantee which enabled a more elaborate course to be established, which could lead to a degree with honours in transport. Other companies made arrangements with University Departments at Manchester, Leeds, Newcastle and Sheffield.

Although the railways were often regarded, and with some basis, as being stuffy, conservative and reactionary, some were pursuing what is now grandly called 'management development' before World War I. It is not easy to think of any other industry in which the training of its future management was given much thought, certainly not as early as this.

Notes to this chapter are on pp 209–10.

CHAPTER 6

COMPLETION OF THE NETWORK

The major era of railway construction ended in the 1860s and 1870s. Though further extensions to the system were made the rate of growth slowed down. In the forty years ending in 1870 just on 15,000 route miles had been built; by the beginning of World War I a further 8,000 were constructed making a total of 23,000. Some of this new mileage comprised important, expensive works: the extension of the Manchester, Sheffield & Lincolnshire to London, the last main line to be built; the construction of the Severn Tunnel to provide a direct link with South Wales; much of the underground system of London; the West Highland Railway, for example. Yet the 'typical' new works were of comparatively short mileage, and, more relevantly, capital expenditures went increasingly on improvements to existing facilities (eg for the quadrupling of tracks).

The period, however, had begun in a state of panic, following the crisis of 1866. As in earlier decades a promotion and construction mania had been succeeded by the revelations of financial mismanagement and ineptitude. During the late 1860s public comment assumed the by now traditional tone. The companies had over-reached themselves; they had spent too much too quickly on unnecessary and unprofitable lines; and their highly geared capital ratios resulted in pitifully small surpluses for distribution to shareholders when rates of interest were high, when costs rose, or when trade was slack.

Early in 1867 *The Economist* spoke of 'the railway disasters of this year', and discussed the problem of dealing with 'insolvent railways'.[1] Some commentators, like Henry Ayres, argued that rates of dividend were fraudulent. In his *The financial position of railways* (1868) he spoke of railway company accounts 'put forth to the public in so complicated a manner, and in such varied forms, as to set at defiance the judgment of the most skilful accountant to determine their actual meaning'. And it was not as though these failings were confined to the small, shady lines. As important a company as the GWR paid no dividend, and in 1867 applied (unsuccessfully) to the Public Works Loans Commissioners for a loan.[2]

Parliament passed two Acts to deal with the situation. The Railway Companies Act (1867) laid down the procedure to be followed when railway companies could not meet their engagements with their creditors; and in the following year the Regulation of Railways Act introduced changes in companies' accounting practices, including the publication of uniform accounts.

But while the events of the late 1860s undoubtedly followed the familiar pattern, the outstanding fact is that the railways recovered extraordinarily quickly. The great boom, centring on 1870, brought immediate benefits to the industry. Traffic continued to grow and at a particularly rapid rate. In 1870 gross receipts were £45 million; by 1875 they were over £61 million. Admittedly working expenses rose fast, too, even faster than the rise in receipts. But for a short time the companies generally did well. In 1871, net receipts rose by nearly 10 per cent.

It was a remarkable change of fortune. Whereas in 1868 Henry Ayres had advocated the closing of capital accounts, four years later the *Report* of the Joint Select Committee on Railway Companies Amalgamation spoke of further railway extension.

> It cannot be supposed that railways have reached their full development. The most important lines have been made, but there is every prospect of a constant demand for branches and feeders.

The committee suggested that these would not be very profitable and that the existing companies would not build them; indeed, they would oppose the introduction of independent lines 'into the heart of their system'. Their discussion about the possibility of financial assistance by local authorities followed logically from their analysis. But they seem not to have been aware that railway promotion had already revived. In 1871 companies applied to Parliament for powers to build nearly 700 miles, and in 1872 for 2,000 miles. The proposed capital in 1872 was nearly £70 million. And in almost every year up to the turn of the century companies applied to build over 400 miles.

Most of this was never built (and the figures are inflated by the repetition of applications). But, despite the pessimism of the 1872 Committee, what was built was done almost entirely without recourse to public authorities. The West Highland Railway, it is true, had a government guarantee, but that line was regarded as a form of public works intended to improve the economy of the region. It was generally recognised also that in some areas the return would be so low as to preclude the building of lines on the traditional scale. The answer was found in light railways, usually built in agricultural areas, and an Act of 1896 provided the legislative mechanism.

Though the rate of extension of the railway system was much slower than in earlier decades the paid up capital of the industry more than doubled, and commentators were not slow to pick on the two sets of figures and to draw alarming conclusions. Mileage had risen from 15,500 to 23,500, but capital had increased from £530 million to £1,318 million. Capital per mile had grown from £34,000 to £56,000.

On the face of it this increase was staggering, and ready explanations were produced. The companies had been wasteful and extravagant; capital accounts had been swollen by unnecessary expenditures; by nominal additions to capital; and by unorthodox accounting practices, whereby items properly chargeable to revenue had been debited to capital.

Such accusations had a ring of truth. The companies continued with their competitive construction and with expensive contests in Parliament, aimed at protecting their territory. Almost every proposed railway scheme was likely to affect the interests of another company, which would necessarily oppose it. The Barry Railway, for example, was a newcomer and interloper of the 1880s. In turn it objected to the Cardiff Railway. In 1908 the latter company promoted a Bill which was opposed by the Barry. Counsel for the Barry company appeared before the Examiner of Private Bills alleging that the Cardiff company had not complied with Standing Orders. The allegations was not upheld and, after one contest between opposing counsel over the inadvertent omission of a word in the documents, the Examiner stated: 'For the last quarter of a century these railway companies have been every year regularly engaged in a fratricidal and suicidal war.'[3]

Perhaps the best-known example of this kind of strife took

place in south-east England. From the 1860s to the 1890s—apart from an occasional truce—two companies, the LCD and the SER—fought a war of construction and operating. The two chairmen, James Staats Forbes and Sir Edward Watkin, both made statements from time to time regretting the competition and pointing to the savings that could be made if the two companies worked together. Instead they built competing lines and speeches to their shareholders contained the military phraseology of 'aggression' and 'defence'. By 1886 the two companies had seven main-line termini serving Kent; two ports for Continental traffic (Port Victoria and Queenborough); and had provided many towns with two separate stations. The SER was not attracted to the idea of working with the poverty-stricken Chatham, which never paid any ordinary dividends and sometimes only part of the preference. Its capital had been issued at large discounts. But Forbes of the LCD had a naïve optimism in the potentialities of his company's network and this Watkin vehemently denied. The gap was too large for terms to be agreed. In any case the two men were personally antipathetic and only when Watkin retired were the two companies able to come together.[4]

Conflicts of this sort undoubtedly added to the growth of capital accounts. And three other sources of expansion can be identified. The first was through nominal additions to capital, mainly in the 1890s, and through stock-splitting occasioned by a number of company reconstructions. In that decade something like £130 million were added to nominal capital. Secondly there was the expenditure caused by the Regulation of Railways Act of 1889 which enforced a number of safety measures. These included the use of continuous brakes on passenger trains; the interlocking of points and signals; and the adoption of the block system of signalling on all passenger trains. And since two types of apparatus were adopted by the companies for their braking systems—one using compressed air, the other a vacuum system—which could not be used together, they had to fit both types to stock required for interchange traffic. This expenditure may have been necessary for reasons of safety, but it is unlikely to have added anything to revenue and might not have been undertaken by the companies except by compulsion. The expenditure under this Act was regarded as additions to capital, a policy encouraged by Parliament which gave the companies powers to finance these works by the issue of debenture stock, on the certificate of the Board of Trade.

The third way in which additions to capital took place was by the debiting of capital account with expenditure which could have been paid out of revenue. This was an old story on the railways—as early as the 1830s there had been complaints that dividends had been paid out of capital by this method. Moreover, there were legitimate differences of opinion about the allocation of individual items of expenditure. *The Economist* in 1903, for example, discussing the companies' expenditure on renewals of carriages and wagons, noted that it was 'one of the departments in which the line between expenditure that ought to be met out of revenue and that charged to capital is apt to become a little shaky and difficult to distinguish'.[5] Nevertheless, H. M. Ross, in his book *British Railways* (1904) wrote of the tendency

> . . . to call upon capital, rather than revenue, to bear the cost of such betterments as replacing old bridges with new and stronger ones, or rebuilding and enlarging passenger stations or goods depots.

And he referred to:

> . . . the usual British practice of treating the cost of widening existing lines as entirely capital expenditure, although such widenings may from some points of view be accounted 'betterments' like rebuilding a station or strengthening a bridge, since they mainly facilitate the conduct of the old traffic rather than of themselves create new business.

He went on to defend this practice on the ground that if the sum available for dividends had fallen, future funds for railway investment would not have been forthcoming.[6]

There was then some justification in the complaints made against the companies, but a great deal can be said in their defence. In a sense the figures were untrue. The annual *Railway Returns* contained three columns relating to mileage: 'Double or more'; 'single'; and 'total'. Thus a mile of double track was equal, in the official statistics, to a mile of six sets of tracks, and one of the essential facts about railway capital expenditure after the 1870s was the building of facilities not for extensions of the network, but to meet the demands of ever-growing traffic on the existing system. There was a widespread provision of extra

TABLE 14

RAILWAY CAPITAL FORMATION 1870-1912 in £ million (UK)

| | Rolling Stock Current prices | | 1869 prices | | Permanent way, Buildings, etc Current prices | | 1869 prices | | Total (excl land and ancillary businesses) Current prices | | 1869 prices | | Land at current prices | Ancillary businesses at current prices | Total gross capital formation at current prices |
	Gross	Net	Gross	Net	Gross	Net	Gross	Net	Gross	Net	Gross	Net			
1870	2.47	0.40	2.39	0.38	5.85	2.40	5.83	2.39	8.32	2.80	8.22	2.77	3.74	0.25	12.3
1871	3.33	1.19	3.26	1.17	7.44	3.79	7.17	3.65	10.77	4.98	10.43	4.82	3.21	0.25	14.2
1872	3.86	1.21	3.18	1.00	8.86	4.90	8.05	4.45	12.72	6.11	11.23	5.45	2.87	0.41	16.0
1873	4.80	1.74	3.58	1.30	10.50	6.08	8.74	5.06	15.30	7.82	12.32	6.36	3.33	0.54	19.2
1874	4.79	1.77	3.80	1.41	13.52	8.97	11.28	7.48	18.31	10.74	15.08	8.89	4.48	0.62	23.7
1875	4.51	1.64	3.94	1.44	14.08	9.44	11.88	7.97	18.59	11.08	15.82	9.41	4.18	0.79	23.7
1876	3.63	0.85	3.32	0.78	14.05	9.34	12.04	8.00	17.68	10.19	15.36	8.78	4.28	0.59	22.6
1877	3.03	0.33	2.81	0.31	12.78	8.02	11.13	6.98	15.81	8.35	13.94	7.29	4.12	0.48	20.4
1878	2.16	-0.30	2.18	-0.30	12.11	7.47	11.12	6.86	14.27	7.17	13.30	6.56	4.09	0.83	19.1
1879	2.05	-0.32	2.14	-0.33	9.61	5.16	9.39	5.04	11.66	4.84	11.53	4.71	2.89	0.71	15.3
1880	2.71	0.12	2.62	0.11	9.05	4.35	8.55	4.11	11.76	4.47	11.17	4.22	2.45	0.91	14.9
1881	3.06	0.53	3.08	0.53	10.70	5.97	10.26	5.72	13.76	6.50	13.34	6.25	2.66	0.80	17.3
1882	3.23	0.57	3.16	0.55	10.47	5.48	9.72	5.08	13.70	6.05	12.88	5.63	3.82	1.36	18.9
1883	4.42	1.76	4.49	1.79	10.88	5.82	10.19	5.45	15.30	7.58	14.68	7.24	3.92	1.24	20.4
1884	3.63	1.03	3.84	1.09	13.80	8.58	12.87	8.00	17.43	9.61	16.71	9.09	3.53	0.99	21.9
1885	3.34	0.73	3.59	0.79	10.57	5.43	10.21	5.24	13.91	6.16	13.80	6.03	2.58	0.69	17.2
1886	2.17	-0.45	2.38	-0.49	9.30	4.20	9.24	4.18	11.47	3.75	11.62	3.69	2.17	0.61	14.2
1887	2.36	-0.29	2.60	-0.32	8.08	2.95	8.10	2.96	10.44	2.66	10.70	2.64	1.90	0.65	13.0
1888	2.71	-0.07	2.90	-0.07	7.66	2.44	7.65	2.43	10.37	2.37	10.55	2.36	1.77	0.64	12.8
1889	3.36	0.47	3.54	0.49	7.90	2.44	7.66	2.36	11.26	2.91	11.20	2.85	2.37	0.71	14.3
1890	4.27	1.07	4.16	1.04	8.74	2.76	7.86	2.49	13.01	3.83	12.02	3.53	2.27	0.58	16.0

Year															
1891	5.10	1.97	5.23	2.02	10.45	4.48	9.58	4.11	15.55	6.45	14.81	6.13	2.65	0.50	18.7
1892	4.73	1.55	4.88	1.60	10.35	4.33	9.57	4.00	15.08	5.88	14.45	5.60	2.33	0.44	18.0
1893	3.56	0.43	3.80	0.46	10.01	3.98	9.40	3.74	13.57	4.41	13.20	4.20	1.85	0.44	15.9
1894	3.22	0.11	3.45	0.12	10.25	4.07	9.54	3.78	13.47	4.18	12.99	3.90	2.18	0.60	16.4
1895	3.18	0.09	3.41	0.09	11.17	4.80	10.27	4.41	14.35	4.89	13.68	4.50	2.37	0.48	17.3
1896	3.91	0.69	4.03	0.71	11.39	4.71	10.16	4.20	15.30	5.40	14.19	4.91	2.55	0.59	18.6
1897	4.72	1.35	4.74	1.36	12.07	5.13	10.54	4.47	16.79	6.48	15.28	5.83	2.85	0.80	20.6
1898	4.88	1.41	4.82	1.35	13.98	6.71	11.89	5.71	18.86	8.12	16.71	7.06	2.87	1.00	22.9
1899	7.15	3.07	6.37	2.74	13.47	5.88	11.17	4.87	20.62	8.95	17.54	7.61	3.68	1.10	25.5
1900	6.83	2.19	5.56	1.82	14.19	6.22	11.42	5.01	21.02	8.41	16.98	6.83	4.00	1.76	26.9
1901	6.32	2.16	5.80	1.98	13.54	5.56	11.06	4.54	19.86	7.72	16.86	6.52	3.48	1.49	24.9
1902	4.83	0.70	4.52	0.66	13.09	5.06	10.81	4.18	17.92	5.76	15.33	4.84	2.48	1.65	22.2
1903	4.28	0.12	3.99	0.11	14.96	6.76	12.32	5.57	19.24	6.88	16.31	5.68	3.88	1.88	25.1
1904	3.74	−0.37	3.52	−0.35	14.97	6.68	12.42	5.54	18.71	6.31	15.94	5.19	2.13	1.78	22.8
1905	4.70	0.46	4.30	0.42	12.53	4.16	10.45	3.47	17.23	4.62	14.75	3.89	2.10	1.77	21.2
1906	5.02	0.55	4.40	0.48	12.12	3.52	9.98	2.90	17.14	4.07	14.38	3.38	1.71	1.59	20.5
1907	5.12	0.50	4.40	0.43	9.47	0.67	7.71	0.55	14.59	1.17	12.11	0.98	1.62	1.51	17.9
1908	3.48	−0.93	3.16	−0.84	7.38	−1.36	6.09	−1.13	10.86	−2.29	9.25	−1.97	1.13	1.29	13.3
1909	3.18	−1.17	2.95	−1.08	6.18	−2.51	5.17	−2.10	9.36	−3.68	8.12	−3.18	0.93	0.82	11.2
1910	2.88	−1.51	2.64	−1.39	5.91	−2.95	4.88	−2.44	8.79	−4.46	7.52	−3.83	0.62	1.11	10.5
1911	3.29	−1.12	3.01	−1.02	5.96	−3.09	4.85	−2.52	9.25	−4.21	7.86	−3.54	0.90	0.81	11.0
1912	4.54	−0.24	3.85	−0.20	6.01	−3.44	4.72	−2.69	10.55	−3.68	8.57	−2.89	0.75	0.82	12.2

H

Source: B. R. Mitchell. The gross figures at current prices are printed in his article 'The Coming of the Railway . . .' The remainder are unpublished.

tracks and sidings, whose mileage was concealed in the official figures. When these are taken into account some of the sting is taken out of the accusations of waste and extravagance. Whereas expenditure per route mile had apparently risen by some £8,500 in the 1890s, expenditure per mile of single track (after deducting nominal additions to capital) was only £1,500.[7]

The response to the growth of traffic has been masterfully summarised by Professor Ashworth:[8]

> More traffic required the rebuilding of some stations on a bigger scale and the running of heavier and more frequent trains; it also involved longer time in loading and unloading at stations, and, if there was to be no deterioration of service, this had to be offset by higher running speeds and longer non-stop runs. The latter change necessitated bigger locomotives and, on passenger trains, more restaurant cars, corridor coaches and lavatories, with a consequent increase in tare-weight. Heavier trains often made it necessary to strengthen the track and bridges; denser traffic, operating at a great variety of speeds, required additional tracks and sidings and often the drastic reform of the signalling system. Much of the high capitalisation of British railways derives not so much from reckless waste in promoting and establishing the railways before 1850, which is popularly supposed to be the fount of most of their subsequent financial ills, but from the enlargement of traffic capacity in the last quarter of the nineteenth century.

A second justification refers to the physical extension of the system. There were clearly some absurd schemes: the Midland & South Western Junction Railway, a contractor's line, which for a time was in the hands of the receiver; and the building of the last main line, the Great Central, in the 1890s. But many others were necessary and essential. The economy was not stationary, and particular regions were expanding rapidly. An area like South Wales, where coal output rose remarkably in the decades before World War 1, required additions to its communications network although one might well wonder whether the numerous competing lines were all needed. Some were expensive to build in the geographical conditions obtaining. Moreover the physical expansion of London would have been greatly retarded without the provision of extensive commuter services, including the electric underground.

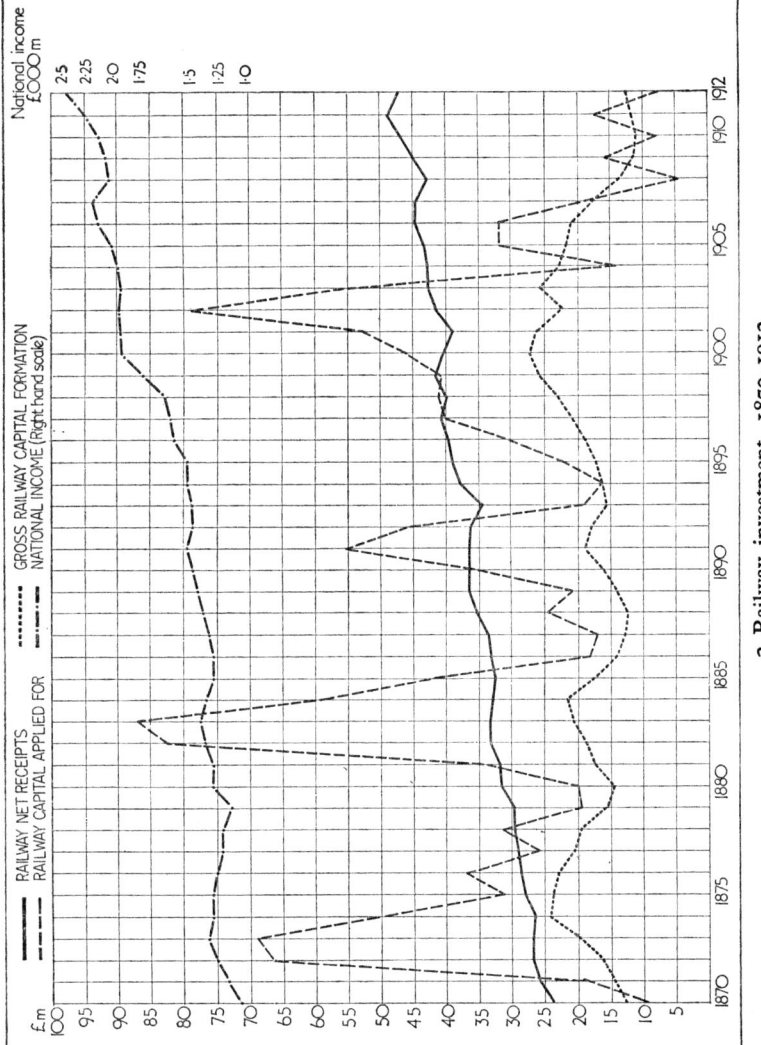

2 Railway investment, 1870–1912

TABLE 15

RAILWAY PROMOTION AND CONSTRUCTION 1870-1912 (UK)

	(1)	(2)	(3)	(4)	(5)
				Gross railway	Route mileage open
		Railway net	Railway capital	capital	for traffic at end
Year	National income £m	Receipts £m	applied for £m	formation £m	of each year
1870	1,083	23.4	9.8	12.3	(15,537)
1871	1,175	25.7	17.5	14.2	15,376
1872	1,254	27.0	66.4	16.0	15,814
1873	1,313	27.0	69.0	19.2	16,082
1874	1,278	26.6	51.0	23.7	16,449
1875	1,263	28.0	31.0	23.7	16,658
1876	1,252	28.7	36.7	22.6	16,872
1877	1,237	29.1	25.3	20.4	17,077
1878	1,220	29.7	31.3	19.1	17,333
1879	1,155	29.7	19.4	15.3	17,696
1880	1,282	31.9	20.1	14.9	17,933
1881	1,281	32.0	33.6	17.3	18,175
1882	1,319	33.2	82.3	18.9	18,457
1883	1,328	33.7	86.9	20.4	18,681
1884	1,302	33.3	59.0	21.9	18,864
1885	1,274	32.8	42.4	17.2	19,169
1886	1,276	33.1	18.2	14.2	19,332
1887	1,329	33.9	17.1	13.0	19,578
1888	1,369	35.1	24.7	12.8	19,812
1889	1,419	36.9	20.9	14.3	19,943
1890	1,454	36.8	35.2	16.0	20.073
1891	1.470	36.7	55.2	18.7	20,191
1892	1,454	36.4	46.1	18.0	20,325
1893	1,460	34.9	19.6	15.9	20,646
1894	1,496	37.1	16.8	16.4	20,908
1895	1,499	38.0	19.5	17.3	21,174
1896	1,557	39.9	30.1	18.6	21,277
1897	1,606	40.7	40.4	20.6	21,433
1898	1,689	40.3	40.5	22.9	21,659
1899	1,806	41.6	41.3	25.5	21,700
1900	1,969	40.1	46.1	26.9	21,855
1901	1,989	39.1	57.3	24.9	22,078
1902	1,992	41.6	78.5	22.2	22,152
1903	1,964	42.3	55.8	25.1	22,435
1904	1,978	42.7	14.2	22.8	22,634
1905	2,043	43.5	31.9	21.2	22,847
1906	2,109	44.4	31.9	20.5	23,063
1907	2,172	44.9	18.5	17.9	23,108
1908	2,072	43.5	4.7	13.3	23,205
1909	2,144	45.1	15.3	11.2	23,280
1910	2,231	47.4	7.2	10.5	23,387
1911	2,328	48.6	17.1	11.0	23,417
1912	2,409	47.3	7.7	12.2	23,411

Note: All in current prices; in £million

Sources: Col (1) Feinstein, C. H., 'National Income and Expenditure, 1870-1963', London and Cambridge Economic Bulletin (June 1964)

(2) Railway Returns

(3) Report of the Board of Trade on the Railway . . . Bills (annual). Figures for Manchester Ship Canal have been excluded.

(4) Mitchell 'The Coming of the Railway . . .' Including expenditure on land and on ancillary businesses. The latter is expenditure on capital account only.

(5) Railway Returns. The figure for 1870 is for number of miles constructed.

The general pattern of railway investment has been established by a number of writers. There was a peak in the mid-1870s, and another at the turn of the century. In 1874 and 1875 gross capital formation by UK railway companies was £23.7 million in each year. In 1900 the figure was £26.9 million. These are at current prices and include expenditure on land and on ancillary businesses. If one takes account of price changes to give a clearer idea of the meaning of these movements, the picture is altered of course by the fact that in periods of high prices they had to be reduced and in periods of low prices to be raised. But it is not altered a great deal. However, it would be unrealistic to think of a slump in expenditure. In no year did the figure fall below £10 million. (See Table 14, pp 112–13.)

In general the year-to-year movements continued as before. That is, as the economy improved in the upswing of the trade cycle, expectations rose and railway net profits rose (before costs increased). New promotions would accelerate, emanating from both old and new companies—the old often reacting to the interventions of the new; applications to Parliament would mushroom, some schemes would be approved and capital expenditures would follow in the downswing of the cycle.

This cycle remained in existence more or less up to World War I. Promotions and applications to Parliament remained of prime importance because it was the expenditure on permanent way and buildings—those items that normally required statutory powers—which fluctuated most and which were greatest in absolute amounts. The lowest sum (in current prices) spent by UK railways on permanent way was £5.85 million in 1870; the highest was £14.97 million in 1904. The amount spent on rolling stock was normally between £2 and £5 million per annum; only on seven occasions was it greater than £5 million; the amount spent annually on land was slightly less than on rolling stock. It was possible for these various categories of expenditure to coincide and consequently produce a high total. Thus total capital expenditure in 1899 and 1900 was £25.5 and £26.9 million respectively. In the first year permanent way expenditure was £13.47 million; the other three categories being high at some £12 million. Similarly in 1900 nearly one-half of the total was on those three. In other words part of the explanation of the investment boom around 1900 was the unusually high

expenditure on locomotives and other rolling stock; even allowing for the high price level of those years the amount spent was
high. Expenditure on land (£4 million) was the highest in any
one year between 1878 and World War I. The amounts spent
on ancillary businesses per year were seldom high but from
1898 to 1908 they were always above £1 million. (See Table 15,
p 116, and Graph 2, p 115.)

These considerations qualify somewhat the notion of emphasising permanent way expenditure as being the main element in
fluctuations in investment activity. But it remained the greatest
individual item. After all the deductions are made for other
kinds of expenditure the fact remains that around 1900 the railways were spending a lot of money on permanent way and works.

We have established that there were peaks of expenditure
in the 1870s and at the turn of the century. But it would be
quite wrong to think that once the effects of the boom of the
early 1870s had worked themselves out, say after 1878, the
railways were doing very little. For some companies, it is true,
it was a period of retrenchment. On the GWR for example the
1870s had been a very busy decade: the boom of the early
years added some 700 miles to its route-mileage (1,321 in 1872
to 2,053 in 1877). In the next ten years only 300 miles were added
(reaching 2,361 in 1887). Similarly there was stagnation in the
growth of the amount of rolling stock in service. The number of
locomotives increased by 50 per cent between 1872 and 1877
(from 1,009 to 1,514). Less than 100 were added in the next ten
years. And the same broad pattern is true of passenger carriages
and wagons: a very rapid increase in the 5 years to 1877, of 50
per cent or more, and then a much slower rate of increase for the
next decade.[9]

There is evidence that while some companies were by no means
moribund, most of their innovations and improvements were experimental. New types of coaches were introduced, eg Pullman
dining cars, but numbers involved were small.

Yet while railway capital formation reached a low level in
the late 1870s, it picked up in 1880, reaching quite high figures
in the years 1883 and 1884. Moreover, in terms of proposed
applications to Parliament for capital powers this was a major
boom. In both 1882 and 1883 companies applied for capital
powers to the order of £80 million, higher even than in the

upsurge some twenty years later. During the 1880s the average annual capital expenditure was lower than in the 1870s and 1890s, but it was never negligible; although it is important to point out that replacement of rolling stock was low, and there was net disinvestment in 1878 and 1879, and in 1886-8. In the 1880s there were some important and expensive works being carried out. There was the Barry Railway; the Inner Circle of the London Underground was being completed; the Severn Tunnel and the Forth Bridge were built.

The purpose of most of this discussion is to see the interconnections between the various economic factors. Whatever the reasons for individual projects, their promotion and expenditures tend to cluster and explanations to account for these general phenomena can be given in economic terms. Thus the comparative stagnation of profits from 1875 to 1879 helps to account for the low level of promotion and for the tailing off of capital expenditure to a low point in 1880. Similarly the rise in profits from 1879 to 1881 was instrumental in the promotion boom and rapid rise in expenditure in the early 1880s. Profits fell from 1883 to 1885, but then rose fast to 1889 and again there was a rise in investment. From 1893 to 1899 profits rose almost every year; this time there was hardly any time lag and investment rose more or less simultaneously. And the level of investment fell as soon as profits fell in 1899-1901. The only real variation from the pattern came in 1903 to 1910. In those years profits were generally moving upwards, but capital formation fell away. Only after 1910 did capital expenditure begin to rise, but it was a small rise from a very low point. Indeed from 1908 to 1912 there was net disinvestment in both rolling stock and in permanent way.

It is important nevertheless to bring into the calculation factors other than the purely economic. Part of the expenditure was determined by public policy. Thus that incurred under the Regulation of Railways Act of 1889 had to be done within a certain time as determined by law and not by economics. Similarly the timing of the building of the extension of the West Highland to Mallaig was determined by Government. In 1892 there had been an inquiry to consider ways of improving communications for the crofting population. In 1894 the railway company obtained powers to build the line and a further

Act in 1896 provided a Treasury guarantee. Construction took place between 1897 and 1901, a peak period for railway investment, but the West Highland's participation was purely coincidental.

Similarly the proposals for new lines sometimes seem to have been based on the shakiest of foundations. In the 1870s and 1880s there were several ideas for building lines between London and the south Midlands, part of the story which culminated in the building of the line from Marylebone. The dates of promotion of these schemes more or less coincided with the general railway promotion booms (early 1870s, early 1880s, late 1880s). The Buckinghamshire & Northamptonshire Railways Union Railway, for example, was a scheme to build some new connecting lines and to link up with a number of existing railways to provide a new line from London to Birmingham. A letter of September 1873 from the Duke of Buckingham sketches some of the details.

> . . . It seems I think clear that to be successful a combination of the following lines must be made

1	London & Aylesbury	21
2	Aylesbury & Buckingham	$12\frac{1}{2}$
3	Princes Risboro & Watlington	9
4	Wotton T.way	$6\frac{1}{2}$
5	Banbury & Towcester about	16
6	East & West Junction	24
		—
		89

To this combination the formation of the following links

1.	Harrow to Rickmansworth	7 or 8 miles
2.	Brill to Oxford	10 miles
3.	Buckingham to Towcester	9 miles
	Wendover to Princes Risboro	4 miles
	Stratford to Alcester	6 miles

would with the use of the L & NW Banbury line Verney Junction to Buckingham $4\frac{1}{2}$ miles
would give the following routes as compared with the L & NW and GW

		new route	L & NW	GT W
London	to Aylesbury	40	43¼	49¼
	to *Oxford*	63	78	63
	to Buckingham	57	61	—
	to Northampton	76	68	—
	to Banbury	78	77	87
	to Stratford on Avon	95	—	110
	to Birmingham via Midland from Worcester	128	113	129

This would bring a valuable traffic from Oxford & Northampton while a northern extension to Birmingham might be developed . . .

Could not a syndicate be formed of a few persons to make agreements with all these independent lines and to promote the missing links—without some such arrangement it seems to me it will be almost impossible to keep the local lines independent under the pressure or temptation of the large Companies.

Such a syndicate would control 120 miles of connected lines having the shortest route from London to Aylesbury

Oxford
Winslow
Buckingham
Stratford on
Avon

and a good route to Northampton

Banbury

& ultimately a probable route via F. Compton & a new line to Birmingham equal in distance to L & NW . . .

This was, admittedly, no more than a preliminary discussion, but it is significant that the letter merely emphasises the distances between London and certain towns, comparing the proposed route with the existing LNWR and GWR routes. In some cases the shorter distances on the new route provided the evidence that it was a viable proposition. There is no mention of cost of construction or of operation and only a vague reference to 'valuable traffic from Oxford & Northampton'. This scheme came to nothing. It got as far as an application to Parliament in 1875, but it was thrown out.[10]

Particularly useful in helping to explain the investment boom around the turn of the century, as well as throwing useful light on the background to investment decisions generally are two studies on the GWR by David Eversley and Humphrey Cole.[11]

The company, having got over the financial calamities of the late 1860s, took part in the promotion and investment boom of the 1870s. Parliament approved several projects and the work on these was carried out despite the deterioration in the economic climate. By 1877 the work was more or less complete. Expenditure then fell, but once the depression of the mid-1880s was over investment picked up and remained at a high level until World War I. The board decided that the final stage of converting the broad to narrow gauge could no longer be postponed—the former was at the end of its useful life; there was the compulsory expenditure under the 1889 Act; new passenger coaches were ordered, each costing more in the 1890s than a decade earlier (over £1,000 as compared with £720); and this in turn meant that new, larger locomotives were required, the monsters, each costing £4,000, were designed by Churchward who took over control at Swindon in 1892.

Cole examines in particular the Churchward period of rapid innovation in locomotive design. He points out that the 1890s was a period of rapid traffic growth, but he argues that explanations for the outburst of new designs and of continuing heavy investment have to be sought elsewhere than in the expansion of traffic. He emphasises the change in personnel at the top, so that while the boom of the late 1880s caught the company short of good locomotives (they had built so very few in recent years) and the shortage had to be met, the extent and duration of the response are to be explained by these personality factors. He notes that the general secretary, the superintendent of the line, and the chairman retired or died between 1886 and 1889; and that between 1889 and 1893, ten out of nineteen directors died or retired. What had been a lethargic company was now jerked into activity with new people at the head.

It may be that this kind of analysis can be extended to other companies. Bell's brief history of the NER in the twenty-five years from 1898 to 1922 vividly describes the atmosphere of life under Gibb.

Towards the close of the nineteenth century, and after the dawn of the twentieth, the North Eastern's executive machinery was driving uncommonly hard. The company had no qualms about taking in hand one important project after another. It either had the funds to meet the cost of each scheme or could raise fresh capital easily.

Receipts were rising all the time, and the growth of operating costs 'caused little anxiety at a time when the coal mining industry was thriving and the demand for goods wagons exceeded the supply.'[12]

There is one major exception to this idea of new people at the top bringing fresh ideas and enthusiasm into their response to the growth of traffic. This was the extension of the Manchester, Sheffield & Lincolnshire line to London. The actual expenditure on this work was in the first part of the investment boom of the 1890s. The company's Act was obtained in 1893 and the line was opened in 1899 (as the Great Central Railway). The leading light here was one of the older generation of railway leaders, Sir Edward Watkin.

The upsurge of capital expenditure at the turn of the century was associated in part with technical innovations. It was a period of intense activity in the introduction of new types of locomotives, especially the large engines which the heavier trains required. As with so much else in locomotive history, 'much argument is possible about the date of its emergence' as Simmons says. He gives four dates between 1894 and 1899 as possible origins. Among the changes were larger boilers and superheaters, and various other improvements were consolidated by Churchward in his designs for the GWR. It is important too—although more important for operating than for investment—that it was in this period that some rationalisation of production took place. The traditionally large numbers of types of locomotive were all very different from each other. Now attention was given to interchangeability of parts so that a variety of locomotives could be used—according to the needs of particular routes and services—but the number of spare parts was reduced.

The most important technical change, in terms of the amount of money spent on it, was the introduction of electricity. Much of the capital requirements of the boom after 1900 went on this new method of traction, notably for the building of the nucleus of the London underground railways.

The first steam underground line in London was opened in 1863. The construction method—the cut-and-cover system, whereby the existing roads were opened up, and the line laid in a ditch just under the surface—was intended to avoid the high cost of acquiring property in the building of urban railways. By doing it this way property would not be disturbed. In practice it did not work out successfully, and where roads were not wide a great deal of costly underpinning of buildings had to be undertaken. The solution was to go deeper, a technique made possible by the development of tunnelling using a circular iron tube driven through the London clay; the ideas came from Barlow and Greathead. The first experiments were with cable traction which proved unsatisfactory, but electrical operation was shown to be possible for surface railways on some short lines in the 1880s (the Giant's Causeway & Portrush, and Bessbrook & Newry in Ireland; and at Brighton, Blackpool and Ryde). This experience enabled the first tube line then being built to adopt electrification for its opening in 1890. It was not particularly successful.

T. C. Barker heads one of his sections; 'The City & South London Railway pays the penalty for being the pioneer'. It was not a well-planned line. 'The undertaking had . . . been promoted on too modest a scale both from a civil engineering and an electrical point of view.' Its traffic hardly grew in the first decade and its dividends were low or non-existent. And no further tube was opened in London until 1898 when the short Waterloo & City was brought into operation. Apart from that there was only the Liverpool Overhead to show what potentialities there were in electric traction.

Yet for London the need for improved transport had become acute. The amount of travelling had grown enormously and had outstripped the facilities supplied by steam railways, by horse buses and horse trams. Social policy was conceived in terms of moving people out of the centre of London, and this suburban housing would necessarily require improved transport to carry them to their work which remained in the centre. Social policies of this kind could be imposed on the railways through the compulsion to provide workmen's fares; but the railways were commerical undertakings and the lack of profit on the c & sl encouraged very few to risk their money in unknown ventures.

Greater certainty came in 1900 when the Central London

Railway was opened: the 'Twopenny Tube'. This was an immediate success, for unlike the C & SL it followed a heavily used route. If anything it was this company's success, coupled with the general boom, which set off what amounted to a mania for electric railway schemes.

In London the tube network was built between 1900 and 1907. The Central London's opening was immediately followed by application to Parliament for powers to raise some £32 million for tube railways. In 1902 the sum applied for was £43 million, the peak figure, but applications remained high until 1906 and 1907. By that time the basic network had been opened and the advent of motor buses, experimental at first but in large numbers nevertheless, helped to end this important tube boom.

The rest of the railway world by no means neglected the new method of traction. From the early years of the twentieth century several companies obtained parliamentary powers to electrify. But in the event only some small sections were changed over to the new form of traction.

The other technical innovation was the internal combustion engine. Some companies were quick to see that the petrol bus was a cheap way of providing feeder services and the GWR made the first move in 1903 (an Irish company had introduced steam buses the previous year).

This diversification into non-railway operation was not new; for example, the industry had acquired canals during the early days. Moreover it owned and operated docks, sometimes built by railway companies as at Barry, South Wales, and Immingham built by the Great Central. Indeed, by 1914 the railway companies had become the major owners of docks and canals in the country. A further extension was into steamboats for both passengers and cargo. From the 1860s many railway companies acquired parliamentary powers to operate their own steamboats. This was an interesting departure; but in the context of investment expenditure, not of great importance. In the period 1870-1912, out of £781 million spent on capital formation (including expenditure on ancillaries and on land and on renewals, financed from both capital and revenue accounts) only £38 million, ie 5 per cent, was devoted to ancillaries.

Notes to this chapter are on p 210.

CHAPTER 7

COLLECTIVE BARGAINING AND MILITANCY

In the 1890s Sidney and Beatrice Webb, using the example of large companies like the railways, spoke of the impossibility of establishing collective bargaining when the employer was powerful and obdurate.

> Against the unlimited resources, the secured monopoly of custom, and the absolute unity of will enjoyed by these modern leviathans, the quarter of a million accumulated funds of the richest Trade Union, and the clamour of even one or two hundred thousand obstinate and embittered workmen are as arrows against ironclads.[1]

In that decade the railway companies' attitude towards trade unions had hardly changed from earlier years. Just before the Webbs published their *Industrial Democracy* the general manager of the LNWR stated to the Royal Commission on Labour, in 1893: 'You might as well have trade unions in Her Majesty's Army as have it in the railway service.' The incident which symbolised with dramatic force the companies' personnel policy was that affecting stationmaster Hood of the Cambrian Railways. This arose out of the evidence given by the general manager of the company to the select committee on Railway Servants Hours of Labour in 1890. He had been asked to explain why the only man on duty when an accident had occurred had been working for nineteen hours. The general manager blamed the stationmaster. In fact he had not been responsible, and the stationmaster, Hood, anxious to maintain his reputation as a conscientious employee, appeared before the select committee to put the record straight. As a result he was dismissed by the company. This was clearly a breach of parliamentary privilege, a direct attempt to interfere with the workings of a parliamentary committee. The four

directors involved were summoned to the Commons and ad-
monished. In this particular case the employers were brought
to book; but only because parliament had been affected. If the
Commons had not been involved—if the man had been arbitrarily
dismissed in some other situation—there was nothing anyone
could do to protect or defend him.

The Webbs had argued that, on their analysis, when companies
were all powerful either the trade union collapsed or, instead of
collective bargaining, the union had to pursue what they called
'The Method of Legal Enactment' ie obtaining their objectives
through legislation rather than by agreement with the employers.
In an important sense they were right. The main railway unions
certainly acted as pressure groups on parliament. But in another
sense they were wrong. In 1907 the unions, although numerically
weak, forced the pace by threatening to call a national strike. The
government, already searching to establish its role in industrial
relations, intervened forcefully and a settlement was reached: the
establishment of conciliation and arbitration boards. Dissatis-
faction with their working was one of the factors in the train of
events which led to the most surprising event of all, the first
national railway strike in August 1911.

At the same time, and as part of this history, the railwaymen
were changing their attitudes. As well as demanding the setting up
of machinery for negotiation and for the settling of grievances the
majority extended their demands by adopting the ideas of industrial unionism, when the National Union of Railwaymen was
formed in 1913. Its forerunner, the Amalgamated Society of
Railway Servants, was instrumental in establishing the Labour
Representation Committee; and it was the NUR (together with the
South Wales Miners Federation) who gave most support to the
Central Labour College, the left-wing breakaway from Ruskin
College. Within a couple of decades the whole atmosphere of
labour relations on the railways had been fundamentally altered.

This is not the place to investigate the whole range of changes
in the economy and in society at the turn of the century. There
were no doubt both general reasons to account for the 'rise of
labour' and the 'strange death of Liberal England' and individual
explanations of the course of events in particular industries and
areas of the country. Nowadays one sees in the fall in real wages
in the years before World War I a convincing reason for industrial

troubles. The railwaymen experienced a fall in living standards since their comparatively inflexible money wages rose only slowly if at all at a time when prices were increasing rapidly. The companies, it will be remembered, could not raise their charges and their attitude to the demand for higher pay was therefore normally negative. Moreover, changes in efficiency seriously affected conditions of work.

At the same time an understanding of the state of labour relations and the growth of trade unionism requires an appreciation of the multiplicity of occupations and the extent of stratification among railway staff. E. A. Pratt noted that:

> . . . the railway service affords employment for a greater range and diversity of talent, skill, ability or effort than probably any other single industry or enterprise on the face of the earth. From the general manager to the railway navvy, and from the chief engineer, working out intricate problems calling for a high degree of skill and scientific knowledge, to the boy who helps in the unpretending but necessary work of cleaning the engines, there is opportunity for almost every possible class or type of labour, whether skilled or unskilled.[2]

These various grades and occupations often imposed a horizontal stratification; the elite footplatemen had little in common with other railway workers. The differentials were quite wide. A top driver in the 1870s might earn 7s 6d (37½p) a day, whereas an unskilled railwayman received less than £1 per week. Moreover, the conditions of work varied greatly. Some worked regular hours, others very irregular shifts. Locomen and guards could more easily keep in touch with each other throughout the country than could signalmen, who worked in isolation. Yet signalmen, whose work was undergoing rapid technical changes in the late nineteenth century, soon found themselves to be in a strategic position. One writer in the 1890s stated:

> . . . knowing as they do their important and responsible position, they have banded themselves together in a very strong union, and of all classes of railway servants, they are the most given to grumbling.[3]

One should add, since freight traffic fluctuated more than did passenger work, that those on the goods side tended to be those on whom economies were made.

Superimposed on this horizontal stratification there were strong departmental loyalties and exclusiveness which followed from the system which had developed of promotion within departments. There were, too, company loyalties and differences in wages structures. Trade union activity was also related to the general movements in the economy. In periods of prosperity, or rising employment, trade unions were active and growing; in periods of depression almost moribund.

One has, therefore, a number of variables in the situation, and at particular moments of time one or more might be the major factors in the examination of the state of labour relations on the railways.

The first permanent railway trade union was formed in the winter of 1871.[4] At a meeting held in December 1871 in London a decision was taken to establish the Amalgamated Society of Railway Servants. It was registered as a trade union in March 1872 and the first delegate meeting was held in June. Conditions were favourable, just as they had been in the mid 1860s. The economy was booming, unemployment was low, the labour market was tight. Recent legislation affecting trade unions now seemed to put them on a secure legal basis.

A 'flood of petitions', according to Bagwell, reached general managers in the autumn of 1871; the companies—this time acting separately, unlike in 1865-6—tended to concede the demands of the men. There were reductions of hours (certain grades on the NER, the Midland, and generally on Merseyside); and increases of pay in various companies. The GNR went so far as agree to grant three days holiday a year for all employees after one year's service.

All of this took place before the union really began to operate and the first dispute in which the union was involved, in June 1872, was a failure. After the LNWR had agreed to a demand for higher pay, the men petitioned for the removal of an official who had dismissed two men for taking part in the agitation. The board refused and the men struck. It should occasion no surprise that the company was obdurate over this issue. It was one thing to grant an improvement in conditions. It was quite another to agree to dismiss an official. This was a matter which the board would not share; it was their function to hire and fire.

The union weathered this setback and survived. If the trade

I

boom was a time when railwaymen could gain improvements, it was also a period when their working conditions deteriorated. The great expansion of traffic in the early 1870s was operated by railwaymen, especially footplatemen, guards and signalmen, working longer hours. It was this issue above all which had led to the formation of the union, and was to be its most important concern for much of its early history.

A peculiarity of the railwaymen's union was that one of its major initiators should be a railway shareholder and a railway customer. On both counts improvements in railwaymen's conditions might have been against his interests. But Michael Bass, the brewer, was also MP for Derby, an important railway centre, and it was natural for him to have regard for the welfare of his constituents, particularly after the changes in the franchise of the 1860s. But it must not be thought that he was primarily thinking of votes for he took a much more active part. In 1871, for example, he employed C. B. Vincent, a railway clerk, and James Greenwood, a journalist, to tour the country to find out the facts about railwaymen's working conditions. They were startling enough. Greenwood wrote of the normal 90-hour week of the guards, for example.

The resulting publicity—Greenwood published his articles in the *Daily Telegraph*, and *The Times* and other publications were sympathetic—helped to establish the union on a permanent basis. The public no doubt supported any move to reduce railway accidents which affected them directly; long hours worked by railwaymen were commonly said to be the cause of accidents.

Yet, successfully established though it was, the early years were not particularly fruitful. A separate Scottish organisation was set up in 1872, and disagreements between London members and the provinces resulted in a weak central body; power tended to rest with the branches rather than with the executive committee. This was perhaps desirable during a trade boom, given the possibility of local improvements being obtained, but the boom collapsed in 1874 and the union, either centrally or locally, could do little to prevent the advances made in the early 1870s being lost. From 1876 onwards there were reductions of wages and some extensions of hours of work. There was nothing the society could do. Its membership fell from 17,000 in 1872 to 6,000 in the trough of 1882.

The union was of the friendly society type, with prominent personalities among its patrons, such as Earl de la Warr. It did not believe in the strike weapon and its power was decentralised. It was weak numerically, even at its peak in 1872 recruiting no more than a few per cent of railwaymen. In 1880 it did set up a protection fund but this evidence of a new determined spirit of militancy came just too late to prevent the formation of a separate union for drivers and firemen, the Associated Society of Locomotive Engineers and Firemen.

The occasion for this seems to have been a worsening of conditions on the GWR. In 1878 the hours of drivers and firemen had been extended to twelve per day, having been ten since 1867. Subsequently a system of payment was introduced which meant that wage increases would not depend on years of service. Nearly 2,000 footplatemen on the GWR signed a petition which was presented to the chairman, Sir Daniel Gooch. There is a pleasing story that his reaction really set in motion the moves towards a union. 'Damn the signatures! Have you got the men to back them up.' This challenge to prove that the petition had wide support was taken up and the union was formed. However, its membership was low and did not exceed 2,000 before the late 1880s. Similarly, another separate union established in 1880, the United Pointsmen's and Signalmen's Society, was small. It was also a craft union, mainly interested in friendly benefits for its members.

These three unions had a ridiculously small membership, but in the gloomy years of the 1880s there was one bright area of railway trade unionism. This was on the North Eastern Railway, where forceful local leadership produced important initiatives; but there were other reasons. Gupta has shown that there was less departmental exclusiveness in the company and there was close cooperation between locomen and goods guards, who formed the bulk of the membership of the ASRS. He says that the reason for this was probably

> . . . the classification system in the wages structure of the locomotive department at Newcastle. There locomen and guards were put into a number of different wage-brackets, according to the types of trains there were attached to—express, passenger, goods or mineral, without any clear principle of promotion from one bracket to another.[5]

This contrasted with the practice of some other companies

which had a uniform wage and a system of annual increments. The NER wage structure thus hindered the development of an exclusive departmental trade union mentality, for it created divisions within the ranks of each grade.

There were also other factors which probably helped to explain the growth of railway unionism in the North East. The company's operations were confined geographically and it had a monopoly in the area—there were no conflicting loyalties to other companies—and there was the local tradition of trade unionism among the Durham miners.

In the later 1880s, in that upsurge commonly termed 'New Unionism', organisations suddenly blossomed among the unskilled and semi-skilled. Even before the dock strike of 1889 the ASRS had adopted a slightly more militant policy. In the previous year the rules had been changed and it was now no longer necessary for a ballot of the whole membership to be taken before a strike was authorised. The new rule of 1888 left the conduct of strikes to the union's head office. It was in one sense, as Gupta says, a defensive response to the depression of the 1880s. But it was also intended 'to enable areas of growth like the NER to press their programmes to a point where a railway strike could be employed as a tactical weapon.'

Yet the ASRS seemed weak, to be derided as a friendly society. Its membership was probably greatest among the better paid, the locomen and guards. There were some lower paid railwaymen in it but they had to wait for the creation of a new body, the General Railway Workers Union, which aimed to recruit the lower paid, who were not interested in friendly benefits and had a definite policy of pursuing its demands by strike action. It very quickly had 10,000 members. And during this great upsurge of trade unionism the ASRS reached 40,000 by 1894 (by which time the Scottish ASRS had amalgamated with it); and ASLEF reached nearly 7,000 in the early 1890s.

Did it amount to anything? There were successful local agitations in Ireland, in South Wales and in the North East. The last two were significant in that union officials were involved in the settlement, giving them a measure of recognition—permanent in the case of the NER, but not in South Wales. However, a six weeks' strike in Scotland was defeated. It led to the Scottish Society joining the ASRS. But, more important, the reason for the strike—the long hours being worked—resulted in the setting up of the Select Committee on Railway Servants Hours of Labour. The committee produced evidence of long hours, and legislation resulted. The Railway Regulation Act of 1893 enabled railway-men to submit complaints of excessive hours to the Board of Trade which was empowered to make enquiries. If appropriate the Board of Trade could order a railway company to submit a revised schedule of duties. The Act had many faults, but it is significant as being the first occasion when Parliament intervened to regulate, in some way, the hours of work of adult males. It may even have been effective in reducing hours; but the evidence is not at all clear.

However, the Act was made use of, which may explain why the membership of the major railway unions continued to grow. The Amalgamated Society launched a national campaign for recognition and there was talk of a national strike. Instead there were sectional and local demands and disputes. A few were successful, but most failed—the Taff Vale dispute of 1900 was only one of many local conflicts. A strike on this South Wales line was successfully fought by the company and resulted in the famous House of Lords judgement of 1901. This granted an in-junction against the union and enabled the company to obtain damages.[6] The case is of major importance in labour history, and equally so for the railways.

The judgement stiffened the resistance of the companies which were suffering from the rapid rise in working costs at the turn of the century. They reacted by introducing economies, by reduc-tions of staff and by a general speeding up. The Railway Com-panies Association was strengthened and a 'scheme was set afoot for the registration of a mobile reserve force of railwaymen for breaking strikes wherever they might occur.' However, while the Amalgamated Society and the GRWU were both weakened by these events, three other unions improved their membership; ASLEF, which was now recruiting electric trainmen and engine cleaners; the Railway Clerks Association (formed 1897); and the signal-men.

It was evident by the 1890s that two decades of attempts to obtain recognition by the companies had been largely unsuccess-ful. The alternative approach was to go outside the industrial situation and into politics. In the first place the ASRS tried to win the support of MPs for their policies, and during the 1890s this was transformed into a demand for independent labour representation. It was this union which proposed the resolution at the 1899 Trades Union Congress calling for a conference to discuss labour representation. This led to the establishment of the Labour Representation Committee and subsequently of the Labour Party.

In the second place, it made sense to make use of parliament since railway affairs were always being examined there, notably during private bill procedure when the companies were asking parliament for powers to extend their functions. The unions tried to have clauses inserted in railway Bills which enjoined the companies to recognise the unions and to improve the conditions of their staff. This method was not particularly fruitful and the lack of success helps to account for the upsurge of militancy in the decade before World War I.

But there was no co-operation between the two main unions and they put forward different programmes. The ASRS mounted an all-grades campaign, in which ASLEF was not interested since it confined itself to the needs of its own members. In particular ASRS insisted on demanding recognition by the companies and it was this that essentially separated the unions.

The companies (except the NER) refused to meet ASRS and they maintained this position from January 1907, when the programme was presented, to October, despite the pressure of public opinion and of the President of the Board of Trade, Lloyd George. The union conducted a strike ballot. Out of 88,000 papers returned 77,000 were in favour of a strike. The government stepped in and after much negotiation a conciliation scheme was introduced. But still the union was not recognised. The 1907 agreement was not between the companies and the unions. It was made separately: between the companies and the Board of Trade; and between the unions and the Board of Trade. The scheme provided for the establishment, within each company, of Sectional Boards to deal with defined groups of employees. Each board was to be composed of elected representatives of the groups and of an equal number of company representatives. Any question not settled at that stage could be referred to a Central Conciliation Board composed of company nominees and of representatives from the employees' side of the sectional boards. If still unresolved, the difference could be referred to arbitration. Two significant features of the scheme were that the subject matter was limited to wages and hours of work only; and that complaints had to originate as petitions and deputations.

This scheme was drafted by Sam Fay, general manager of the GCR; it was not, as is commonly thought, the result of a brilliant idea of Lloyd George's. It does not follow, however, that the companies were happy with the scheme, even though the unions were left outside. There is plenty of evidence, for example, of attempts to influence the election of representatives in order to keep out any who were trade unionists. They were largely unsuccessful. A very high proportion of those elected to sectional boards were union members. One kind of management response can be illustrated by a letter which G. J. Churchward, the locomotive superintendent of the GWR, wrote to the secretary of a sectional board: 'If you and those you represent are not satisfied with the conditions in my department, I shall be pleased to receive your notices.'

If the management objected to the scheme because it interfered with their prerogatives, the men objected because it did not provide them with many useful results. In the first year or so, years of depression, the companies were able to resist demands successfully and to pursue policies which circumvented the arbitrator's awards. The managements resorted to 'cheeseparing economy at the expense of men', eg through the manipulation of hours of work, and the regrading of men to avoid paying higher rates of pay. At the same time, railway workers were adversely affected by the various changes made by the companies, such as agreements for reducing competition.

> Whilst economies in traffic operation were welcome in the national interest and were not opposed at any time by the union, they reduced the security of employment of railwaymen in areas where there had been an overlapping and duplication of services, they reduced the prospects of promotion for younger men and they increased the pace and intensity of labour.[7]

On the other hand if one consequence of the (limited) participation by railwaymen in the running of the industry was to force managements to become more efficient, then this can be welcomed. What was missing was the attention which ought to have been given to those whose employment was adversely affected.

In addition the new locomotives being introduced were often physically difficult to operate, the needs of the footplate crews not having been considered by the designers. Subjects like these could not be discussed in the conciliation machinery, whose scope was limited to wages and hours. In any case the arbitrators' awards were not regarded by the men as being very favourable. The (incomplete) Board of Trade returns of railway wages showed that the results of all this had not resulted in higher pay. Indeed, the figures for 1910 demonstrated that average weekly earnings were slightly lower than they had been in 1907, before the scheme started. (See Table 16 below.)

TABLE 16

EARNINGS OF RAILWAYMEN, 1901-10 (UK)

	Average weekly earnings per head	
	£ s d	(Decimal £)
1901	1 5 0¼	(1.25)
1902	1 4 11¼	(1.24½)
1903	1 4 10½	(1.24)
1904	1 5 0½	(1.25)
1905	1 5 3½	(1.26)
1906	1 5 5¼	(1.27)
1907	1 5 10	(1.29)
1908	1 5 0	(1.25)
1909	1 5 4½	(1.26½)
1910	1 5 9	(1.29)

Source: Board of Trade, *Report on Changes in Rates and Wages and Hours of Labour in the United Kingdom in 1910*. Quoted Pratt, *History of Inland Transport*, 435.

Note: The figures refer to manual workers only in twenty-seven companies which employed over 90 per cent of all railway employees. The earnings are those obtained in the first week of December each year. Actual earnings as in original; decimal equivalent to nearest ½p.

The railwaymen, therefore, could argue that the 1907 scheme was working badly, and that their unions were not even recognised by the companies (except for the NER). In the three or four years before World War I the world of labour was transformed and there began that period of intense militancy which did not end until the early 1920s, of which the general strike of 1926 was a final fling. Even so one should not exaggerate the actual extent of the conflict. Thus in the period 1911-14 the number of working days lost per year in strikes by those employed in all forms of transport was only 1.51 per man. But those who look back on these years as years of excitement and enthusiasm and of change cannot be faulted. There was a national railway strike, with some loss of life. There were important changes in union policy and structure.

The explosion came in 1911. There are always many reasons why strikes take place and it is not necessarily possible to establish the real causes. What can be said about 1911 was that following two successful major strikes in shipping and on the docks which brought gains through militant action, the lessons were absorbed quickly by other transport workers including railwaymen. At first all the action was unofficial. In July and August railwaymen in various parts of the country left work before the union leadership took action; 50,000 were on strike before the leadership took over control.

The storm centre had been Liverpool and the executive committees of four unions met there to decide on concerted action. They quickly agreed 'to offer to the railway companies twenty-four hours to decide whether they are prepared to immediately meet the representatives of these societies to negotiate a basis of settlement of the matters in dispute affecting the various grades.' The government at once intervened, firstly by meeting the railway managers and assuring the companies 'that they will give ample protection to enable them to carry on their services'. Secondly the union general secretaries were invited to meet the President of the Board of Trade. The unions explained that the causes of their action were the shortcomings of the conciliation scheme and the absence of recognition by the companies.

The Prime Minister, Asquith, was then involved and he suggested that there should be set up a Royal Commission to investigate impartially the statements made by the unions about the working of the conciliation scheme. The unions rejected this. The proposed commission might have taken months or years to report; the government was already on the side of the companies; and the real issue was not the actual workings of the conciliation boards: it was recognition by the companies. The four union executives agreed on a strike and telegrams were sent out on 17 August, instructing their members to strike.

It was by no means a complete strike, nor did it last long. Probably 200,000 men took part, less than half the labour force, and it was virtually over in two days. On 19 August the government got management and union representatives together for the first time, sitting at the same table. The union leaders agreed to instruct their members to return to work having been promised the reinstatement of the strikers, the speedy convening of the conciliation boards to examine the men's claims, and the establishment of a Commission of Inquiry whose purpose would be to examine the machinery of collective bargaining in the industry. None of this seemed to be an advance on what the unions had rejected a few days before and in some parts of the country meetings of railwaymen rejected the settlement. But generally it was accepted and the railways worked again.

The major consequence was the new conciliation scheme of 1911. The major stumbling block remained the recognition of the unions. The company representatives continued to oppose it, their views being summarised by the commission in these terms:

> The apprehensions of the companies are that recognition, as they interpret it, would seriously affect discipline and interfere with the management if men in approaching their officers or directors on any subject of grievance or complaint had the right to bring a Trade Union official with them. We think that with their great responsibilities the companies cannot and should not be expected to permit any intervention between them and their men on the subject of discipline and management.

But they went so far as to recommend that 'the members of each Board shall be at liberty to elect a secretary from any source they may think proper'.

Obviously the word 'recognition' had a very restricted meaning by modern standards and the demand for it seemed to be no more than asking that union representatives should assist railwaymen when they appeared at the Conciliation Boards or before officers or directors of the companies. The new scheme did not come into existence straight away. The unions did not accept all the recommendations and sought to discuss the problems with the companies, but this the managements refused to do. The unions decided to ballot their members about a further strike and after much pressure the companies and the union representatives met in December and the new scheme, slightly amended, was agreed.

Essentially it included a speeding-up of the procedure and removed some of the ambiguity of the 1907 scheme; conditions of employment as well as wages and hours could be discussed but matters of discipline and of management were this time explicitly excluded (previously their exclusion was implicit). Despite the appeals of the ASRS, sectional boards were retained (the society naturally preferred not to maintain a structure which crystallised divisions between grades); but central boards for each company were abolished. The impartial chairman was transferred from central to sectional boards and his decision was to be final, as before. The significance of this was that where a sectional board could not agree, instead of referring the matter to a board composed of all grades it could now be settled bindingly by the chairman. The procedure was more rapid, and this was a gain. But it meant greater isolation between grades and therefore between unions.

The companies no doubt thought they had made great concessions. In essence though it was only a primitive kind of collective bargaining. The unions were recognised only insofar as it was possible for the men to elect as secretary to their side someone not in the employment of the companies. Union officials could thus take part in the scheme. But other representatives of the men could be elected by any employee whether unionist or not.

In 1917 Cole and Page Arnot could point out that in the years following the new scheme wages rose slightly, but

> . . . the gains from the settlement were so small that they stimulated rather than quietened the unrest. Indeed, despite the existence of a scheme designed to prevent disputes, no industry was, during the three years before the war, subject to so frequent upheavals as the railway service, and, while there was no national stoppage, there were many occasions on which such a stoppage threatened, as well as many actual strikes within confined areas.

The mood of many railwaymen remained militant as two major events illustrate. The first was the establishment of the National Union of Railwaymen. This could be regarded as purely a constitutional matter, a simple case of union amalgamation. It was certainly this; it was also more than this. For the railways were the first major industry in which an industrial union was established, intended to cater for all workers within that industry. In particular it was formed at the time when the ideas of industrial unionism were being propagated and the need for workers to be organised on an industrial basis was part of the theme of those advocating workers' control. One cannot say, of course, that the

NUR was established mainly because they wanted workers' control. But it is certainly reasonable to argue that the amalgamation, while clearly influenced in its timing by the experience of joint action in 1911, cannot be divorced from the background of new ideas then current in the labour world.

The railway unions had talked about closer working for years. They had examined the possibility of federation and of amalgamation. Inevitably there was the real difficulty of combining craft and occupational unions with general unions, the fear of a loss of identity and of their special needs being swamped within a larger organisation. Moreover as one reads the events of the first decade of the twentieth century, one can almost feel the bitter divisions, notably between ASRS and ASLEF, which were manifested in a real rivalry and hostility between their general secretaries. At any rate the actual fusion of 1913 was between ASRS, the General Railway Workers, and the Signalmen, ASLEF and the railway clerks remaining separate organisations.

The second illustration of pre-war militancy was the formation of the Triple Alliance. The experience of the major strikes in the basic industries was that taking strike action at different times was costly and that simultaneous action would be more effective. The miners in 1913 decided to approach other major unions 'with a view to co-operative action and the support of each others' demands'. They then approached the NUR and the National Transport Workers' Federation and the scheme was approved in December 1915.

Notes to this chapter are on pp 210–11.

CHAPTER 8

WORLD WAR 1 AND ITS AFTERMATH

Writing of the period which ended in 1914 Professor Simmons avers that:

> For all the uncertainties and occasional gloom of these years, the student of British railways is bound to look back to them as, in most respects, the climax of the story . . . the railways have never since enjoyed so strong a position, or offered so good a service, as they did in the years before 1914.[1]

The railways were one of the staple industries on which so much of Britain's prosperity rested in the nineteenth century, but which in the last half-century have experienced stagnation and decline, and supersession by newer technologies. The war itself did not cause the change over: its origins can be found in earlier years, but it undoubtedly greatly speeded up the process. Thus if recent railway history can be summarised as consisting of competition from new forms of transport, of greater centralisation and control, and of a highly unionised labour force, then one can readily trace the trend back to some time before 1914.

But the war was a forcing house of change without which the changes may have taken much longer to be put into operation. One example will suffice. The use of motor lorries by the army provided a remarkable testing ground in the worst possible conditions. They provided experience in their use and maintenance for many thousands of men, an extensive and rapid training unlike anything which could have happened—at that period—outside the necessities of war. Such men were well equipped to enter the new motor transport industry after the war, unregulated as it was, and needing only small amounts of capital.

This unexpected by-product of the war was external to the railways, as were the interruptions to international trade which severely affected the industry's traffic. Equally important were events peculiar to it, not least those which had significant consequences for management and control. In 1914 the industry was taken over by the government under the powers of the Regulation of the Forces Act, 1871. Unlike the experience of other government control during the war, characterised by the sudden need to improvise, there had been some preliminary planning occasioned by the alarmed reaction to the Agadir crisis of 1911. A Railway Executive Committee, established in 1912 and consisting of the general managers of the major companies, was charged with the duty of managing and operating the industry during the period of control. The government took over the railways but the companies remained in private hands.

They received no payment for the services they were called upon to perform for the government, but since it was assumed that they would make losses they were guaranteed their net income for 1913. The eventual practice was for the government to pay sums based on the companies' monthly estimates, which included an allowance for that maintenance which the companies had been unable to perform. In addition the government met the cost of all wage increases (except that it met only three-quarters of the first wage increase) and paid 4 per cent on all capital expenditure incurred since 1913. The justification of that payment was that the companies had built various works which could not benefit them because they had not been opened and producing revenue in 1913, the year taken as the base for their guaranteed income.

The really important aspect of war-time control—which lasted until 1921—was the experience of unified operation. Most of those interested in the subject looked at the work of the REC and concluded that a railway system worked better this way, and there should be no return to the old type of competition.

In 1917 Sir Herbert Walker, chairman of the REC, said:

I cannot think that our railways will ever revert to the independent and foolish competitive system which obtained before war broke out . . . If we are to get the really useful and tangible results of what has been done in the war—if we are to prove that the experience gained has been beneficial—there must be

vastly more co-ordination between the various lines and companies. Overlapping must cease, and waste of material, stock,
manpower and energy must be done away with.

Sentiments of this kind were a commonplace but not all voices
were in harmony. In the third edition of *The History and Economics of Transport* by Kirkaldy and Evans, published in 1924,
the authors were not enthusiastic.

> The experience gained has been of no value to the student of
> that perplexing problem, the State ownership of railways. Every-
> thing was subordinated to the requirements of war. Passenger
> services were curtailed and withdrawn; ordinary goods and
> minerals traffic was delayed because the requirements of the
> Government were so large that it could not be moved; and as
> a consequence industrial establishments were sometimes brought
> to a temporary standstill.

It was perfectly possible to come to opposing conclusions
since the statistics were not complete. Those for operating
receipts and expenditure were published but there was no information available on the amounts of traffic carried. On balance
it seems likely that the traffic increased, despite the reduction
in services as the war went on. Rolling stock and even track
were sent overseas for war purposes and passenger fares were
raised in 1917 primarily to discourage civilian travel. The staff
was also depleted for the needs of the armed forces and maintenance was reduced.

The railways were able to institute pooling arrangements for
certain kinds of wagons—something never before achieved—
which must have made for more efficient working. But the
management had the advantage of not having to worry much
about finance and costs and in certain matters they had the
power of the state behind them. Thus in 1916 powers were taken
under the Defence of the Realm Act by which users of wagons
were given time-limits for their loading and unloading, so that
shortages, due to the traditional detention of wagons, were reduced.

The fact that the railways, despite all the difficulties they
faced, could do the increased work was helped by two other factors. As the pre-war companies were lavishly supplied with equipment, this enabled them—at the beginning of the war at any rate

—to meet sudden demands and to continue to run normal services. Then, ironically, the work of the Railway Executive Committee was undoubtedly helped by the very existence of competing companies with their variety of routes. A comparatively smooth flow of services, including fitting in trains demanded suddenly, was facilitated by the duplicated routes which had been built under a competitive system.

The experience of war shattered what was left of a belief in competition between the railways and led to massive changes in organisation in the 1920s. The immediate economic effect was a physical deterioration of the industry's assets. On the one hand maintenance was reduced while the amount of work done was growing; on the other, investment was at a low level. During the war gross investment ran at about one-half of the average expenditure of the immediate pre-war investment. It is true that investment had been rising from 1910 and reached a peak in 1913, so that a comparison with those years may be somewhat misconceived and may overstate the actual fall. Nevertheless, it is quite clear that capital expenditure fell to the lowest figure since the 1840s, and that the amount of renewals could not have been sufficient to meet depreciation. The industry was therefore in a poor position to meet the demands of the post-war world.

In labour relations, too, the war brought new challenges and a changed circumstance. During the war, it is true, the strike weapon was hardly used; the unions and the companies agreed, soon after the war began, to continue existing arrangements, and this 'truce' continued for the period of hostilities. But when prices rose the unions demanded wage increases to maintain their members' living standards. One company, the South Eastern & Chatham, agreed to this late in 1914 and the other companies fell into line in February 1915, by agreeing to flat-rate increases. It was highly significant that for the first time there was an industry-wide agreement, a move away from the earlier company bargaining. This was new; it became permanent. Since then collective bargaining has continued at national level.

By the end of the war the various increases amounted to 33s (£1.65), which just more than doubled the average earnings of July 1914. This method of compensating for price increases naturally enough resulted in differentials being narrowed. Those who gained most proportionately were the low paid, whereas the higher paid staff such as footplatemen gained least relatively. It was a situation possessed of all the ingredients for trouble after the war. The standard increases were added to a variety of basic pre-war rates (numerous grades in different companies). The attempt to standardise them led to acrimonious conflict, ending in the national railway strike of 1919.

The government was still in control of the railways, and an agreement was reached as the war was ending to institute the eight-hour day, to operate from early 1919. The companies had to take on extra staff and the unions negotiated for various improvements. In particular they wanted 'standardisation upwards', ie standardisation of the basic rates at the level of the highest rate in the grade. A separate settlement for the footplatemen conceding this principle was made in August. The absence of a settlement for the rest produced a nine-day strike in September, in which the footplatemen participated.

Subsequently negotiations took place with the first Minister of Transport, Sir Eric Geddes, who proposed a reduction in the number of grades and a scheme for wages to be based on the cost of living index. At the same time a new system of bargaining was established by the institution of Central and National Wages Boards consisting of representatives of management and unions.

In the conditions of the immediate post-war period these improvements for the staff could not easily be offset by economies and efficiencies. Prices were high; wages were at least double the pre-war figure and the cost of many materials used by the railways had risen. But charges, as ever, were not flexible and apart from the passenger fare increase of 1917 there was no general rise until 1920 when increases of goods rates were permitted. Thus post-war inflation resulted in a familiar situation for the railways. Their increased traffic did not bring in sufficient revenue to meet the great rise in costs. In 1920 their net profits fell; in 1921 they actually made a loss. In that year the period of control by the government came to an end, as did so many other war-time controls.

The three years since the end of the war had been partly filled by an intense discussion about the future of the railways, during which several parliamentary committees examined different

K

aspects of that industry and other forms of transport. The acute financial conditions of the railways made the search for a policy an insistent urgency, given also the demands for a much greater participation by employees in the running of industry.

The first change was the establishment of a new government department to take over certain transport functions of the Board of Trade to which were added duties with regard to road transport. In 1920 it published a white paper *Outline of proposals as to the future organisation of transport undertakings in Great Britain and their relation to the State.* This policy, much of it to be embodied in the Railways Act of the following year, implicitly rejected nationalisation and instead proposed the grouping of the railways of England & Wales, and Scotland. It envisaged up to seven groups, five or six for England & Wales, and one for Scotland: Southern, Western, North Western, Eastern, North Eastern, London, Scotland.

> It is recognised [said the white paper] that a more logical grouping of the existing systems might result if regard were had exclusively either to geographical or to operating considerations; but the amalgamation of complete undertakings as the initial step will avoid many of the difficulties which would arise if undertakings had to be divided. It would be open to the new group companies to exchange between themselves lines which project from the territory of one group into that of another, and at a later stage it may become necessary to require them to do so.

This was the first significant change, the compulsory merging into groups, and in a slightly different form it was eventually put into operation. The white paper also suggested that each board should be limited in number to twenty-one, 'in order to secure efficiency and uniformity, and avoid undue cost'; it went further and proposed that 'the workers—both officials and manual workers—should have some voice in management'. Thus the boards should be composed of representatives of shareholders, who should be in a majority, and of employees. The employees should be one-third 'leading administrative officials of the group, to be co-opted by the rest of the Board', and two-thirds 'elected from and by the workers on the railway'.

Other proposals were equally far-reaching. The white paper thought that 'with due care and economy' the groups should be able to improve on their pre-war return—the road transport industry was not thought of as a major competitor—'but, in that event, the Government is of opinion that such surplus revenues should not accrue entirely to the companies'. The government should participate in them as a quid pro quo for 'very materially extending the "charter" of the companies'. This share going to the State would not be part of the country's revenue. 'The intention is that the Government's share of these surplus profits should be funded for development purposes, to assist backward districts, to develop light railways, and for other appropriate purposes in connection with transportation.'

The white paper, indeed, in discussing the 'Future powers of the State in relation to Railways' proposed quite sweeping powers. Among them was the state's right to require adequate services and facilities; to impose standards of permanent way, rolling stock and equipment; to require greater operating co-operation, eg running rights, the pooling of traffic and receipts, and the common use of plant. Moreover, 'the railways should be required to submit for approval their proposals involving capital expenditure and also their plans for raising capital required.' And the state should have the power to require that adequate reserves for renewals and depreciation be made before dividends were distributed.

The outcries from those who thought the proposals were a kind of backdoor nationalisation were balanced by those who had looked forward to workers' control. The actual legislation was the Railways Act of 1921 which was a watered down version of both the white paper and of the subsequent Bill. The grouping was altered and only four main-line companies emerged. The actual number of directors was fixed but it was not a uniform number for each board; there was no mention of employees participating in board matters. Instead of the state appropriating any surplus revenue the general requirement was that charges should be adjusted to revenue and a new body, the Railway Rates Tribunal, was established with a general oversight of these matters. Charges initially were to be fixed to enable companies to earn a standard revenue, based on their 1913 figures. Any excess net revenue earned could be reduced by the tribunal modifying the charges.

Of special importance was Part 4 of the Act which dealt

with wages and conditions of service. This laid down the machinery to be established, based on existing procedures. The Central and National Wages Boards were re-constituted and put on a statutory basis. The former was to consist of representatives of the companies and the unions, but the assumption of the Act was that 'all questions relating to rates of pay, hours of duty or other conditions of service' should be settled by agreement between the companies and the unions. Only if no agreement was reached at this stage were the matters to go to the Central Wages Board. From this body there could be an appeal to the National Wages Board, which was to be composed of representatives of the companies and the unions, plus four representatives of railway users (one each nominated by the Trades Union Congress, the Co-operative Union; the Association of British Chambers of Commerce; and the Federation of British Industries).

In addition the Act provided for the establishment of councils for each company, consisting of officers of the company and representatives of employees. Each council was to have functions which 'shall generally be such as are mentioned in paragraph (16) of the Report of the Reconstruction Committee on the Relations between Employers and Employed, dated the eighth day of March, nineteen hundred and seventeen'. This was a reference to the famous Whitley Committee which had advocated that management and workers should establish machinery for negotiations and for the avoidance of disputes.

One can recapture how novel and unusual these changes in labour relations were from the reaction of Kirkaldy and Evans in their book written just after the Act was passed.

From the moment the Act came into force and the various boards were established in working order, there ceased to be any excuse for a strike on the part of the men, or for retaliatory action on the part of management.

Here the industrial world has been given a great object lesson in how to do it. Friction and class warfare have cost our country dear. The eyes of all engaged in our industries and commerce should be fixed on the working out of this great experiment. It will doubtless cause great searching of heart among those who desire industrial unrest. Foreign propagandists will realise the bulwark this new policy raises, not only in the safeguarding of the best interests of labour, but against the chances of strife, both internal and external. They and those who think with them will undoubtedly do their worst to make the machinery unworkable. But the good common sense of all true Englishmen will welcome Part IV of the Act as a statesmanlike attempt to keep our industries sane and healthy. The policy will be watched and its success will be acclaimed. May this great attempt to find an avenue, by means of which organiser and worker, employer and employee, may work harmoniously together, be crowned with success. Should this be the outcome, we as a great industrial community will, indeed, find ourselves at the outset of a new epoch in our history well equipped for a prosperous future.

On second thoughts, these sentiments could well have been expressed at any time in the last fifty years. Here is the assumption that the establishment of machinery to negotiate and settle disputes will somehow reduce industrial conflict. Implicitly, the absence of strikes will raise output. And an important cause of strikes is the importation of foreign ideas. Nevertheless, whatever the relevance of these innovations for industry as a whole, for the railways they were pretty revolutionary. Moreover, implicit in the Act was the obligation on the part of the companies to undertake collective bargaining with the unions—before the nationalisation Acts of the late 1940s probably an unique example of such legal duty.

Note to this chapter is on p 211.

Part Three:
The End of Monopoly

CHAPTER 9

TRADE DEPRESSION AND COMPETITION, 1920-39

In one sense or another the railways in the last half-century have been a problem. Apart from World War 2 with its special circumstances, the industry has experienced a decline in the demand for its services. If the nineteenth century was the age of steam, the twentieth is that of the internal combustion engine, and the varying attempts to accommodate the old with the new provide the basis of recent history. The background has not been constant: in the inter-war period trade depression and changes in industrial structure and location were significant determinants of the industry's fortunes. In the post-war years high operating costs have been important. But throughout, chipping away at the traffic has been the rapid growth of road transport.

Whatever problems there may have been for the railways in the first two decades of the century, the year 1921 had all the ingredients for a disaster. The year of the Railways Act also saw the ending of the post-war boom, and a major coal strike. Railway traffic and receipts fell catastrophically.

This shock came just as the companies were preparing themselves for massive organisational changes. Under the Act some 120 separate companies were compulsorily merged into four, each more or less with a territorial monopoly. A check was placed on the possible abuse of this monopoly power by the regulation of rates and charges and also of profits. The railways' charges were to be fixed at levels which would provide the companies with a 'standard revenue' based on the level of profit of 1913.

The pricing system, embodied in the 1921 Act, found its origin in the deliberations of the Railway Rates Advisory Committee which had been established by the Ministry of

Transport Act of 1919. The Minister had to consult the committee before making any changes in railway rates. Its most important function was to examine, at the request of the minister, the whole basis of railway charges. After a public inquiry the committee reported and its recommendations formed the essence of Part III of the 1921 Act.

Standard rates were to be fixed, implying a uniform scale of charges for the whole country, thus maintaining the traditional notion of equality of treatment for the railways' customers. This uniformity, together with the idea that each of the four new companies should pay their way, was instrumental in determining the details of the mergers. Each company had to take a share of the poorer paying areas as well as the more profitable ones; for this reason the badly-off Scottish companies were not able to form a separate company. Naturally this principle implied cross-subsidisation, the profitable parts of each company supporting those making losses.

At the same time the policy replaced the system of the 1890s. Instead of maximum rates, actual rates were fixed, settled at levels which would enable the companies to earn their standard revenue. (If they failed to earn it the rates could be altered.) Flexibility was introduced by the permission given to companies to make 'exceptional' charges, below the standard rates; but if they were more than 40 per cent below they had to be approved by a new body, the Railway Rates Tribunal.

The Railway Rates Advisory Committee was also given the task of determining the classification of goods, after negotiation with the traders. The classification, agreed by 1923, followed from the principles laid down in the Act. Merchandise was to be allocated to a particular class according to 'value, to the bulk in relation to weight, to the risk of damage, to cost of handling, and to the saving in cost which may result when merchandise is forwarded in large quantities.' The negotiations led to the establishment of twenty-one classes (as against the eight previously existing), plus a number of special classifications (eg for dangerous goods). In practice, the principles of the classification were those used by the railways in the past.

> Value, more than any other characteristic, determined whether a particular sort of goods was placed in a high class, paying a high rate per ton-mile, or a low class paying a low rate. Of the

remaining principles, bulk in relation to weight received most consideration.[1]

The final stage in these preliminaries was the settling of the charges themselves, to be done by the Railway Rates Tribunal, again after discussion with the traders. These negotiations were concluded by 1927 and the new scheme came into operation the following January.

The Act, it is commonly said, was a piece of legislation for the nineteenth rather than for the twentieth century. The assumption behind it was that each company would be a monopoly and therefore there should be some safeguards to prevent abuse. This notion was buttressed by the continued operation of various obligations towards society inherited from the past: to publish charges, to act as a common carrier, to show no undue preference, for example. Each of the four companies was possessed of a geographical monopoly (apart from a few competing routes) and regulation was therefore legitimate. But in an important sense their monopoly was being undermined by market forces which placed constraints on the industry. The road transport industry had come of age. In 1920 the number of goods vehicles with current licences reached 101,000, thus surpassing the previous peak of 85,000 of 1915. Expansion was rapid, the numbers doubling by 1924, and reaching nearly 350,000 by 1930. The increase in motor cars was even faster, from less than 200,000 in 1920 to over 1 million by 1930.

It is right and proper to place at the forefront of discussion the new role of the internal combustion engine in its effects on railways. This has been the major long-term factor in recent railway history in Britain as in all advanced industrial countries. More immediately relevant to the 1920s, just when the industry was undergoing organisational change the economy was hit by the post-war slump.

Despite the alarms of any particular year the railways, up to then, could look forward to greater activity—all the indices of the work they were doing (tons hauled, passengers carried, gross receipts, profits) moved upwards. That epoch was now finished. The figures demonstrate the inter-war situation unequivocally (see Table 17, p 156).

If one examines the actual amount of traffic carried it is clear that it was the freight side of the railway's activities which

TABLE 17

FREIGHT TRAFFIC, 1920-38 (GREAT BRITAIN)
EXCLUDING FREE HAULED

Year	Merchandise (million tons)	Minerals	Coke and coal	Total (excluding livestock)
1920	68.7	68.1	181.2	318.0
1921	50.5	39.1	128.3	217.9
1922	52.8	48.7	200.1	301.6
1923	59.0	62.1	222.2	343.3
1924	60.9	65.4	209.2	335.5
1925	59.7	62.6	193.7	316.0
1926	53.4	48.1	114.1	215.6
1927	60.6	65.6	199.3	325.5
1927	60.2	65.8	195.8	321.8
1928	57.2	61.6	187.3	306.1
1929	57.6	64.9	207.1	329.6
1930	53.2	57.8	193.3	304.3
1931	47.6	47.1	173.7	268.4
1932	42.5	39.9	167.2	249.6
1932	42.5	39.9	167.2	249.6
1933	42.5	43.1	165.5	251.0
1934	45.2	50.8	174.0	270.0
1935	45.3	50.7	174.8	270.9
1936	48.3	54.9	177.5	280.7
1937	50.3	58.7	188.1	297.2
1938	44.3	47.4	172.8	264.5

Notes :   (1) The figures for 1920 are not strictly comparable as they include some
duplication.
          (2) Changes in compilation occurred in 1928 and 1933, and for both 1927 and
1932 figures on the old and the new basis are given. Up to 1932 the figures
relate to all railway companies; from 1933 they exclude the railways taken
over by the London Passenger Transport Board. The LPTB carried little
freight and its exclusion makes little difference to the series.

Source :   *Railway Returns.*

was hit harder than the passenger side. In 1913 the total of all freight (excluding livestock) was some 364 million tons. In no inter-war year was the figure approached, although in most years up to 1930 more than 300 million tons were carried. From 1931 to 1938 the amount was usually between 250 and 300 million tons a year, rising each year from 1932 to 1937. In those classes of goods where the railways had the advantage, coal and minerals, the decline was due to depression in industry; road competition can be discounted. But the fall in the quantities of merchandise carried must be attributed largely to road competition (Table 18 p 157). The railways were better able to maintain their passenger traffic. The figures are comparable for the period 1928 to 1938 and although there was a decline to a trough in 1932, the recovery was rapid. The movement of receipts reflected these changes in volume (Table 19, p 158).

Operating expenses followed a similar pattern. They almost

TABLE 18

PASSENGER TRAFFIC, 1920-38 (GREAT BRITAIN)

Year	Ordinary full fare	Reduced	All	Passenger journeys (millions) Workmen	Season	Total
1920	n.a	n.a	1,120	459	607	2,186
1921	843	79	923	307	557	1,787
1922	747	148	895	300	554	1,749
1923	701	224	925	310	536	1,772
1924	663	263	926	310	511	1,747
1925	618	306	923	309	511	1,743
1926	532	277	809	260	473	1,542
1927	527	361	888	287	476	1,651
1928	236	373	609	238	402	1,250
1929	201	427	628	242	398	1,268
1930	183	429	613	232	394	1,238
1931	159	422	581	244	377	1,172
1932	139	432	571	206	364	1,141
1933	98	493	591	207	360	1,159
1934	89	520	609	221	370	1,200
1935	88	541	630	227	375	1,231
1936	88	550	638	237	381	1,257
1937	93	567	559	247	389	1,295
1938	82	523	(604)	(244)	387	(1,236)

Notes: (1) The figures for 1920 are not comparable as they include duplications
(2) Up to 1927, all railways. From 1928 excluding London underground and tube railways. In 1928 these amounted to 417m passenger journeys, ie, 25 per cent of *all* journeys in Great Britain
(3) Season tickets calculated on basis of 600 journeys a year
(4) 1938. The figures in brackets are estimates.

Source : *Railway Returns.*

halved between the extraordinary heights during the immediate post-war boom and the depression of the early 1930s. This downward movement was arrested in 1933-4 but, as the economy improved, thus bringing benefits to the railways, the extra income was absorbed by higher costs. The worst years were 1932 and 1933 when net receipts fell to between £18 and £21 million. By 1937 receipts were up to £170.3 million but expenses rose to £142.6 million.

While road competition and trade depression account for a good part of the industry's difficulties, another major factor was the generally higher level of costs, both in absolute and in relative terms. The operating ratio in the inter-war period was normally around 80 per cent. Once the immediate post-war inflation was over operating costs tended to be about 100 per cent higher than pre-war. A significant part of the increase was the rise in the cost of labour. Wages were higher and the shorter working week added to costs. Wages made up about

TABLE 19

RAILWAY INCOME AND EXPENDITURE 1920-1938 (GREAT BRITAIN)

Year	Receipts (a) £m	Operating expenses (a) £m	Net receipts £m	Other net receipts £m	Total net revenue £m	Receipts (b)			
						Passengers £m	Mails and parcels £m	Freight £m	Total £m
1920	251.2	244.2	7.0	42.4	49.4	90.1	17.9	125.7	244.8 (c)
1921	227.8	236.8	−9.0	53.0	44.0	85.5	20.4	109.6	215.5
1922	227.2	182.7	44.4	6.9	51.3	82.8	19.0	115.6	217.4
1923	213.3	173.5	39.8	9.5	49.3	77.0	17.1	109.8	203.8
1924	211.1	174.6	36.5	8.4	44.9	78.5	16.6	106.4	201.5
1925	207.4	172.7	34.6	7.7	42.3	77.1	17.0	103.7	197.8
1926	179.1	161.2	17.9	6.1	24.0	68.6	16.5	85.0	170.2
1927	208.5	168.7	39.8	6.9	46.7	72.3	17.3	109.6	199.1
1927	208.7	167.1	40.6	6.1	46.7	72.3	18.0	110.4	200.7
1928	199.0	159.8	39.2	6.0	45.2	71.1	17.8	103.3	192.2
1929	200.6	157.9	42.7	6.6	49.3	69.1	17.9	106.7	193.6
1930	189.8	153.8	36.0	6.0	42.0	65.8	17.9	99.4	183.1
1931	174.8	142.5	32.3	5.2	37.5	70.0	17.2	90.4	168.6
1932	160.6	134.8	26.0	4.4	30.4	57.3	16.2	81.3	154.9
1932	153.9	130.5	23.4	3.8	27.2	50.9	16.2	81.2	148.2
1933	154.1	128.3	25.8	3.7	29.5	51.1	16.3	80.8	148.2
1934	160.4	132.3	28.0	4.2	32.2	52.3	16.4	85.5	154.1
1935	162.6	133.1	29.5	4.2	33.7	53.8	16.3	86.2	156.2
1936	169.2	136.6	32.5	4.0	36.5	55.8	16.4	90.2	162.4
1937	179.8	142.6	34.2	4.5	38.7	58.6	16.6	94.6	169.8
1938	169.9	143.9	25.9	3.9	29.8	58.6	16.7	87.8	163.1

Source: *Railway Returns*

Notes:
(a) Receipts and Operating Expenses include Collection & Delivery receipts and expenses
(b) Excluding Collection & Delivery and some miscellaneous receipts
(c) Including £1.2 estimated value of services to HM Government and not allocated between passengers, parcels, etc.

Changes in compilation occurred in 1928 and 1933, the second being the exclusion of the railways taken over by the London Passenger Transport Board. In 1932 these railways accounted for £6.4m out of £57.3m of passenger receipts (11 per cent), but less than £200,000 out of £97.5m of all freight receipts.

two-thirds of costs and although the total wage-bill fell, because of reductions in the number of staff and because of wage-cuts, they remained rather more inflexible than other costs. Thus while total expenditure fell by nearly one-half between 1920 and 1933 (the highest and lowest years), the total wage bill fell by only about one-third.

What could be done to meet the situation depended on the diagnosis and the actions taken. The companies could do nothing about the state of trade but they could reduce their cost of operation and a main target was labour. The numbers employed were reduced and so were wages. Another approach was to improve efficiency by investing in new types of machinery or by better utilisation of resources. The Royal Commission on Transport (1930-1) heard some vague evidence about efficiencies following the amalgamations of the 1920s (but it was impossible to distinguish between savings due to greater efficiency and those which had come about through falling prices). It is certainly true that fewer types of locomotives were built and the average weight rose. Some signalling systems were modernised which produced savings in labour. There is also some general evidence that labour was being used more effectively; the number of man-hours per train-mile fell between 1923 and 1926 from 4.08 to 3.02. The Southern Railway pursued an active policy of electrification and improvement of train services. The 1930s indeed were years when major attempts were made to retain traffic. Passenger fares were reduced and fast train services were brought in. Many exceptional rates were granted to freight customers.

In all these ways and others, the railways tried to fight back. Could they have done more? Such innovations as were made were useful but hardly fundamental. It is possible that if the companies other than the Southern had vigorously pursued a policy of electrification they might have so improved their services that traffic could have been won back. But against the railway managements were the weight of tradition and their pricing policy. In the environment of the inter-war period the way to fight competition was through restriction and help came from the state.

In the late 1920s the companies obtained powers to enter the road transport industry and acquired interests in bus and haulage companies. They even ran a few air services. The industry obtained tax concessions. In 1929 the railway passenger duty was abolished and in 1930 the Railway Rating and Valuation Act gave the railways the benefits that the Local Government Act of the previous year had bestowed on agriculture and industry.

These measures brought some relief but the main question which was tackled was how to deal with road competition. Parliament's assistance was to place restrictions on the road industry. Licence duties and petrol taxes were introduced or raised and the Road Traffic Act of 1930 and the Road & Rail Traffic Act of 1933 had the effect of limiting entry into the haulage industry. Part of the purpose of these Acts was to raise standards of safety, a perfectly legitimate function for parliament. But the advantage was to the railways. Perhaps the best indication of public thinking at the time was the creation of the London Passenger Transport Board in 1933. The London underground railways were not included in the reorganisation of British railways under the 1921 Act but competition between them and independent bus operators as well as with tramways produced problems almost as acute as for the main-line railways. The solution was to bring into existence a public corporation charged with the duty of running public passenger transport in the London area. (The suburban services of the main-line companies remained with those companies.)

As well as these two government objectives—regulating the growth of road transport and unifying London's passenger transport—a third aim was to enable the railways to compete more effectively by granting them powers to set 'agreed rates'. The principle was

> . . . that of a charge per ton or per consignment, or even a percentage of the purchase price of the goods carried, irrespective of the distance or the places to which the goods are consigned.[2]

This was an attempt by the railways to win traffic and arose from an agreement made in 1931 between the GWR and Robinson's of Bristol. However, the Railway Rates Tribunal adjudicated against it on the ground that it conflicted with the 1921 Act. As a result a clause was inserted in the 1933 Road & Rail Traffic Act which enabled such agreed rates to be made.

It is not likely, though, that this new system brought in much revenue to the railways.

Some assistance therefore came from the state but it hardly touched some of the main problems. The companies still had to publish their rates and to avoid undue preference. They were thus understandably wary of reducing rates to one trader since others might demand the same; and the tradition of being a public service was pervasive. Services had to be run and cost was secondary. It was unthinkable to close lines.

The law, then, imposed a certain habit of mind which un-fitted the industry for the severe competition from road transport. It also led to other problems. Gilbert Walker's researches in the 1930s demonstrated that while the railways' charges were broadly based on the value of the goods carried, those of the competing road hauliers were based rather on cost. This meant that the most valuable goods—those which attracted the highest railway rates—were usually carried by road, whose costs were lower than the rates charged by the railways. Conversely the less valuable commodities were carried at cheap rates by the railways, at rates below the costs of the road hauliers. He argued that the general level of road charges was about the same as the standard railway rate for class 7. So that classes 1 to 6—coal, minerals and heavy merchandise—remained virtually the monopoly of the railways, whose rates were low. The road hauliers mainly concentrated on carrying goods in classes 7 to 21, general merchandise. His general conclusion was:

> The haulier is certainly taking the best paying traffic when he runs only along the heavy traffic routes and competes only for the larger consignments. These are the traffics for which costs are low and railway rates in comparison correspondingly high.

It followed that to put road and rail on an equal competitive basis it was essential for their charges to be on the same basis, whether value or cost. It was no remedy to bring their costs into line with each other (taxation of road vehicles, or by raising the wages of road transport workers) so long as they operated different systems of rate-fixing.[3]

This kind of thinking was more in line with the approach of the 1950s and 1960s. Public discussion in the 1930s centred rather on co-ordination of transport in which the emphasis was

L

on changes in organisation and control. The Final Report of the Royal Commission on Transport (1931) was entitled 'The Co-ordination and Development of Transport'. The London Passenger Transport Act of 1933 was a demonstration of the way in which such thoughts were put into practice. And Professor H. M. Hallsworth, speaking to Section F of the British Association meeting in 1934 on 'The Future of Rail Transport' ended:

> ... to meet modern requirements [the railways] need to be sup-plemented by other modes of transport. This, I venture to think, can be done most effectively and economically when the different modes of transport are under one management.[4]

He was only one of many saying the same kind of thing. Whatever other reasons there may have been for the post-1945 Labour Government's decision to nationalise certain industries, including much of the transport industry, there was already a strong body of opinion arguing for some form of centralised control.

One of the major arguments for the Railways Act of 1921 had been that of greater economy and efficiency. In the process of building up unified organisations out of a heterogeneous collection of companies, opportunity was taken to re-examine the management structure. There were, of course, immediate problems at the top but these were largely of personalities. When several large companies were brought together to form one undertaking arrangements had to be made to accommodate the several senior officials. What is to be done where there are two or more secretaries, general managers, and so on? Temporary solutions were found, for the problems were not particularly acute or long-lasting. Thus the Southern Railway had three joint general managers at first. More interestingly changes were made in the way the companies were organised. The LNER went furthest in delegation in that it created

> ... three independent sources of energy, at Edinburgh for the Scottish lines, at York for the North Eastern, and at Liverpool Street, London, for the lines of the 'Three Greats' (Great Eastern, Great Northern, Great Central). Each area was to be in charge of a divisional general manager, assisted by area officers dealing with commercial matters, operating, locomotive

running, engineering and signalling, estate questions, and hotels. Each divisional general manager had authority to settle cases affecting only his own area; he could not commit the company to any large expenditure. Large schemes had to be submitted to the chief general manager and, if he approved, went forward to the appropriate directorial committee.[5]

Other companies retained the traditional chain of command by specialised functions. The officials at local level reported to their own departmental chiefs and not to any person having general supervision over an area. On the Southern Railway centralisation was manifested in that not even the general manager could approve anything above £250 of capital expenditure (although 'the G.M. could always obtain an interim approval from the Chairman or his deputy, or any of the committee chairmen, which was later reported to the Board for confirmation').[6]

The LMS was a highly centralised organisation, rather surprisingly for the largest company of all (employing something like a quarter of a million people). As was traditional on the railways

> . . . the various aspects of railway work . . . were administered by separate departments, inside which there was a continuous chain of delegation from the national departmental head down to the lowest ranks. At first the national departmental chiefs were responsible to a General Manager, but the strain on him was too great and from 1927 this function of overall general management was exercised by a President and four Vice-Presidents who formed an executive Committee responsible to the Board of Directors. Each Vice-President controlled and acted as the head of a major Department or group of Departments.

Frank Pickstock, from whom these quotations come, argues: 'The main weakness of this organisation was the lack of any authoritative co-ordination except at national level.' But it did secure standardisation and it achieved many economies. However,

> The LMS was undoubtedly the over-centralised organisation of a bureaucratic kind, unrelieved by the pressures of Parliament and public opinion which can check the worst faults of similar manifestations in Government Departments.

Before and during the second world war this centralisation was reduced by a greater delegation of authority to local officials, but this 'did not alter the main pattern, nor did it meet the criticism of the failure to provide for co-ordination except at the very top.'[7]

Felix Pole's autobiography gives some interesting details about management problems on the GWR. Even before the merger of the early 1920s there had been some alterations, eg the transfer of certain electrical matters to the chief mechanical engineer. (The purpose of this was to encourage electrification and this could best be done if one department was responsible for both steam and electric power, so avoiding inter-departmental rivalry.) Pole notes that the GWR was organised on the departmental rather than the divisional system. He too refers to 'evidence of over-centralisation'.

> For example, the distribution of rolling stock was arranged at headquarters by the Superintendent of the Line. Theoretically, if not actually, no station master or local officer could make use of a wagon or coach without authority from headquarters; the Divisional Traffic Officers had no control over the Rolling Stock Inspectors, who, although located at various stations throughout the line, were responsible direct to headquarters.

Changes were made in the twenties; eg Rolling Stock Inspectors were transferred to the control of the various Divisional Superintendents. And the various divisions and districts of the Traffic, Goods, Locomotive and Engineering Departments were made co-extensive.

Pole tells a beautiful little story which brings home some at least of the deficiencies of railway management. He describes the use made of local conferences; each month in each division meetings of the various officers would be held. They examined everything to do with the efficient running of the company. 'It was my desire,' he wrote, 'to have a divisional profit and loss account, and it may be of interest to recall the inception of the idea.'

> In the Spring of 1925, a tree blew down across my drive . . . My neighbour very kindly telephoned to tell me what had happened and offered to send a car to take me to the station. I was driven by his son who, with his father, was interested in a road

motor service then running between Newbury, Reading and London. I thought I might get some useful information about this service, so I asked what was the cost per mile. The reply was: 'I don't know.' I then asked: 'Do you know your receipts per mile?' Again the reply was 'No.' Perhaps I was reflecting that this particular bus concern could not be very efficient when the remark was made 'I tell you what I *do* know; that is what each bus earns and what it has to earn to make a profit.' What more was there to say, but I often reflected sadly on the fact that a railway does not know what each coach or each train or each division earns.[8]

In the unsatisfactory years of the 1930s the railways continued to press for greater freedom from their legal obligations. Their 'Square Deal' campaign proposed changes in the law to permit them greater flexibility in charging, including the duty of publishing rates, and to be rid of the prohibition of undue preference. They might have been successful. The Transport Advisory Council (set up under the Road & Rail Traffic Act of 1933 to advise the minister) agreed with many of the companies' views and there was the possibility that legislation would result. But the war intervened and thinking on the subject changed. A conference of the railways and the major road hauliers presented, after much examination and discussion, a joint memorandum to the Minister of Transport. This paper on the *Co-ordination of road and rail freight traffic* appeared in 1946. Among its proposals was the suggestion that road and rail charges should be brought into line with each other. It was too late. This attempt to organise the activities of two major sections of the transport industry in the context of private enterprise could not commend itself in the post-war atmosphere. For too long the discussion had been about co-ordination in terms of a single control, preferably under the state. The Labour government of 1945 was of the appropriate political complexion to bring these discussions to a legislative conclusion.

Notes to this chapter are on p 211.

CHAPTER 10

FROM NATIONALISATION TO COMMERCIAL OBJECTIVES

In the present context the events of World War 2 need not detain us for long. In general the financial and economic arrangements were similar to those of World War 1 with the state taking over control. Under great difficulty—shortage of staff, bombing, little maintenance—miracles of operation were performed. During the war the railways reached new heights in the amount of traffic they carried, and given the shortage of rolling stock apart from locomotives, efficiency improved. But the war did not have the cathartic effect that the previous war had produced. The changes that were introduced in the late 1940s were due, perhaps, less to the experience of the war than to so many years of discussion of the need for change and to the existence of a Labour government.

At the end of the war the railways were in poor physical shape. Investment had been very low and maintenance had been reduced to levels which would have been unthinkably unsafe according to the earlier traditions of the industry. For the first decade after 1945 the position did not change materially. The railways were low on the priority list for investment but their traffic remained high. Full employment enhanced the demand for transport because wartime restrictions on the road transport industry remained up to the early 1950s. Once petrol rationing was abolished and motor vehicles became available again for the home market, the downward movement in rail traffic gathered strength. In 1956 the industry made an actual loss on operating and the urgency of finding remedies now became acute. This is a brief background to the legislative and organisational changes and the policies which accompanied them.

In 1947 the Transport Act nationalised all inland transport

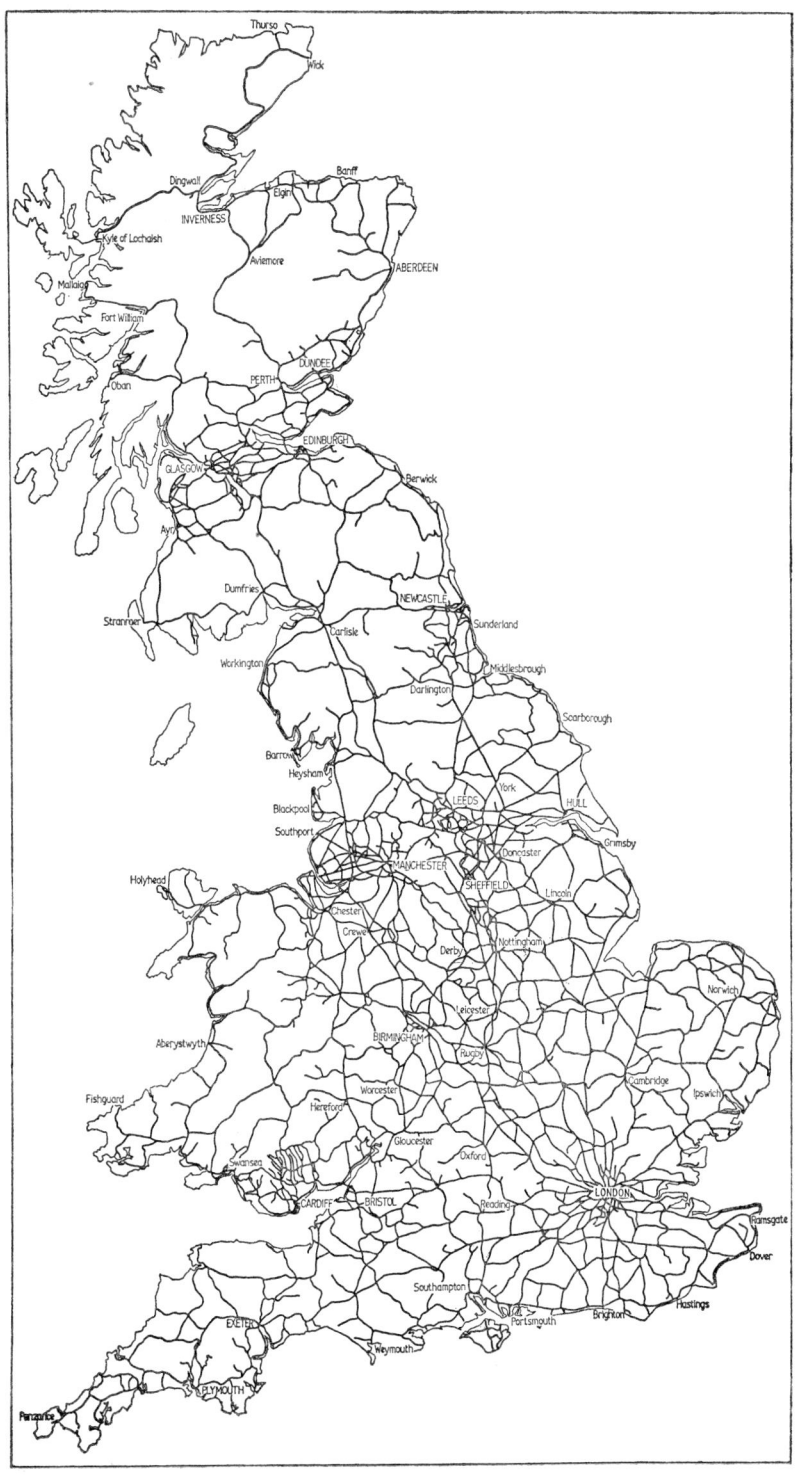

Railway network in 1952

except private cars, 'own account' lorries and roads. A British Transport Commission was established under which there were a number of executives, of which one was for the railways and another for London Transport. As critics were quick to point out, this was a rather curious structure for an organisation whose function was to operate an integrated transport system. The BTC was organised functionally, according to different kinds of activity, with little attempt at co-ordination between them. Only in London Transport was there a single control over a number of different types of transport operation. Apart from this exercise in what might be called the 'divisional' type of organisation there was little attempt to relate the various parts of the commission's work to each other. The BTC reorganised the railways into six regions: Southern, Western, London Midland, North Eastern, Eastern, and Scottish. These were administrative arrangements for operating convenience; the individual regions were not intended to be viable economic bodies.

On the contrary: as with other nationalised industries the Act which placed transport under public ownership did not really provide adequate guidance for management. The BTC was instructed 'to provide . . . an efficient, adequate, economical and properly integrated system of public inland transport'. It had to ensure that its revenues were at least sufficient to meet the outgoings which were properly chargeable to revenue account (which included repayment of loans and interests and amounts debited to a reserve fund). Moreover, this injunction was to apply, 'taking one year with another'. Finally, it was the BTC's accounts as a whole to which these instructions applied; there was no obligation on road operations or railway working to break even. This was made quite clear in section 3 sub-section 4:

> All the business carried on by the Commission, whether or not arising from undertakings or parts of undertakings vested in them by or under any provision of this Act, shall form one undertaking, and the Commission shall so conduct that undertaking and, subject to the provisions of this Act, levy such fares, rates, tolls, dues and other charges, as to secure that the revenue of the Commission is not less than sufficient for making provision for the meeting of charges properly chargable to revenue, taking one year with another.

It is true that the various parts of the BTC kept and published separate accounts. The important fact was that it was perfectly legitimate, quite in accordance with the law, for one executive to make a loss, provided any such losses were counterbalanced by surpluses of other executives. Thus, cross-subsidisation was permitted; indeed, it was encouraged.

All of this had a major bearing on the pricing policy adopted by the BTC. The two injunctions to break even and to cross-subsidise, when added to the obligation to act as a public service, meant that prices need not be based on costs. In the late 1940s and early 1950s there was an acute controversy about these policies and their implications, culminating in the deliberations of the Ridley Committee on Fuel Policy, whose report was published in 1952. There were opposing prescriptions to charge prices according to average or to marginal cost where displayed. This discussion subsequently led to significant changes in policy; but they took some years to be brought into operation and in the meantime the railways had undergone another organisational change.

The Conservative government of 1951 produced the Transport Act of 1953. Apart from denationalising road haulage, the Act abolished the Railway Executive. Its members had been appointed by the minister, a situation which had resulted in conflict between the Executive and the BTC. The Act obliged the BTC to propose a scheme of reorganisation which was to include area bodies instead of the Railway Executive (including the publication of certain statistics pertaining to each area).

In the following year the BTC produced a Railway Reorganisation Scheme. Six regions were established, each under an area board composed of a chairman and up to six part-time members appointed by the BTC. The Select Committee on Nationalised Industries, which examined British Railways in a report published in 1960, stated that:

> ... each Area Board manages its railways, improves its facilities and cuts its costs, sees that the needs of transport users are met, and ensures the safety, health and welfare of its employees.[1]

At the same time the BTC retained a large number of railway functions. They submitted details to the select committee which commented: 'After a first reading of this catalogue of controls, it seemed hard to form a picture of decentralisation'. But they readily understood that the division of functions between the area boards and the BTC was sensible. Generally the commission took decisions on matters which affected more than one region, while the area boards had some power to pursue their own ideas within the general framework. They had a great deal of freedom in fixing charges and they had power to authorise expenditures of up to £100,000.

Each region pursued its own type of reorganisation. The Eastern Region, for example, set up three Lines each with a number of districts below them. The Western Region had Divisions (not Lines) together with districts. At the same time there were changes in internal management structure. In particular, traffic departments were established which combined the work of the previously existing operating, commercial and motive power departments. 'This ensures that the man who sells the traffic is also responsible for seeing that the trains to carry it are available and running well.'[2]

The select committee however was rather less impressed with matters of regional accounting. They noted the vast improvements made in cost-accounting, beginning with the Traffic Costing Service, established early in the history of the BTC. But while these innovations enabled the railway management to identify the costs of a particular service—a very important advance for the railways—it was still not possible for the region to know what its finances looked like.

> The system relies on the Region, in whose area the service originates, to see that the costing is done, notwithstanding the fact that the service may involve other Regions. The result is that the costs, and the receipts, of a particular stream of traffic may be ascertainable; but to go further and get the profit and loss of a geographical area is much more difficult, unless the area is fairly self-contained, or unless an apportionment of costs and receipts between Regions is arbitrarily made.[3]

It was an advance from the days of Sir Felix Pole in the 1920s but not a very great one.

Other problems, some of which it shared with other nationalised industries, afflicted British Railways in the 1950s, such as that of accountability to parliament—how far should there be interference by the state in the operation of these large organisations. Another was the nature of the pricing policy to be adopted. Because of the railways' historical background, the method used was that of average costing. When one examines the railway situation in these terms one is really moving away from the emphasis on organisational matters towards a much closer identification of the economic factors. As well as the continuing discussion of these problems in the 1950s it was important that the 1953 Transport Act belatedly realised the absence of a railway monopoly in inland transport and removed some of the historical obligations on the railways. The prohibition on undue preference went as did the duty to publish charges.

In 1955 a new freight charges scheme was proposed and was examined by the Transport Tribunal, a body established under the 1947 Act which took over the functions of the Railway Rates Tribunal; notably it had the power to approve or refuse alterations in charges. The hearings lasted forty-four days and the transcript of proceedings ran to some $1\frac{1}{4}$ million words. It was a major document making public for the first time the details of costing data and of methods, but essentially the object of the exercise was to arrive at a new charges scheme. The scheme sought approval for a classification of charges based on the concept of 'loadability', a move towards the idea of basing price on cost. The arguments before the tribunal were lengthy and this delayed the introduction of the new scheme until July 1957, but at maximum levels of charges below those applied for.

At this point the railways' difficulties became so acute that changes in policies became imperative. The railways had just started on their modernisation programme, a belated attempt to bring the system up to date, but whereas the railways had up to then made a surplus on operating activities, in 1956 there was a deficit which yearly became larger (Table 20, p 172). It is important to emphasise that the loss was on actual working; it was not 'a financial mirage'. The reality has been a decline in traffic.[4]

All traffics did not decline equally. Passenger traffic has been fairly static; it is on the freight side that the large reductions have occurred. The reduction in coal production after 1957 hit the railways hard, since coal provided a high proportion of the freight carried. The real disappointment was in the carriage of merchandise. If the reduction in coal-carrying was outside the control of the railways, the same cannot be said of general merchandise for this was a rapidly growing market. (See Table 21, p 173.)

TABLE 20

OPERATING UNDER NATIONALISATION 1948-69

Year	Passenger receipts £m	Mails and parcels £m	Freight £m	Total receipts £m	Operating expenses £m	Operating surplus and deficit £m	Other activities (net receipts) Miscellaneous receipts (net) central administration charges £m	Net revenue £m	Interest £m	Overall surplus £m
1948	122.6	29.4	180.9	346.3	322.5	23.8	13.8	37.6	42.3	-4.7
1949	114.0	28.8	179.2	335.7	325.1	10.6	4.9	15.5	43.9	-20.8
1950	106.6	30.7	198.9	351.3	326.1	25.2	5.7	30.9	45.0	-14.1
1951	107.0	33.1	227.9	384.9	351.6	33.3	11.6	44.9	44.8	0.1
1952	111.9	36.0	250.5	416.3	377.7	38.7	11.8	50.5	46.0	4.5
1953	114.8	38.6	263.1	434.7	400.1	34.6	20.1	54.7	50.4	4.2
1954	116.6	40.8	272.8	449.3	432.9	16.4	24.2	40.6	52.4	-11.9
1955	118.1	41.9	274.2	453.9	452.1	1.8	21.4	23.2	53.8	-30.6
1956	127.5	47.6	284.1	481.0	497.5	-16.5	17.6	1.1	54.7	-54.7
1957	138.9	51.4	283.5	501.4	528.6	-27.1	18.9	-8.2	61.9	-70.1
1958	138.0	51.9	259.1	471.6	519.7	-48.1	15.8	-32.3	72.5	-104.8
1959	140.0	53.4	242.7	459.2	499.5	-40.3	23.6	-16.7	82.8	-99.5
1960	151.3	55.5	247.3	478.6	546.2	-67.7	27.0	-40.7	92.7	-133.4
1961	157.5	56.4	236.8	474.7	561.6	-86.9	32.4	-57.5	102.8	-160.2
1962	161.1	57.4	235.7	465.1	569.1	-104.0	32.1	-71.9	110.7	-182.6
1963	161.8	57.5	235.4	468.7	550.2	-81.6	5.9	-75.7	59.9	-135.6
1964	167.2	58.6	233.0	474.1	541.6	-67.5	5.0	-62.5	60.8	-123.3
1965	173.5	58.1	225.5	472.6	545.7	-73.1	1.5	-71.6	63.2	-134.8
1966	179.4	58.3	216.9	470.4	542.1	-71.7	1.2	-70.5	65.0	-135.5
1967	179.7	55.5	194.8	445.5	536.1	-90.6	4.1	-86.5	66.5	-153.0
1968	185.2	58.1	204.3	463.7	547.1	-83.4	3.3	-80.1	67.3	-147.4
1969	266.6	60.1	195.5	539.2	491.7	48.6	7.6	56.2	41.5	14.7

Notes: (1) Total Receipts include miscellaneous gross receipts plus net revenue from letting of non-operational property, advertising and catering
(2) Various changes were made in the compilation and presentation of the statistics. Where figures on both the old and new basis are given the new figures have been used
(3) 1969. Passenger receipts include £61.2m in grants for unremunerative services. Operating expenses reduced by £15m grant for maintenance and certain track and signalling equipment. Both authorised by the Transport Act, 1968.

Sources: *Annual Reports and Accounts* of the British Transport Commission (1948-1962) and British Railways Board (1963 onwards)

During 1956 the BTC examined their financial situation as it would appear to develop over the following few years, which included the fact that the effects of modernisation would take some time to accrue. The estimates were based on various assumptions including the availability of all the necessary resources for modernisation and the granting of reasonable freedom in charging. 'The conclusion was reached', wrote the BTC in its report for 1956, 'that, subject to these assumptions, the Commission's annual net revenue should be in balance by 1961 or 1962.'

TABLE 21

TRAFFIC 1948-69

Freight (million tons)

Year	Passenger miles (millions)	Iron and steel	Minerals	Coal and coke	Merchandise	Other
1948	21,022		59.1	158.5	54.7	
1949	20,902		60.8	164.6	54.0	
1950	19,952		60.3	167.1	53.0	
1951	20,561		61.2	169.4	53.3	
1952	20,459		63.0	170.8	50.3	
1953	20,578		64.4	175.3	48.7	
1954	20,712		62.5	173.5	46.7	
1955	20,308		64.0	166.2	43.4	
1956	21,133		65.7	168.2	42.5	
1957	22,591		65.4	166.7	41.6	
1958	22,150		52.9	153.2	36.3	
1959	22,270		52.2	144.2	37.1	
1960	21,547		60.4	148.1		
1961	21,061		54.3	145.7		
1962	19,728	37.1	47.1	145.0		46.3
1963	19,230	39.3		151.4		44.1
1964	19,874	45.9		147.4		46.2
1965	18,713	46.0		138.3		44.2
1966	18,453	38.8		131.7		43.0
1967	18,089	35.7		122.2		42.8
1968	17,681	38.7		122.7		45.9
1969	18,400	39.4		119.3		42.4

Notes: (1) Changes were made in 1963 in the calculation of passenger miles
(2) The classification of freight was changed in 1962

Sources: *Annual Reports and Accounts* of the British Transport Commission (1948-62) and British Railways Board (1963 onwards).

The government accepted the BTC's proposals and subsequently the Transport (Railway Finances) Act of 1957 was passed. This authorised the commission to borrow any deficit on the railways (less any surplus on the BTC's other activities) during the period 1956 to 1962, the maximum being £250 million. It also enabled the commission to borrow the interest to be paid on these advances and also on the advances to meet the interest, as well as the interest on borrowing for capital purposes. The clear intention was that these loans should be repaid; they were not to be a subsidy.

But the deficit on operating grew larger and in 1959 the Transport (Borrowing Powers) Act increased the limit of borrowing to £400 million. As yet the modernisation programme had not much to show despite the brave list of projects which the BTC reports showed to be under way. Similarly the changes in organisation—to get away from the traditional form of railway management structure—were taking time. This is not to belittle what was being done; rather it demonstrates that the railway deficit outweighed whatever improvements were being made.

In the late 1950s a number of changes in policy had been put into operation, but such increases of traffic as had been stimulated by improved services, and such costs as had fallen because of greater productivity and the cutting out of unprofitable services, were small beer compared to the loss of traffic and the constant rise in costs through wage increases and from other sources.

In the late 1950s and early 1960s a decade or so of discussion and argument about the problems of the nationalised industries culminated in a number of highly significant policy changes. In particular there were difficulties about the financing of capital requirements and the complicated relationships between the appropriate ministers and the nationalised boards. The BTC, for example, could quite rightly claim that part of its deficit had arisen because much needed fare increases had been postponed by the minister, thus losing revenue. Similarly—and this was an equally awkward problem—the nationalised industries' capital investment plans had been slowed down or speeded up according to the needs of the country in general, to help carry out government economic policies.

The revolution in thinking and in policy really boils down to a few simple propositions. The first essential was to define the basic objectives of the nationalised industries. Were they to be commercial undertakings or were they to continue to act as providers of public services? Were they to be used by government to carry out economic policies which had relevance for the national economy but not necessarily for the industry involved? What should be the basis for their pricing policies? How should their capital requirements be financed?

In 1960 the report of the Select Committee on Nationalised

Industries strongly argued against the policy of the BTC acting in ways which were not strictly commercial; ie in making decisions about charges and investment based not on the economic return which would ensue but rather on the desire of the commission to meet the needs of the public.

> If . . . there are other considerations which make it desirable for members of the public to travel or freight to be carried on some routes at prices below the cost, it should be for the Government and not the Commission to decide . . . This confusion in judging between what is economically right and what is socially desirable has played an important part in leading to the situation in which the Commission now find themselves.[5]

In a sense this was unfair. The Transport Acts of 1947 and 1953 had certainly spoken of the need not to make losses; they had also obliged the BTC to provide 'an efficient, adequate, economical and properly integrated system of public transport'. They had not stated that where there was a conflict of aims one should take precedence over the other.

Inevitably, given the history of railways in this country, the changes in policy were associated with alterations in organisation. In March 1960 the prime minister committed the government to a policy of regionalisation and announced the setting up of an inquiry, the Stedeford Committee, whose report provided the basis for a white paper published in December 1960 as *Proposals for the reorganisation of nationalised transport undertakings.* Broadly this envisaged the break-up of the BTC by the creation of separate boards to manage railways, London Transport, docks, inland waterways and various other transport undertakings under a holding company—road haulage, hotels, buses for example.

This separation necessarily meant a further move away from the possibility of 'co-ordination' in the old-fashioned sense and the organisational changes were accompanied by the appointment of a member of the Stedeford Committee, Dr Richard Beeching of ICI, to take over as chairman of the BTC in 1961 and subsequently of the British Railways Board when it was established.

A further relevant change of policy was heralded by the publication of a white paper in 1961 on *The financial and economic obligations of the nationalised industries.* The changes here included the obligation that the undertakings had to cover deficits on revenue account over a five-year period, rather than vaguely 'taking one year with another'. Indeed the five-year period was chosen as the appropriate length of time for governmental approval of projects. This would prevent abrupt alterations in investment at the behest of government reacting to sudden changes in the economic climate. In general the white paper was intended to make the industries more commercially minded, including greater freedom and flexibility in pricing policies.

The Transport Act of 1962 established the Railways Board to manage British Railways and hived off certain functions historically associated with railway undertakings to be run by other bodies. Beeching had taken over in 1961 and became the Railways Board chairman. In the meantime studies had been initiated into the cost of handling traffic by existing methods, into the kinds of traffic which the railways could handle better than other forms of transport, of the pattern of traffic flows to establish the profitability of particular parts of the system, and into the methods of freight carrying.

These resulted in the board's report, published in 1963, as *The Reshaping of British Railways*. This 'Beeching Report' introduced a new name into railway history, a new title for a policy. 'Beeching' came to be identified as synonymous with 'closure' but this was only one part of the proposals. The report did certainly accelerate the reduction in size of the industry, but the essential fact is that it aimed to clarify the principal characteristics of rail transport and to base the board's activities on them. Thus, it argued, the railways' specialised track provides certain advantages, such as high speed and dense flows. But the track is costly (about one-fifth of total costs in 1961 were for maintenance of track and signalling). So that,

> . . . the art of operating a railway system [consists] of providing such facilities and securing such traffics as would enable a dense flow of high capacity units to be handled at high speed, in order to spread the overhead to the fullest possible extent.[6]

The purpose of the report was to make clear which categories of traffic were particularly suitable to rail transport and the implications followed logically. The highly unprofitable services and routes would be reduced or cut out and improvements would be made to retain and recover that traffic which 'ought', according to this analysis, to be carried by rail. Thus the liner train idea

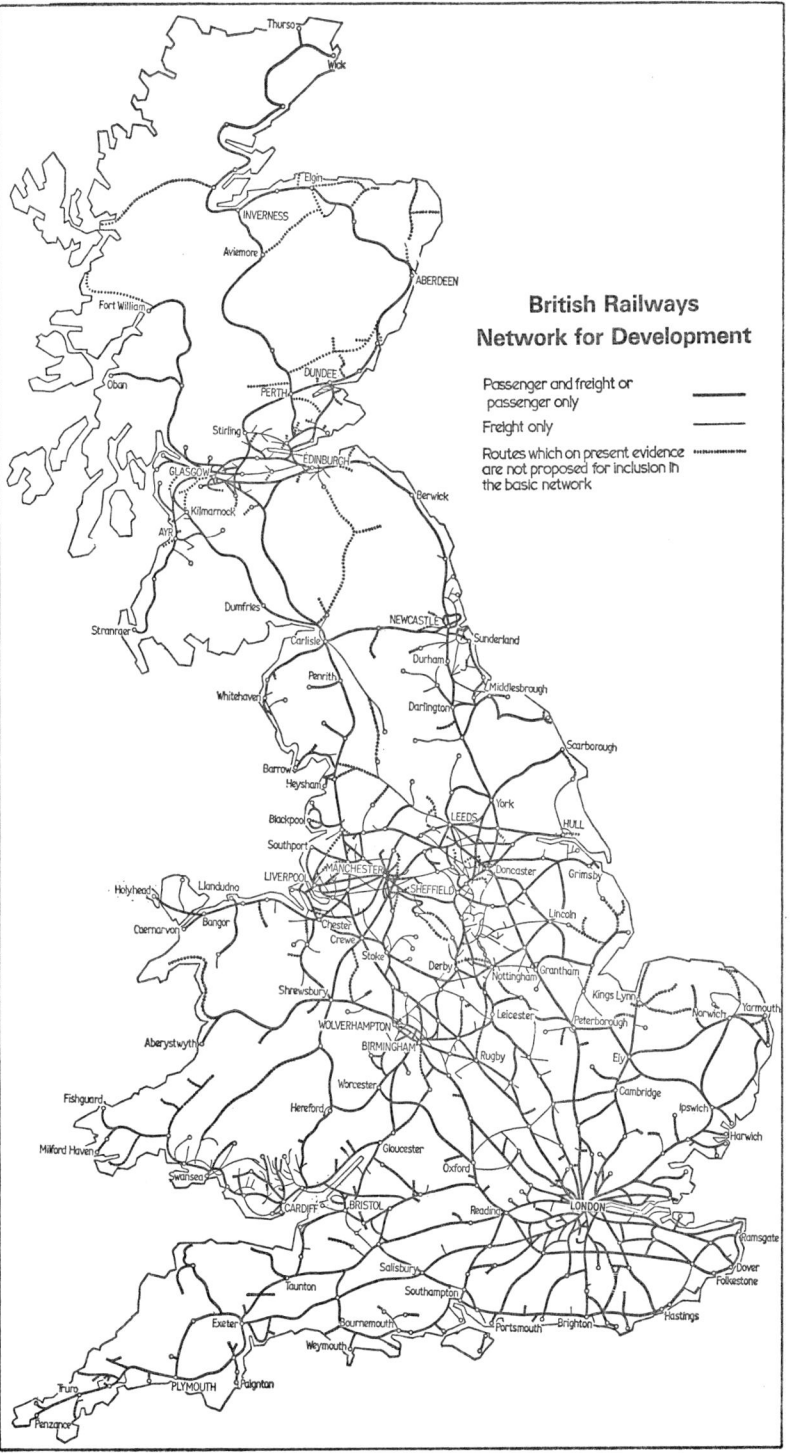

British Railways
Network for Development

Passenger and freight or
passenger only ——————

Freight only ——————

Routes which on present evidence ·········
are not proposed for inclusion in
the basic network

Railway network in 1967

was intended to meet the problems of carrying small consign-
ments of general merchandise. These would be loaded into con-
tainers which could be fed to depots by road vehicles, transhipped
on to permanently-coupled flat wagons and carried swiftly over
the major routes. Thus the proposals envisaged much higher
productivity of both labour and capital. A smaller undertaking
would cut costs and raise revenues.

To some extent it happened. Closures of lines, stations and
depots rapidly accelerated and the labour force was quickly run
down. Services were improved for passengers: there were more
and faster express trains. And in freight fast services between a
small number of main terminals conveyed an increasing number
of full train loads of commodities arranged with companies on a
long-term basis. Similarly there was a significant growth in
liner-train operation despite initial hold-ups through labour
disputes.

At first things seemed to be going well. The deficit fell because
costs fell and some revenue rose. Broadly, receipts from passenger
services rose more than did their costs; but freight receipts fell
more than did the fall in costs. In 1965 passenger receipts surpassed receipts from freight and thereafter the position deteriorated. The general economic climate adversely affected receipts
and increases of charges were not allowed. Thus after five or so
years of the board's operations the railway position was no better
than it had been when it was set up. In a comparison of the years
1961 and 1966 D. L. Munby showed that 'receipts fell by 2 per
cent and costs by 3 per cent, leaving the loss more or less the
same'. (To be clear, costs had been reduced markedly through
greater utilisation of resources, but increases in the price of
factors, especially of labour, had largely wiped out the reduction.)[7]

In the meantime there had been a change of government and
almost inevitably different policies for transport came to be expected. A White Paper was published in 1966 which among other
suggestions advocated the making of grants to passenger services
making heavy losses provided these were essential for social
purposes. It also proposed the establishment of a national freight
organisation. In the meantime a Steering Group was set up to
report on various matters including the identification of loss-mak-
ing services, possible changes in pricing policy, investment criteria
and the suitability of the railways' management structure.

Early in 1967 the Minister of Transport issued a statement which revised the railway network. Some 3,000 route miles would not be closed, thus leaving the network at some 11,000 instead of the 8,000 proposed by the Beeching report. And subsequently towards the end of 1967 transport policy was elaborated in a series of White Papers, three of them affecting railways, together with a White Paper on the nationalised industries.

The White Paper, *Railway Policy* also included the report of the Joint Steering Group and necessarily concentrated on financial and management questions. Thus it was made quite clear that since the railways 'have no hope of supporting from profits on their other passenger services and on freight work, the many non-paying passenger services which they are expected to retain', the latter should be separately costed and the decision whether or not to retain them should rest with the minister, not with the Railways Board. The White Paper advocated the need to reconstruct the railways' finances; this meant the end of deficit financing and was to be associated with a capital reconstruction. Capital assets should be revalued on a lower level 'to correspond with the revised capital liabilities'. The White Paper also spoke of the need to alter the railways' organisation structure. Instead of board members having functional responsibilities they should concentrate on board policy decisions.

The recommendations on organisational change were much less concise for the lower levels of the railways. The Joint Steering Group referred to:

> . . . a need for dispersed management. Both the scale of railway operations, and the geographical dispersion of the system require local managements with authority to make decisions on day-to-day matters.

This policy statement dealt specifically with the railways. The other two white papers, on freight and urban transport, looked on their topics comprehensively, bringing other forms of transport into the picture. Thus the white paper *Public Transport and Traffic* took into account all forms of urban transport and at the same time endeavoured to relate them to the problems of town planning. Organisationally, the responsibility for the transport needs of particular areas was to be placed on the localities. The four conurbations—Greater Manchester, Merseyside, the West

Midlands and Tyneside—were each to have a Passenger Trans-port Authority, appointed largely by local authorities, to control policy and finance. Each would appoint an executive to manage the operations (although with power to delegate the running of bus services to subsidiaries).

As far as the railways were concerned it was envisaged that the actual operation would remain with the railways but that agreements would have to be made with the Authorities about services and fares. The ultimate financial arrangement was for the executives to be responsible for any subsidy for services making losses. At the same time the central government was to provide grants for capital purposes for public transport (in the same way that this has been done over many years for roads). (London Transport was not included in these proposals. Subsequently arrangements were made for it to be incorporated into the authority of the Greater London Council.)

The third White Paper dealt with freight transport. Here again the railways were only part of the policy. In outline, the proposals were to eliminate 'wasteful and inefficient competition' between road and rail in the public sector and to encourage the transfer of traffic from road to rail.

The first aim was to be achieved by setting up a National Freight Corporation to take over the road haulage services of the Transport Holding Company and also railway depots and collection and delivery services as well as freight liners. These last were to be run by a Freightliner Company in which the British Railways Board was to have a 49 per cent shareholding and seats on the board.

In general this meant that the NFC would be responsible for certain road haulage services and for some railway services associated with road. In the words of the white paper:

> This will enable it to take commercial responsibility for all the movements which originated by road leaving the B.R.B. responsible for both the marketing and operation of freight traffic—full train loads, company trains and wagon-load traffic —originating by rail.

In these various ways the carriage of freight in the public sector was to be integrated and rationalised. At the same time the regulation of private road haulage was to be altered by the first major changes in the licensing system since the early 1930s. This was the new proposal for 'quality licensing', a difference in kind from the older 'quantity licensing', and applying only to the heavier vehicles. The applicant for such a licence would need to satisfy the licensing authorities that, among others, he could provide adequate maintenance facilities, had sufficient financial resources, and held a new personal licence (a 'transport manager's licence') issued by the licensing authority.

Quantity licensing was to remain, but in a different form from the past. In its favour the white paper stated:

> It is on the long distance general merchandise traffic and on the bulk traffic now moving by road that quantity licensing needs to be concentrated in order to promote the fullest economic use of rail.

An operator would apply for a licence to a licensing authority, but objections to its granting could be made only by the British Railways Board and the National Freight Corporation (Freightliner Company).

The white paper emphasised that the criteria to be adopted in these cases were economic ones.

> It is not the Government's intention that the licensing system should be capable of being used as a means of diverting traffic to rail uneconomically.

The only basis for an objection to a licence was that the service provided by the BRB or by the NFC was 'as satisfactory as that of the applicant, taking into account a combination of speed, reliability and cost in relation to the need of the consignors and the nature of the particular traffic concerned. (Cost in this connection will mean cost to the consignor.)'

Finally, the white paper proposed that goods vehicles over 3 tons unladen weight should pay an annual charge to meet costs of road construction and maintenance, The charge was to be related to weight, from £50 up to £190.

The last white paper was that which laid down policy for the nationalised industries in general: *Nationalised Industries—A review of economic and financial objectives*. Broadly, this emphasised the need for nationalised industries to be commercial undertakings, aiming to reach given financial targets. It was an extension and elaboration of the policies adopted since the earlier white papers in 1961.

The Transport Bill was hard fought in Parliament, but its essential features remained and the new organisations came into existence. Once again there was to be reorganisation in the transport world, but this time it was policies rather than the structures that were the centre of attention. For once there was some sort of coherence in the objectives that the government was pursuing, at any rate in the economics of the allocation of resources.[8]

Perhaps the differences of very recent years can be seen by the juxtaposition of two statements. The first is from the last annual report of the Transport Holding Company, a body set up in 1962 to run certain non-railway activities of the British Transport Commission (including road transport and shipping). The company was abolished under the 1968 Transport Act, and this extract comes from its final report.

Section 8 of the report is called 'Retrospect' and refers to the twenty-one years since the Transport Act of 1947 which nationalised much of the transport system.

> Approximately thirteen years out of the twenty-one were spent waiting for major Transport Acts of Parliament, whether good or not-so-good, and in re-organising after them.
>
> The years 1948 and 1949 were occupied with the vast job of acquisition and rationalisation, and if possible of reconciliation, which had to be undertaken as a result of the Act of 1947 setting up the British Transport Commission. The years 1952 to 1954 were spent either in a state of deep-freeze prior to the Act of 1953 or in cleaning up subsequently. The next period of organisational and developmental stasis occurred over the four years prior to the Act of 1962. Finally there was the period 1966 to 1968, to which unfortunately the year 1969 must presumably be added, since at the time of writing it is confidently asserted that a different Government, if and when it came to power, would probably upset a great part of the basis of the Act of last year.

The second quotation is from the Report of the British Railways Board for 1968. This speaks of that year being 'a climacteric year, marking the end of deficit financing and the preparations for the new relationships with other branches of nationalised

public transport created by the 1968 Transport Act'. In chapter
II, headed 'Prospect', one reads phrases like these:

> The financial arrangements set up as a result of the Transport
> Act 1968 introduce a new realism into the Board's financial
> targets and provide assistance toward their attainment . .
> The changes introduced by the 1968 Act are a great assistance
> in the achievement of viability in the short term . . .

In 1969 the board did, in fact, make a profit, but this arose
largely because of a reduction in the amount of interest paid
(following capital reconstruction), and the receipt of grants for
certain unremunerative services and towards operating expenses.
This was a welcome change, but it cannot be said that the
railways' problems are solved. The industry remains labour-
intensive and the continuing rise in wages and salaries (and in the
price of other factors) leads inevitably to pressure on costs and
thus on fares and charges. These can be contained to some extent
if productivity rises, but the difficulty for the policy makers is that
economic factors may not be crucial. It is now fairly well recognised that consumer choice between different forms of transport
is only partly a question of price.

> Railways have had an advantage in both price and speed over
> the motor-car and in speed over coach services, and the decline
> in the share of public road and rail passenger services must be
> explained by other non-price factors, such as door-to-door
> service, flexibility and the general increase in motor-car owner-
> ship, which outweigh considerations of both price and speed.[9]

This applies too to freight charges by rail which are lower for
many commodities than are charges by road. Again, the loss of
traffic by the railways 'does suggest that factors other than price
may have a considerable bearing on consumer choice of freight
transport mode'.[10]

This is a depressing conclusion, for it means that railways may
not be able to provide the services for which they are peculiarly
suited. If consumers prefer convenience, flexibility, or door to door
service, the task of the railways in competing is that much more
difficult.

Notes to this chapter are on pp 211–12.

CHAPTER 11

CAPITAL FORMATION AND NEW TECHNOLOGIES

In his article on 'Economic Problems of British Railways' published in 1962 D. L. Munby examined a number of possible explanations to account for the industry's difficulties. 'If we were asked to choose in order of importance, we would be tempted to lay most stress on the lack of investment and the attempt to run too large a system as the two most important of all.'[1] He was referring in particular to the period since the end of World War 2, or more precisely to a period which includes the war itself. Redfern's investigation into net investment in fixed assets for the years 1938-53 had shown that the industry had disinvested by about £440 million (at constant 1948 prices), most of this being attributable to the neglect of permanent way. It was not until the modernisation plan of 1955 that investment picked up, so that for over a decade and a half capital formation by the railways was low.

In general this might be expected. During the war the railways' investment was necessarily low and even maintenance was reduced to what had traditionally been thought dangerous levels. After the war the railways were low on the list of priorities, the explanation of the railways' difficulties which stresses the enormous net disinvestment since the late 1930s is very persuasive.

In fact the recent investigations by Feinstein enable us to carry the story back further. He shows that between 1920 and 1938 the railways' gross capital formation was less than depreciation in every year except one (1938). Thus insufficient was spent to replace the assets which, in economic terms, were wearing out and needing replacement. Given also that during World War 1 there was disinvestment, as might be expected, and that Mitchell shows that for several years before 1914 the same was happening, one concludes that a shortfall in capital formation has been a major feature of railway history during the twentieth century.

The concept of net disinvestment depends of course on the convention that assets have a life of so many years after which they are replaced. This 'life' is to some extent arbitrary. Thus the life of rolling stock is assumed to be thirty-three years; but it does not follow that the stock has to be replaced after that period, nor that stock of an age greater than thirty-three years is useless. Despite these calculations of 'deterioration' the railways were still making a profit in the inter-war period and if the revenue of an asset, no matter how old, is greater than its cost, it is still economically useful. In the long run, though, if it is not replaced it may no longer make a profit and the accumulated cost of replacement may eventually be very high. We may legitimately, therefore, ignore the question of depreciation and replacement, particularly in the case of an old and declining industry.

After 1918 the pattern of investment was not likely to continue in the nineteenth-century way. There were no longer the stimuli of further territorial expansions or protection from intruders; only London Transport could really talk of building new lines and in total their expenditure was small. Instead of having to meet the needs of growing traffic, the railways faced competition from the roads and the loss of income through trade depression. The level of investment would thus be low. On the other hand the state now began to intervene and its actions affected both the amount and the timing of expenditure.

In essence—using expenditures at current prices—expenditure on rolling stock and permanent way was high in 1920 and 1921 (but in real terms, taking into account the massive price inflation, it was rather lower than the average for the 1920s). There was a reduction in 1922 and 1923, followed by a rise to a peak in 1925. This was followed by a fall (apart from 1927) until a low point in 1929, to be succeeded by three years of higher expenditure. The lowest point of all was reached in 1933 and then expenditures rose each year up to 1938. (Table 22, p 186.)

The experience of the 1920s looks like the familiar railway pattern of investing in the downswing of the trade cycle. Thus investment was high in 1923-5 and again during the great depression of 1930-2. But the explanation for this contra-cyclical pattern is not the same as for the pre-1914 years. A study published during World War 2 concluded: 'it was in fact mainly the result of State interference and assistance.'[2]

The first such assistance came under the Trade Facilities Act of 1921, passed 'to enable new enterprise, which was calculated to promote increased employment in this country, to borrow more cheaply than was normally possible in that period of extremely high interest rates.'[3] The method was by a Treasury guarantee of capital or interest—the guarantee reducing the risk and therefore the cost of borrowing. Because of the continued high unemployment the Act was renewed annually until it expired in 1927. Of the £65 million for which guarantees were given, some £12 million were for the railways, for extensions to the London underground. (The South Eastern & Chatham applied to use the Act for raising £6½ million but did not proceed.)

TABLE 22

INVESTMENT 1920-38 (UK)

Gross railway fixed capital formation in rolling stock and permanent way

Year	Rolling stock	Permanent way at current prices (£m)	Total	Rolling stock	Permanent way at constant (1930) prices (£m)	Total
1920	13.4	6.2	19.6	6.9	3.7	10.6
1921	13.7	8.0	21.7	7.0	5.5	12.5
1922	5.8	7.3	13.1	2.9	6.4	9.3
1923	4.9	8.9	13.8	3.9	8.4	12.3
1924	8.5	8.3	16.8	7.1	7.7	14.8
1925	10.6	8.0	18.6	9.0	7.5	16.5
1926	9.1	6.3	15.4	8.2	6.0	14.2
1927	8.9	9.2	18.1	9.1	8.8	17.9
1928	8.3	6.8	15.1	8.3	6.6	14.9
1929	8.1	4.5	12.6	8.1	4.4	12.5
1930	7.3	7.6	14.9	6.8	7.6	14.4
1931	4.8	11.2	16.0	4.5	11.3	15.8
1932	3.6	10.2	13.8	3.4	10.8	14.2
1933	3.1	4.8	7.9	2.9	5.2	8.1
1934	5.9	5.2	11.1	5.5	5.6	11.1
1935	8.5	5.7	14.2	7.6	6.1	13.7
1936	9.9	7.5	17.4	9.0	7.8	16.8
1937	11.0	9.1	20.1	10.3	8.9	19.2
1938	9.8	12.3	22.1	8.8	11.4	20.2

Source: Feinstein, C. H., *Domestic Capital Formation in the United Kingdom 1920-1938* (1965), Table 9.10
The figures are for the UK, but the inclusion of Northern Ireland only marginally affects the totals.
The current prices here quoted are those in his table headed 'Historical Prices'.

In 1929 there were two government initiatives which acutely influenced railway capital formation: the abolition of the railway passenger duty and the Development Act. These primarily affected investment in permanent way and in railway docks. The Southern Railway, for example, was enabled to electrify the line to Brighton and Worthing—previously their electrification had been mainly of suburban lines. The work began in 1931 and was completed in 1933.

It is important to emphasise the fact that permanent way expenditure did not decline during the depression; indeed two of the three years in which expenditure was greater than £10 million were 1931 and 1932. The draught was felt in rolling stock. The amount spent fell by something like one half of what it had been in the late twenties.

In other words in the early 1930s the railways were economising because of the fall in receipts and since so much of their capital formation came from revenue account it was here that cuts were made. Without some form of government assistance— including the beginnings of restriction of road transport—their total expenditures would have been much less.

As the economy moved out of depression the opposite situation obtained. Permanent way expenditure rose less rapidly than that on rolling stock. The lowest point of expenditure for rolling stock was in 1933; by 1935 the amount had more than doubled, most of it financed from revenue account. In that period permanent way expenditure rose but at a slower rate. Yet again the state intervened. In 1935 two Acts of Parliament were passed which set up the London Electric Transport Finance Corporation and the Railway Finance Corporation. These were Treasury companies formed to re-lend funds to the railways to carry out electrification. The first was devoted to the electrification of lines in the London area, and the second for main-line company purposes. Something like £70 million were thus made available for railway purposes, of which rolling stock expenditure played a larger part than in the early 1930s.

This being so, could the railways have done more? Was there much more scope for investing in order to meet competition, by cutting costs and becoming more efficient? To some extent they did. There were important improvements in signalling, eg by the use of coloured lights, and by the mechanisation of signal boxes— the continuation of a long-term process. There was some standardisation of steam locomotives, aimed at reducing the bewildering variety of types still in existence when the companies merged in the 1920s. The 24,000 steam locomotives of that date were reduced to just under 20,000, and from 1920 to 1938 about

9,000 new locomotives were built, in general more powerful and heavier than those they replaced. Similarly large numbers of wagons and coaches were built, the wagons on average being weightier than the old ones. There were important changes in passenger coach design but only the LMS introduced new techniques of construction—standardised mass-production methods using light alloys to reduce weight.

Investment was concentrated on those projects which would have an immediate impact on operating and thus produce higher revenues quickly. But at the same time the fact that the industry on the whole neglected to take advantage of new technologies can be explained only in part by its financial condition. By the end of the 1930s only about 5 per cent of the total route mileage had been electrified and the amount of diesel operation was negligible. One has to attribute a large part of this to the continued delight in steam-power, an attitude which was still in evidence after World War 2.

Virtually the only electrification took place in the London area, comprising the efforts of the London underground system, still expanding into new suburbs, and the transformation of the Southern Railway. Ursula Hicks wrote that the Southern found electrification to be a paying proposition and, on the government financial assistance of 1935, commented that 'it is thus possible that the railways are being aided to do what they could have done unaided and would probably do later.'[4] This is probably unlikely. The London area was prosperous and had the stimulus of a growing commuter traffic, which had to be accommodated in some way. For railways in other parts of the country the conditions were extremely unfavourable.

In fact, electrification was being advocated strongly. In 1931 the report of the Weir Committee on main line electrification estimated that the net cost to the railways would be about £260 million (other capital costs would be incurred by the Central Electricity Board). About £17½ million would be saved on operating and maintenance, ie providing a return of just under 7 per cent. This was quite a reasonable figure, but since the work would have to be carried out over say 20 years, the net return after allowing for interest charges would only be 2 per cent. Such a figure was clearly most unattractive to the companies in the middle of a depression.

The net effect of all this was that on the eve of the second world war there had been some useful developments in rolling stock and in certain other departments such as signalling. Every year from 1933 to 1938 investment rose. But then the war intervened and the amount available for these purposes fell drastically. At its end there were very heavy arrears of maintenance and of renewals and in the immediate post-war period the only important works undertaken were left-overs from the pre-war programme, such as the completion of the extension of the Central line of the London underground and the electrification of the Manchester-Sheffield-Wath line.

The railways came low, as did the transport industry generally, in the list of investment priorities. The early reports of the BTC reveal the severe limits placed by the government on capital investment and even the permitted figures were sometimes not reached because of physical shortages of materials. In its 1950 report the commission stated: 'In the main, assets are being patched rather than replaced', and two years later, in 1952:

> The effects of limitations upon either capital investment or use of materials have been constantly felt since the Commission took over the railways in 1948, and have enforced in many directions a policy of 'make-do-and-mend' which, whilst it may have been inevitable, has proved harmful both to efficiency and economy.

Thus the shortage of steel compelled the railways to repair carriages which were forty or fifty years old. Similarly with wagons which 'are always liable to fall out of traffic for repairs'. The proportion of carriages and wagons under or awaiting repair rose.

The sad tale continued into 1953, but the BTC was able to report some major new works including the start on widening the main line between New Barnet and Potters Bar, the modernisation of Crewe North motive power depot and the building of a new depot near Middlesbrough.

Everything changed with the publication of the Modernisation Plan in 1955. In essence the plan comprised

   a. improvements in the permanent way and in signalling and other devices to permit higher speeds;

   b. the replacement of steam by electric and diesel traction;

c. improvements of stations and rolling stock (passenger and freight).

These proposals were part of a larger set of policies which find their origin in the Transport Act of 1953. This had freed the railways from some of their historical obligations and, as the commission's 1953 report stated, 'a decisive point was reached in the history of the Commission's undertaking and it became necessary to review the basic conceptions which had formed the background to the Commission's policy during the first five years of their existence.' Chapter 7 of the report was entitled 'Future Objectives' and these included: 'An equipment, in the widest sense of the word, of modern design and fit to give reliable and speedy transport on a large scale.'

The modernisation plan was the result. It is quite fair, looking back, to comment that it was really no more than a draft. The BTC's report for 1954 noted that:

> The main technical details of the Plan, which is designed to transform virtually all the forms of service now offered by British Railways, are the result of six months' intensive work by a Planning Committee, set up by the Commission in May 1954, composed of headquarters and regional officers, and working in close conjunction with the Chief Regional Managers.

This half years' work was welcomed by the government with virtually no examination of the details and put into operation straightaway. If the schemes were not as meticulously planned as they ought to have been, there would have been problems enough. But in addition the railways, like other nationalised industries, found themselves used as instruments of policy in the government's attempts to regulate demand. Although the investment plans were of a long-term nature the government—which after 1955 provided the funds for capital works—only permitted expenditure one year at a time. In its evidence to the Committee on the Working of the Monetary System (1957-9) the BTC stated that: 'The Commission's investment expenditure is . . . secured for one year ahead, though many of the investment schemes take much more than a year to carry through, and though in practice the orders must often be placed well before the year begins if the expenditure programmed is to be effective in that year.'

This was difficult enough, but, as the BTC also pointed out to the committee, sudden contractions or expansions in programmes caused numerous difficulties. The Select Committee on Nationalised Industries reported on the events of 1957:

> In September 1957 the Commission were informed that they would have to restrict their total spending for 1958 to £170 million, and for 1959 to £175 million—these figures being respectively £15 and £19 million less than the sums that had been provisionally agreed earlier. The effect of this was that at least one major scheme had to be cut back—causing the loss of the direct penalties paid to the contractors, a slowing down of work in their own shops in order to avoid paying compensation in other jobs, and the wasting of a considerable amount of planning work that had been done; the total cost of this action was impossible to identify, but it might have been considerable.

Thus the ministry had not at first exercised sufficient control at the outset of the modernisation plan, and had then changed its policy—to meet other governmental objectives—which had interfered considerably with long-term plans.

Further, hardly any attempt was made by the ministry to examine together and relate to each other the capital schemes of all the forms of transport. Thus the building of the M1 motor-way between the London area and the North West coincided with the electrification of the main railway line between those points. And although various calculations were made by the railways on the financial implications of their schemes there was some difference between the commission and the ministry on the definitions of the terms employed. The Select Committee, looking back at the electrification of the Euston, Liverpool and Manchester line, reported:

> One can only assume that these schemes costing very many millions of pounds were put forward in the early days of modernisation by the Commission and allowed to go forward by departments, on the basis of figures which apparently meant completely different things to the two sides.

(The Committee spelled out the details of this, which concerned the rate of return to be expected from the expenditure.)

Finally the inception of the modernisation plan coincided with the beginning of railway deficits. Something new needed to be done. Despite some significant developments the plan was not

producing great benefits very quickly and it was absurd for the
BTC to be borrowing money to finance the interest payments on
earlier borrowed money.

The change in thinking and in policy came in the early 1960s
in a series of white papers and reports on the nationalised industries, on the control of public expenditure, and the Transport
Act of 1962. At the same time there was the significant innovation of using cost-benefit analysis to test whether London
Transport's Victoria line should be allowed to go ahead. London
Transport had obtained parliamentary powers in 1955 to build
the line but its calculations that it would not pay, naturally held
things up. The Minister of Transport employed an Oxford
economist to examine the social costs of the line and its social
benefits—that is, the costs and benefits which would accrue outside as well as inside London Transport. The conclusion that the
scheme would on balance be of benefit to London provided the
justification for going ahead.

At the same time the events already described which led up to
the Transport Act and the Beeching Report seemed to put things
on a much clearer basis. The Act wiped out the loans which had
been made since 1956 to cover deficits, and reduced the capital
liability on the debt with which the BTC had commenced. This
amounted to some £1,200 million and naturally greatly limited
the amount of interest the railways had to pay. Of this total about
£500 million were the accumulated deficits and £700 million
were written off the commencing debt.

The actual physical work of modernisation meanwhile went
on rapidly. The last steam engine was delivered to the railways
in 1960. In 1966 the electrified main-line from Euston was completed. In that year the British Railways Board, in their Report,
spoke of 'the beginning of a railway resurgence with many people
recapturing or experiencing for the first time the thrill of a long
distance journey'. There were important experiments and research
going on at the Derby research centre. But new policies came with
the White Papers of 1966 and 1967, and the Transport Act of
1968.

The first was the further writing down of the railways' capital.
The £700 million of suspended debt under the 1962 Act was not
written off. The commencing capital debt was reduced to £330
million (from over £1,500 million). The £300 million were to be

paid off in sums of about £15 million per year beginning in 1970 and ending in 1994, the interest being of various amounts, mostly of around 5½ per cent (but about one quarter of the total paying rates higher than this, the maximum being just over 8 per cent). The second was the introduction of the technique of discounted cash flow, a method of establishing the relative merits of investment schemes. Broadly the system provides means of estimating the return to be expected of projects, and thus their worth as against alternative schemes.

The capital reconstruction was a tidying-up operation and valuably assisted the railways by reducing their interest burden. At the same time it marks the end, together with the other events of the 1960s, of the discussion about the reasons—on the capital side—for the railways' decline. To summarise them as insufficient capital formation and unpredictable government intervention is valid, certainly for much of the period since 1945. Either funds were not available or permission was not forthcoming to undertake necessary works and the wider needs of the economy sometimes took precedence. Moreover, the criteria adopted for evaluating investment projects were seldom very rigorous. But overriding these questions was the major one: what should be the role of railways in the economy? How big should the network be? These questions were not really faced until the early 1960s, an answer being given in the Beeching Report (subsequently modified). The use of new techniques in the examination of investment projects is a major innovation; it will be of supreme interest to see how they work out in practice. The unknown factor, however, remains. Will the railways (and other nationalised industries) continue to operate fairly independently or will government intervention and, more particularly, abrupt changes in policy, return to bedevil the industry's long term plans?

Notes to this chapter are on p 212.

N

CHAPTER 12

REDUNDANCY AND EFFICIENCY

During a half-century when the railway industry has been comparatively unprofitable and when closures rather than extensions have dramatised its decline, one might expect that relations between management and employees would be tense. In the 1920s the numbers employed declined rapidly, unemployment was high and wages were reduced. During the inflationary post-1945 years the unions have pressed almost continuously for higher pay and labour has been in short supply. These circumstances could well have produced continuing tension but in terms of overt conflict, of strikes, the industry is best described as peaceful.

One possible explanation is that once the unions had been recognised by the companies and collective bargaining had been established, and when there were agreements on the guaranteed week and on promotion, many of the reasons for the bitterness of the generation before the Railways Act of 1921 had gone. The institutionalisation of conflict had performed its major function of providing mechanisms for its peaceful solution.

Further, whereas in 1907 and 1911 a railway strike was a major disaster for the economy since so much of industry was dependent on rail services, once the road transport industry had been established the impact of a rail strike was much less. Even in the early days of the new industry, during the national rail strike of 1919, *The Times* could refer to 'The Triumph of the Lorry'. The possibility of substitution of transport facilities could be an inhibiting factor. In 1934 when there was a demand, based on the improvement in the industry's gross receipts, for a restoration of earlier wage cuts, the newly appointed general secretary of the NUR, John Marchbank, told a delegate meeting that 'he was willing to fight "if what they were going to fight for was there to be got", but the railway returns were not the sort of figures they could be "over jubilant to fight on". If they struck work there "would be no road stoppage" and many of their members would be walking the streets after it was over."[1]

But this was in the 1930s. Although the Triple Alliance of 1915 had not in fact operated in 1921, a major preoccupation of the government in the early 1920s was the possibility of a general strike of miners, railwaymen and other transport workers. Moreover, although a railway stoppage is no longer the disaster to the economy that it once was, the NUR's strategy in the post-1945 period of playing on government fears has been notably successful. For a time in the 1950s and 1960s threatened railway strikes involved the intervention of successive prime ministers, brought in, uniquely, to act as conciliators. The railway unions have not often used the strike weapon, but they have known how to deploy its potential use.

Railway staff had indeed made great advances after 1918. Wages rose, hours of work fell, collective bargaining procedures were firmly established, and machinery for the settlement of grievances was in operation. They had, it is true, been frustrated in their demands for nationalisation and there were some detailed points to be settled (eg workshop staff had no grievance procedure until 1927). Nevertheless there had quite obviously been a massive change in terms and conditions of work and the Railways Act of 1921 provided the legal framework for the enhanced prestige of the railway unions.

To some it looked like a revolution, an appropriate part of the ferment in the labour world in that period. And certainly many of the changes were permanent. Yet for most of the 1920s, and in the early part of the next decade, the whole picture changed. Instead of demanding improvements the unions were normally on the defensive faced with the companies' proposals for wage cuts and other reductions in conditions. Instead of greater numbers being employed there were massive reductions in manpower. Even the collective bargaining machinery itself was abandoned for a short time.

The figures tell their own story. There were nearly ¾ million railway employees in 1921. In the early 1930s the number was some 200,000 less. In 1921-2 the number fell by 60,000 and in 1930-1 by about 40,000 (during the 1920s the numbers employed fluctuated; there was no continuous reduction). In the 1930s there was a slight increase in staff. The obverse of this was the degree of unemployment among railwaymen. Between 1923 and 1939 the percentage of insured railwaymen who were unemployed was never below 6. The worst years were between 1931 and 1935 when the percentage was 10 at its lowest and 16.7 at its highest.

Wages also fell. Mitchell's index (1924 = 100) starts in 1920 with a peak figure of $127\frac{1}{2}$; by 1922 it had fallen rapidly to 108, followed by a slow decline to 94 in 1932, a fall of just over one quarter. Chapman & Knight's figures of earnings are slightly different: wages fell in that period by about 20 per cent and salaries by about 9 per cent. However, both show a definite downward movement until the 1930s when there was a slight increase.

For those employed on the railways the inter-war period was one of insecurity and of falling money wages. The trade union histories which record these developments, especially the unions' attempts to ward off attacks on their members' conditions, quite rightly speak in terms of 'Backs to the Wall' (Bagwell, NUR) and 'Into Battle' (McKillop, ASLEF).

Trade unionists measure the effectiveness of their organisation by its success in negotiation. When railwaymen saw that their unions had to accept wage reductions for ten years or so, many withdrew from membership. The NUR had recruited over 480,000 members in 1919; by 1933 the figure had fallen to 275,000 and not all the reduction can be accounted for by a smaller labour force. The number in the latter year included members in the road passenger transport undertakings associated with the railway companies; and membership in the later 1930s and in the 1940s rose more rapidly than did the rate of increase of employment on the railways.

The unions had to operate in an environment which necessarily meant that they would be weak and on the defensive. Yet despite the bitterness of the period, notably during the General Strike the companies were able to demand and obtain concessions from their employees with remarkably little overt conflict. One can sensibly compare this industry with coalmining, whose long-drawn-out strikes over wage cuts were a feature of the period. It is impossible to imagine a miners' leader speaking—as did the general secretary of the NUR after the unions had agreed to a temporary $2\frac{1}{2}$ per cent wage reduction in 1928—of the agreement as 'the best ever made'.[2] The railway unions agreed to the reduction after the companies had given them information about their financial situation (in 1928 gross receipts fell). The executives of the three unions met and, as the historian of ASLEF puts it:

> The result of these deliberations was possibly unique in the history of trade union negotiations: the unions agreed to accept a provisional agreement whereby all railwaymen, from the highest to the lowest, would accept a $2\frac{1}{2}\%$ reduction in wages and salaries, pending endorsement by a specially convened delegate meeting representing the total rank and file. This delegate meeting not only endorsed the Executive's decision, but did so with an overwhelming majority.[3]

Yet the unions were not so unsuccessful as the figures might suggest. Despite their apparent weakness they still retained sufficient bargaining power to whittle down the companies' demands. The 1928 reduction was accepted, moreover, partly because it was to be temporary—and it was so—and partly because the major gains of the post-war period were not lost. Similarly when the companies withdrew in 1934 from the collective bargaining machinery after the unions had rejected an award of the National Wages Board, the breakdown was short-lived. The employers proposed a new system, including the replacement of the NWB by the Railway Staff National Tribunal. After hard bargaining the unions were able to obtain the companies' agreement to withdraw some of the more obnoxious innovations proposed (eg that the findings of the proposed tribunal should be binding on both parties).

While earnings fell in the 1920s and early 1930s the standard of living of those at work did not. Wage rates fell by about one-quarter between 1920 and 1933 but the cost of living fell by 45 per cent. Railwaymen were earning less but the remarkable fall in the cost of living was to the advantage of those in work.

At the same time the companies continued with their paternal attitude. For example, after World War I the GWR was approached by its employees to help meet their housing needs. Railwaymen often had to move round the country and could not, therefore, buy their own houses, and local authorities, at that date, were giving priority to those who had lived in the localities before the war. The company advanced £1,400,000 in direct loans, enabling over 3,000 to buy their houses, and also formed Public Utility Housing Societies of whose capital nearly £¾ million were provided by the company. These sums were not grants and the schemes were expected to pay their way. The idea, though, must have been useful to hard-pressed employees whose circumstances required special treatment.

Railwaymen's wages proved to be more flexible downwards than upwards. When railway traffic began to improve the unions put forward demands for the restoration of wage cuts. The companies resisted strongly in their contests before the Railway Staff National Tribunal. The unions, however, were in a difficulty. Their wage policy was a combination of two types of argument, (apart from the occasion in 1936 when improved labour productivity was emphasised). On the one hand it was based on the financial condition of the companies. This was the justification for their acceptance of wage cuts in the late 1920s, when profits were low. Yet at the same time, and naturally enough, they were anxious to safeguard and improve their members' standards, so they produced arguments about railwaymen's low pay. When the unions, in the mid-1930s, demanded the restoration of earlier wage cuts, the companies were able to retort that their net profit position was worse than it had been when the unions accepted cuts.

> The weakness of a policy of basing wages on the fluctuating net revenues of the companies, instead of on the need for railway men for a reasonable standard of living was thus revealed.[4]

Even so, the union continued to base demands on the companies' revenue, often on the figures of gross receipts.

The cuts were restored and in 1939 the tribunal examined a demand for a 50s (£2.50) minimum wage. The tribunal was unsympathetic and gave only some limited concessions which were rejected by the union. This was in April and the arbitrators had at the back of their mind the fact that gross receipts for the first quarter of the year were some £¼ million below those for the corresponding period of 1938. In the second quarter of the year traffic rose rapidly and by the late summer it was producing a revenue of £1 million per week above the previous year. The demand for a 50s minimum was reiterated by the NUR (the RCA dropped it and ASLEF had its own programme) and in July the companies agreed to a 45s (£2.25) minimum. The full demand was granted in October but only for those working in the London area.

The important thing here is that the NUR was still to a large extent basing its policies and tactics on the companies' income. Such a policy would make sense in a period of prosperity for the industry. The industry was not prosperous or expanding and wage increases tended to raise operating costs which in turn reduced net profits. The circle was closed.

During the war wages rose to meet the rising cost of living. A number of flat-rate increases were granted, as in the first world war. These could be justified but the result was to reduce differentials, thus sowing the seeds of trouble in future years.

Nationalisation came in 1947. The unions had advocated it for years and,

> . . . the transfer of these great industries to public ownership raised high hopes in the employees.
>
> These hopes were both ideological and material. Ideologically, public ownership was regarded as the gateway to a new society, in which there would be greater plenty and less hardship for the toiling masses, and in which co-operation would supplant competition. Materially, the unions and their members expected better treatment in every respect from nationalised industries than they received under private enterprise. They hoped that the elimination of profits would bring them higher wages and better working conditions; that State control would ensure full employment; and that industrial democracy would be brought appreciably nearer.[5]

This is not the place to attempt a balance sheet of the effects of nationalisation on railway labour. Certainly many of the more extravagant hopes were not realised. In some senses the change of ownership and organisation made little difference: the railways had had collective bargaining for three decades. The expectations of those who anticipated much greater control by railway employees in the running of the industry have been dashed. The functions of management and those of unions have remained separate and distinct and the establishment of joint consultative procedures at all levels exemplified the division. For while all manner of topics could be discussed in consultative committees, the final decision for their acceptance or rejection remained with management. In the final report of the BTC, for the year 1962, we read that

> At national level joint consultation was carried out through the medium of either the British Transport Joint Consultative Council or the British Railways Productivity Council, on both of which bodies senior representatives of the Management and the Trade Unions served. Discussions took place during the year on various aspects of the Commission's undertaking including the closure of unremunerative lines and the withdrawal of uneconomic services . . .

But these discussions did not succeed in that on 3 October the NUR and the engineering unions called a one-day strike 'as a protest against the closing of branch lines, withdrawal of services and the closure of railway workshops'.

In a period when railways have been declining and when operating losses have been extraordinarily high one would expect relationships to be poor. And in 1960 the chairman of the BTC told the Select Committee of Nationalised Industries that 'I would not pretend for one moment that we are as good at this as we should be'. Nevertheless it is right to point out the changes and improvements which occurred.

In the early reports of the BTC references to productivity are rather vague. In 1954, for example, the unions are described as having made pledges of greater co-operation. 'Provided a satisfactory wages structure for all grades on the railways could be agreed, they would do everything possible to secure the co-operation of all concerned in revised methods and the more effective deployment of effort.' Sentiments of this kind were common in collective bargaining sessions; they were easily made and imposed no commitment on the unions.

The first change came soon afterwards with the Modernisation Plan. In May 1955 the British Railways Productivity Council was established and the BTC's Report for 1956 stated that:

> . . . much progress has been made both in the study on modern lines of the problems involved in securing greater productive efficiency and also in the practical application of work study methods to particular sectors of activity and in the consequent development of incentive bonus schemes.

At first progress was slow but by the end of its life, in 1962, the BTC was able to state that on British Railways 57,000 employees were under work study schemes (just less than 12 per cent of the total). About three-quarters of them received an incentive bonus.

In the 1960s the emphasis changed to productivity bargaining. The background to this needs describing, involving some consideration of the development of negotiation and of the role of the state in industrial relations generally. Broadly it is right to say that up to the 1950s the state's main function was to maintain industrial peace. It was less interested in the economic consequences of any resulting settlements. During the 1950s as governments were faced with the problems of demand management, the unreality of this approach became evident. At the same time, as far as nationalised industries were concerned, the government was inevitably involved in wage settlements. In the final analysis the state would have to find the money.

We can see the changes of policy and attitude in the history of railway wage bargaining. In 1953 railwaymen were offered a small increase by the Railway Staff National Tribunal. A threatened strike was followed by a Court of Inquiry offering nearly twice the original amount.

> Some employers (including, understandably, the boards of the nationalised industries) preferred to support industrial co-operation and its established institutions at almost any cost.[6]

The award was a stop-gap until railway wage structures were fully investigated. The result of the review was not satisfactory to the NUR and a further court of inquiry was held. It included in its report the statement that:

> . . . the employees of such a national service should receive a fair and adequate wage, and that, in broad terms, the railwaymen should be in no worse case than his colleagues in comparable industry.

This view was in line with thinking in the late 1950s, the idea that 'fair comparisons' would provide a sensible and rational basis for wage determination. This method requires the wages of people in one industry to be settled by direct comparison with those of people, doing comparable jobs, in other industries. It was applied to the railways in 1960, and was an attempt to be rid of the constant pressures for higher pay and of the quarrels between the three unions. For the separateness and rivalry of the unions led to problems which seemed incapable of solution. Thus the negotiations, awards, threatened strikes and courts of inquiry during the period 1953-5 were in large part a reflection of the differing policies of the NUR and ASLEF. And these in turn depended on the different membership of the unions. The footplatemen aimed to maintain their differentials, whereas the NUR, more of a general union, had to have regard to the interests of the bulk of its members.

Worse still, after 1956 the railways had no money and the BTC's rejection of the wage demands of 1958 was upheld by the Railway Staff National Tribunal. A threatened railway strike was called off after a small increase had been granted, together with an agreement to establish an independent inquiry into wages and salaries. This was the origin of the Guillebaud report. The BTC and the three railway unions agreed to set up an independent body whose terms of reference included:

> To conduct an investigation into the relativity of pay of salaried and conciliation staff in British Railways covered by the machinery of negotiation for Railway staff with the pay of staff in other Nationalised industries, Public Services, and appropriate Private Undertakings, as agreed between the Parties or on the instigation of the Independent Body, where reasonable and useful comparisons can be made, and in relation to any such comparisons—
> (i) to establish the degree of job comparability;
> (ii) to ascertain the rates of pay and such other emoluments of the jobs compared as may be properly taken into account; and
> (iii) to take account of all such other factors as the Body may consider relevant in assessing the comparability of the jobs.

The investigation was very full and elaborate. It comprised a systematic examination of earnings and other conditions in a variety of occupations, in different industries, which were considered to be comparable with those on the railways. It showed that generally railwaymen's wages were lower than those of people doing comparable work elsewhere and detailed recommendations were made to increase them.

Thus railway wages were not to be based on the industry's capacity to pay them; nor were they related to the cost of living. Instead, what mattered was the actual content of the job, in terms of skill, responsibility, mental and physical effort. The comparison of jobs used these criteria; when it was seen that a certain occupation on the railways was similar in its content to outside occupations, then it was possible to argue that the pay should be similar.

The exercise took a long time and could not be repeated frequently. But despite the enthusiastic reception for its methods —they seemed to be a way out of endless wrangling and irrational wage determination—drastic changes soon altered the whole background. On the one hand the industry's objectives became more specific and clear-cut, the purpose being to try to get its finances straight and to avoid constant government subvention. On the other, from 1961, collective bargaining itself now became a major interest of the state. Instead of concentrating on peace-keeping, the state became involved in the substantive content of collective agreements, in the details of what the parties agreed. Incomes policy was now more important than industrial peace since the containment of inflation (given the adverse balance of payments position) had to be tackled seriously.

The relevance of all this for the railways was that fair comparison, as a method of wage settlement, was no longer acceptable in terms of public policy. The railway unions argued for its continuance but they were faced with the railway management's statement that the Guillebaud exercise had been a once-for-all effort. There were pay increases in 1962, 1963 and 1964, but the 1965 settlement, an offer by the Railways Board accepted by the unions, was referred to the National Board for Prices and Incomes established in that year. Their report came out strongly against fair comparisons, partly for technical reasons (eg the Guillebaud committee had not identified the sources of many of its non-railway statistics; the unions in 1965 could base their arguments only on the identifiable ones, the outside labourers' rates). Moreover, and more important, comparability was regarded as inflationary in that wage increases were granted even if there had been no increase in productivity, so that costs would rise and railway charges would have to be increased.

Some pay increases were recommended. The 1966 Report of the Railways Board commented:

> Subsequent developments were rapid and dramatic—the NUR's rejection of the report and threat of strike action; the series of meetings between the Railway Board and the unions and members of the Government; and the ultimate withdrawal of the strike threat by the NUR after a meeting with the Prime Minister.
>
> At that meeting the Prime Minister undertook to inaugurate discussions about the basis for future negotiations on pay and conditions, including the problems of devising a new pay structure which would relate pay to productivity.

This was the beginning of the new phase in collective bargaining on the railways—one notes that this section of the Report is headed 'Pay and Productivity', whereas in previous reports the equivalent section had been headed 'Staff Negotiations'—in which pay discussions are related directly to costs and efficiency. The phrase 'productivity bargaining' had come into currency in 1964; under the incomes policy one of the criteria for obtaining increases was that they should be related to certain changes in working practices aimed at raising output.

> The prime purpose of productivity bargaining is to raise labour productivity and lower unit labour costs, and this is achieved by the exchange of alterations in working practices for increased leisure, higher remuneration for labour, more comprehensive fringe benefits and a general increase in the status of the manual employee.[7]

In an industry like the railways, where labour costs account for 60 per cent or more of total costs, even a small *per capita* rise in wages, no matter how justified, can raise total costs alarmingly. Charges would then have to be raised but this might lead to a drop in traffic. If costs are contained by higher productivity, wages can rise without serious consequences for the industry's finances.

Of course, productivity had improved. New techniques like work study began to be introduced in the 1950s. The British Railways Productivity Council had continuing discussions. A major agreement was made in 1957 about the future manning of diesel and electric locomotives. Broadly, the unions agreed that there should be one driver or motorman, subject to certain safeguards; and this was combined with provisions for any men made redundant.

Not everything went smoothly. The London International Freight Depot at Stratford (London) was due to be opened on 19 June 1967 but the NUR declared it 'black' and there was an official strike between 22 June and 3 July. The union claimed that all the traffic should be handled by railwaymen, whereas forwarding agents who rented premises there wanted to use their own staff. There was a further inter-union problem in 1967 over the duties of goods guards. The dispute first concerned the NUR and after much difficulty an agreement was reached, part of which involved the transfer of guards to the rear cabs of locomotives. ASLEF then argued that this now broke their manning agreement.

Moreover, even the negotiations over the productivity agreement—the Railways Board put forward its proposals in February 1968, in itself an interesting indication of a management preparing a positive programme rather than waiting for the unions to make claims—were not straightforward. As well as discussing problems of pay and efficiency, the NUR and ASLEF put forward claims for higher pay, a general rise not connected with productivity. One curious result of the dispute which ensued was that a team from the board went to Penzance, where the NUR was holding its annual conference, and reached a settlement.

This was regarded at the time as a defeat for the government's incomes policy. But for the railways the subsequent events were of major significance. The board's Report for 1968 put it thus:

> There followed a period of concentrated discussions at New Lodge, Windsor, where representatives of the NUR, ASLEF and the Board lived and worked together to the exclusion of all other problems in order to find a solution to the productivity bargain which had been under discussion since 1966.
>
> These discussions led to a productivity deal being concluded with effect from 12 August for footplate staff and other railway conciliation staff as Stage 1 of the pay and efficiency review. The agreement reached makes provision for the joint monitoring of results flowing from this first deal, the outcome of which will

clearly influence the timing and extent of the next round of productivity bargaining talks.

It would be absurd to pretend that changes of this kind are going to mean the end of conflict on the railways. There will always be scope for disagreement on major and minor matters. The significant feature is that the new shape of the industry, and the stricter requirements of its financial and economic objectives have been matched by parallel developments in labour relations. It is now possible for the unions to be completely involved (in the jargon of the day to 'participate') in managerial decisions; and the mechanisms of productivity bargaining enable them to continue to represent the special interests of the members, in their dealings with management (to improve their members' standards) at the same time as the management can pursue, in collective bargaining, their main objective of improving efficiency. In such a situation industrial conflict can produce positive results. It is no longer necessary, therefore, to measure the state of labour relations by the existence of conflict. What is important is that the conflict can be used so that both sides can achieve their objectives.

Notes to this chapter are on p 212.

NOTES

Chapter 1 (pp 17–34)

1 Quoted Pratt, E. A. *History of Inland Transport and Communications in England* (1912 reprinted 1970), 220-1.
2 Rolt, L. T. C. *George and Robert Stephenson* (1960), 36.
3 Pollard, S. *The Genesis of Modern Management* (1968), 82.
4 Simmons, J. 'For and Against the Steam Locomotive', *Journal of Transport History*, 2 no 3 (1956).
5 See Broadbridge, Seymour. *Studies in Railway Expansion and the Capital Market in England 1825-1873* (1970), 160ff; also Lee, Joseph. 'The provision of capital for early Irish railways, 1830-53', *Irish Historical Studies*, 16 no 61 (1968); and Vamplew, Wray. 'Sources of Scottish Railway Share Capital before 1860', *Scottish Journal of Political Economy*, 17 no 3 (1970).
6 Matthews, R. C. O. *A Study in Trade Cycle History* (1953), 110.
7 Pollins, Harold. 'The Marketing of Railway Shares in the first half of the nineteenth century', *Econ Hist Rev*, 7 (1954).
8 Ward, J. T. 'West Riding Landowners and the Railways', *Journal of Transport History*, 4 no 4 (1960).
9 *Railway Times*, 28 January 1843, 83.
10 These details are taken from the minutes of the Eastern Counties Railway.
11 For a recent discussion of some of these points see: Hawke, G. R. and Reed, M. C. 'Railway Capital in the United Kingdom in the Nineteenth Century', *Econ Hist Rev*, 22 no 2 (1969).
12 Pollins, Harold. 'A Note on Railway Constructional Costs 1825-50', *Economica* 19 (1952). The subsequent discussion comes from the same source.

Chapter 2 (pp 35–54)

1 Clapham, Sir John. *An Economic History of Modern Britain. The Early Railway Age* (2nd ed 1930), 389.
2 *The Economist*, 17 August 1844, 118.

3 Parris, H. W. *Government and the Railways in Nineteenth-century Britain* (1965), 61.
4 Broadbridge, *Railway Expansion*, 32. Italics in original directors' *Report*.
5 Simmons, J. *The Railways of Britain* (2nd ed 1968), 11.
6 Pollins, Harold. 'Aspects of Railway Accounting before 1868', in Reed, M. C. (ed) *Railways in the Victorian Economy* (1969).
7 Barnes, E. G. *The Rise of the Midland Railway 1844-1874* (1966), 147.
8 Robbins, M. *Points and Signals* (1967), 82.
9 See: Pollins, Harold. 'Contractors and the Finance of Railways in Great Britain', in Reed (ed) op cit.

Chapter 3 (pp 55–73)

1 Mitchell, B. R. 'The Coming of the Railway and United Kingdom Economic Growth' in Reed, M. C. (ed) *Railways in the Victorian Economy* (1969).
2 Jackman, W. F. *Transportation in Modern England* (1916, reprinted 1966), 572-3.
3 Lardner, D. *Railway Economy* (quoted Mitchell).
4 Hart, H. W. 'Some Notes on Coach Travel, 1750-1848', *Journal of Transport History*, 4 no 3 (1960), 148-9.
5 Williams, R. A. *The London and South Western Railway*, 221.
6 Hadfield, C. 'The Grand Junction Canal', *Journal of Transport History*, 4 no 2 (1959).
7 Turnbull, G. L. 'A Note on the Supply of Staff for the early railways', *Transport History*, 1 no 1 (1968), 4.
8 Bagwell, P. *The Railway Clearing House in the British Economy 1842–1922* (1968), 72.
9 Bagwell, 79ff.
10 This discussion owes much to Hawke, G. R. *Railways and Economic growth in England and Wales 1840-1870* (1970), originally a DPhil thesis, Oxford, 1968.
11 Dunlop, J. T. *Industrial Relations Systems* (1958), 20.
12 Bonavia, M. R. *The Economics of Transport* (1955), 82.
13 *Felix J. C. Pole. His Book* (1968), chapter 8.
14 See: Hawke, op cit; and Gourvish, T. R. 'British Railway Management in the Nineteenth Century, with special reference to the career of Captain Mark Huish (1808-1867)', PhD, London (1967). Also Gourvish, T. R. 'Captain Mark Huish: a Pioneer in the development of Railway management', *Business History*, 12 (1969).
15 The best study is by Hawke and is contained in Reed (ed),

Railways in the Victorian Economy as well as in *Railways and Economic Growth*. A useful examination of a limited field is by Channon, G. 'The Aberdeenshire Beef Trade with London: a Study in Steamship and Railway Competition, 1850-69', *Transport History*, 2 no 1 (1968). See in general, Milne, A. M. and Laing, A. *The Obligation to Carry* (1957).

16 BTHR: LNW 1/50, 1.
17 BTHR: LNW 1/716.
18 Ibid.

Chapter 4 (pp 74–84)

1 This chapter owes much to Kingsford, P. W. *Victorian Railwaymen* (1970).
2 Marquess of Anglesey (ed). *Sergeant Pearman's Memoirs* (1968), 21-2.
3 Kingsford, P. W. 'Labour Relations on the Railways, 1835-1875', *Journal of Transport History,* 1 no 2 (1953).
4 For a discussion of relevant aspects of labour law in this period see: Simon, D. 'Master and Servant' in Saville, J. (ed) *Democracy and the Labour Movement* (1954), chapter 6.
5 The North Midland episode is described in Parris, H. *Government and the Railways* 47ff, and Robbins, M. 'The North Midland Railway and its Enginemen, 1842-3' *Journal of Transport History,* 4 no 3 (1960).
6 Parris, *Government and the Railway* 47-8.
7 Kerr, C. and Siegel, A. J. 'The Interindustry propensity to strike' in Kerr C. *Labor and Management in Industrial Society* (1964).
8 Kingsford, P. W. op cit (1970), 19.
9 Bagwell, P. *The Railwaymen* (1963).
10 Kingsford, 'Labour Relations on the Railways' 1, 70.
11 Ibid, 79.
12 See Kingsford, 'Labour relations . . .'; and Bagwell, P. S. 'Early attempts at national organisation of the railwaymen, 1865-1867', *Journal of Transport History,* 3 no 2 (1957).

Chapter 5 (pp 87–106)

1 Robbins, M. *The Railway Age* (1965), 105.
2 Aldcroft, D. H. *British Railways in Transition* (1968), 7-8. See also his 'The Efficiency and Enterprise of British Railways, 1870-1914', *Explorations in Entrepreneurial History,* 5 no 2 (1968).

o

3   Barker, T. C. and Robbins, M. *A History of London Transport,* I (1963), 214ff.
4   Campbell, C. D. *British Railways in Boom and Depression* (1932).
5   Tomlinson, W. W. *The North Eastern Railway* (1915, reprinted 1967), 662-3.
6   Ross, H. M. *British Railways* (1904), 40.
7   Rowe, J. W. F. *Wages in Practice and Theory* (1928), 40.
8   Aldcroft, especially *British Railways in Transition,* 15.
9   Ross, 127.
10 Ross, 119-20.
11 Ellis, C. Hamilton. 'Lewin Papers concerning Sir George Gibb' *Journal of Transport History,* 5 no 4 (1962).

Chapter 6 (pp 107–25)

1   *The Economist,* 16 February 1867, 30 March 1867.
2   Roberts, G. K. 'The development of a railway interest, and its relation to Parliament, 1830-68'. PhD, London, (1966), 287.
3   BTHR: PYB 1/2373, 79.
4   Bagwell, P. S. 'The Rivalry and Working Union of the South Eastern and London Chatham & Dover Railways', *Journal of Transport History,* 2 no 2 (1955).
5   Pollins, Harold. 'Aspects of Railway Accounting before 1868', in Reed (ed) *Railways in the Victorian Economy.*
6   Ross, H. M. *British Railways* (1904), 227.
7   Ross, 221.
8   Ashworth, W. H. *An Economic History of England, 1870-1939.* (1960), 121-2.
9   Eversley, D. E. C. 'The Great Western Railway and the Swindon Works in the Great Depression' in Reed (ed) *Railways in the Victorian Economy.*
10 Pollins, Harold. 'The last main railway line to London', *Journal of Transport History,* 4 no 2 (1959).
11 Eversley, op cit. Cole's work is discussed in Kindleberger, C. P. *Economic Growth in France and Britain* (1964), 138-9.
12 Bell, R. *Twenty-five years of the North Eastern Railway* 1898-1922 (1951).

Chapter 7 (pp 126–40)

1   Webb, S. and B. *Industrial Democracy* (1897), 554.
2   Pratt, E. A. *Inland Transportation,* 406.
3   Anon. *Railways and Railwaymen* (1892), 96.
4   See: Bagwell, P. S. *The Railwaymen* (1963); McKillop, N. *The Lighted Flame* (1951).

5 Gupta, P. S. 'Railway Trade Unionism, in Britain, c. 1880-1900',
   Econ Hist Rev, 19 no 1 (1966). See also his thesis: 'History
   of the Amalgamated Society of Railway Servants, 1871-1913',
   DPhil, Oxford, 1960.
6 For a discussion see: Clegg, H. A., Fox. A., and Thompson, A. F.
   A History of British Trade Unions since 1889. Vol 1. 1889-
   1910 (1964), 315ff.
7 Bagwell, *Railwaymen*, 285.

Chapter 8 (pp 141–9)

1 Simmons, J. *The Railways of Britain* (2nd ed 1968), 33.
GENERAL NOTE TO CHAPTER 8. The course of events from 1914 to
1921 can be readily obtained from a number of sources, including
Aldcroft, *Railways in Transition,* and Hamilton, J. A. B. *Britain's
Railways in World War I* (1967) among the most recent.

Chapter 9 (pp 153–65)

1 Savage, C. I. *An Economic History of Transport* (1959), 103.
2 Walker, G. *Road and Rail* (2nd ed 1947), 82.
3 Walker, 115.
4 Hallsworth, H. M. 'The Future of Rail Transport', *Econ Journal*
   (1934).
5 Bell, R. 'The London & North Eastern Railway. 1. Sixteen Years,
   1923-38', *Journal of Transport History*, 5 no 3 (1962), 134.
6 Elliot, J. 'Early Days of the Southern Railway', *Journal of Transport History*, 4 no 4 (1960), 202.
7 Pickstock, F. *British Railways—The Human Problem* (Fabian
   Pamphlet, 1950).
8 *Felix J. C. Pole. His Book* (1968), chapter 14, especially 78 and
   80-1.

Chapter 10 (pp 166–83)

1 *Report from the Select Committee on Nationalised Industries.
   British Railways.* H. C. 254 (1960), para 21.
2 Ibid. para 40.
3 Ibid, 49.
4 Gwilliam, K. *Transport and Public Policy* (1964), 169.
5 *Sel Comm on Nationalised Industries Transport and Public
   Policy,* paras 415, 417.
6 Gwilliam, 182.
7 Munby, D. L. 'Mrs Castle's Transport Policy', *Journal of
   Transport Economics and Policy*, 2 no 2 (1968), 20.
8 I am not suggesting that the policies are optimal, in a welfare
   sense, but rather that they are unambiguous and consistent.

9 Deakin, B. M. and Seward, T. *Productivity in Transport* (1969), 67.
10 Ibid, 63.

Chapter 11 (pp 184–93)

1 Munby, D. L. 'Economic Problems of British Railways', *Bulletin of the Inst of Stats* (1962).
2 Bretherton, R. F., Burchardt, F. A., and Rutherford, R. S. G. *Public Investment and the Trade Cycle* (1941).
3 Vernon, R. V. and Mansergh, N. *Advisory Bodies, A Study of their uses in relation to central government, 1919-1939* (1940), 114.
4 Hicks, U. K. *The Finance of British Government 1920-1936* (1938), 71ff.

Chapter 12 (pp 194–206)

1 Bagwell, *Railwaymen,* 545-6.
2 Ibid, 512.
3 McKillop, *Lighted Flame,* 188.
4 Bagwell, 550.
5 Robson, W. A. *Nationalised Industry and Public Ownership* (1960), 321.
6 Knowles, K. G. J. C. 'Wages and Productivity' in Worswick, G. D. N. and Ady, P. H. *The British Economy in the Nineteen Fifties* (1962), 505.
7 Golding, J. and Jones, K. *Productivity Bargaining* (Fabian pamphlet 1966), 2. There is now a vast literature on this subject. See, *inter alia,* Towers B. and Whittingham, T. G. *The New Bargainers. A Symposium on Productivity Bargaining* (1970), and National Board for Prices and Incomes, *Productivity Agreements,* Report no 123 (1969).

GUIDE TO FURTHER READING

Despite the daunting size of George Ottley's *A Bibliography of Railway History* (1965)—nearly 700 pages—the reader wishing to pursue the topics discussed here need not be deterred by the potential vastness of the task. He may be comforted by reading Kellett, J. R. 'Writing on Victorian Railways: an Essay in Nostalgia', *Victorian Studies*, 13 no 1 (1969), a brief review article which rapidly dismisses a great deal of recent railway historiography. Nevertheless much useful work has been published and this note is a guide—in no way comprehensive—to some of the more interesting studies.

The reader might wish to place railway history in its general transport context and for this we have Dyos, H. J. and Aldcroft, D. H. *British Transport: An economic survey from the seventeenth century to the twentieth* (1969). It goes up to World War 2 (with a brief epilogue on events thereafter) and its annotated bibliography will be found extremely helpful.

Nineteenth century to World War 1

All kinds of statistics are to be found in the parliamentary papers (for convenience called *Railway Returns*) but they have to be handled with care. (A guide to the sources is to be found in Menzler, F. A. A. 'Rail and Road Statistics', *Journal Royal Stat Soc*, Series A, 113 (1950), reprinted in Kendall, M. G. *Sources and Nature of the Statistics of the U.K.* [1951].) Hawke, G. R. and Reed, M. C. 'Railway Capital in the United Kingdom in the Nineteenth Century', *Econ Hist Rev*, 22 no 2 (1969) provides new series on paid-up capital up to 1912. Mitchell's figures on capital formation (Mitchell, B. R. 'The Coming of the Railway and United Kingdom Economic Growth', in Reed, M. C. *Railways in the Victorian Economy* [1969]) go up to 1919; another series is Kenwood, A. G. 'Railway Investment in

Britain, 1827-1875', *Economica*, 32 (1965). The differences between these two sets of figures are examined by Hawke, G. R. *Railways and Economic Growth in England and Wales, 1840-1870*, (1970). The raw material on which this kind of work is based is to be found in the records of the individual companies. The nature and difficulty of accounting practices are discussed by Pollins, Harold, 'Aspects of Railway Accounting before 1868', in Reed, *Railways in the Victorian Economy*, and by Broadbridge, S. *Studies in Railway Expansion and the Capital Market in England 1825-1873* (1970). The latter performs, for the L & Y, the useful exercise of disentangling the published accounts to produce new series on a consistent basis.

It would be wrong, however, to conclude that one can dismiss earlier works. Some of the contemporary publications are very much worth reading, and several have recently been re-issued. Lardner, Dionysius, *Railway Economy* (1850: reprinted 1968) has been used by some writers but its significance has now been firmly established by Hawke, *Railways and Economic Growth*. Tooke, T. and Newmarch, W. *A History of Prices* V (1857) is well worth looking at, and so are some of the writers at the turn of the century, such as Ross, H. M. *British Railways* (1904), and Pratt, E. A. *A History of Inland Transport and Communications* (1912, reprinted 1970).

It is probably true that most attention has been devoted to the early period, before 1870, and to construction. In addition to the works on capital investment already mentioned, reference should be made to Matthews, R. C. O. *A Study in Trade Cycle History* (1953) and Lee, Joseph. 'The provision of capital for early Irish Railways, 1830-53', *Irish Historical Studies*, 16 no 61 (1968). Both of these deal with the cyclical aspect of investment. Costs of construction are discussed in Pollins, Harold, 'A Note on Railway Constructional Costs, 1825-50', *Economica*, 19 (1952); in Lee, Joseph, 'The Construction Costs of Irish Railways 1830-1853', *Business History* 9 no 2 (1967); and in Kellett, J. R. *The Impact of Railways on Victorian Cities* (1969).

The parliamentary aspects of railway company promotion and construction are examined by Williams, O. C. *History of Private Bill Procedure* (2 vols, 1948, 1949), by Parris, H. *Government and Railways in Nineteenth Century Britain* (1965)—mainly up to 1867; and by Cleveland-Stevens, E. *English Railways: their development and their relation to the State* (1915).

On the sources of railway capital there is useful information in Broadbridge, *Railway Expansion*, and in Lee, Joseph, 'Provision of capital . . .' On the capital market there are Pollins, Harold, 'The marketing of railway shares in the first half of the nineteenth century', *Econ Hist Rev*, 7 (1954), Broadbridge, *Railway Expansion*, Reed, M. C. 'George Stephenson and W. T. Salvin: the early railway capital market at work', *Transport History*, 1 no 1 (1968) and his other article 'Railways and the Growth of the Capital Market', in the volume he edited, *Railways in the Victorian Economy*.

Promotion and construction are now well covered, but operating less so. Among recent relevant work are Hawke, *Railways and Economic Growth*; Milne, A. M. and Laing, A. *The Obligation to Carry* (1956); and Bagwell, P. S. *The Railway Clearing House in the British Economy 1842-1922* (1968); Aldcroft, D. H. 'The Efficiency and Enterprise of British Railways, 1870-1914', *Explorations in Entrepreneurial History*, 5 no 2 (1968) and chapter 1 of his *British Railways in Transition* (1968) critically examine the record of the industry. The earlier work of Campbell, C. D. *British Railways in Boom and Depression* (1932) is different in being rigorously statistical and is primarily concerned with the relationship between the trade cycle and the railways' revenues and costs.

A great deal of work has been done on railway labour, Kingsford, P. W. *Victorian Railwaymen* (1970) goes up to the 1870s, to which can be added a short piece by Turnbull, G. L. 'A note on the supply of staff for the early railways', *Transport History* 1 no 1 (1968). Bagwell P. S. *The Railwaymen* (1963) is the official history of the NUR (usefully to be compared with Gupta, P. S. 'Railway Trade Unionism in Britain, c 1880-1900', *Econ Hist Rev*, 19 no 1 (1966), a piece intended as a corrective to Bagwell). For an aspect of the major upheaval just before and during World War 1 see: Pribicevic, B. *The Shop Stewards' Movement and Workers' Control, 1910-1922* (1959).

The work on organisation and management is probably the least satisfactory, although Hawke, *Railways and Economic Growth* has useful material, and the examinations of financial and accounting practices, as well as of labour relations, are obviously relevant. The unpublished thesis by Gourvish, T. R. 'British Railway management in the nineteenth century, with special reference to the career of Captain Mark Huish (1808-1867)', PhD, London 1967, is of interest. Ross, *British Railways* has a chapter on organisation, and the changes made by the NER at the turn of the century are described by Ellis, C. Hamilton, 'Lewin Papers concerning Sir George Gibb', *Journal of Transport History*, 5 no 4 (1962).

Post-1914

Railway statistics improved in the twentieth century but they still need to be used with caution because of numerous changes of definition and coverage. D. L. Munby has been working on the figures for the period since 1900 and it is to be hoped his work will be published.

The inter-war period has not, surprisingly, been well researched yet. Two earlier discussions of investment contain useful analyses (Bretherton, R. F., Burchardt, F. A. and Rutherford, R. S. G., *Public Investment and the Trade Cycle* (1941), and Glover, K. G. 'The recent course of gross investment in inland transport and the influence of government upon it', MSc [Econ], London, [1949]). The most recent compilation is by Feinstein, C. H., *Domestic Capital Formation in the United Kingdom, 1820-1938* (1965). Some of his statistics are used by Aldcroft in his *British Railways in Transition*. Aldcroft's article 'Innovation on the Railways: the lag in Diesel and Electric Traction', *Journal of Transport Economics and Policy*, 3 (1969) has interesting material on the industry's slowness to innovate.

Operating in the 1920s and 1930s is examined in Aldcroft's book and there are useful earlier discussions by Sherrington, C. E. R., *The Economics of Rail Transport in Great Britain* (2 vols, 1928; vol 2, 2nd ed 1937), and Walker, Gilbert, *Road and Rail* (2nd ed 1947). Savage, C. I. *Inland Transport* (1957) while mainly on the second world war contains relevant material. Sherrington has a chapter on management organisation and the descriptions of the Southern Railway and the LNER by Elliot, John, 'Early Days of the Southern Railway', *Journal of Transport History*, 4 no 4 (1960) and by Bell, R. 'The London & North Eastern Railway. 1. Sixteen Years, 1923-38', ibid 5 no

3, (1962), are illuminating. Two autobiographies throw fascinating insights into railway management. *Felix J. C. Pole. His Book* (1968) is particularly useful for the discussion of his work as general manager of the GWR in the 1920s (the material on pre-1914 life adds considerably to our knowledge too) and Fiennes, G. *I tried to run a railway* (1967), a livelier book, describes life on the LNER from 1928.

The new atmosphere in labour relations in the inter-war years can be caught from Bagwell, *Railwaymen*, and from Martin, R. M. *Communism and the British Trade Unions* (1970). Clegg, H. A. *Labour Relations in London Transport* (1950) and Knowles, K. G. J. C. *Strikes* (1952) have useful material. McKillop, N. *Lighted Flame* (the history of ASLEF) includes some documents.

It is convenient to distinguish between the inter-war and the post-war periods, although some studies cover the whole period. There is now a mass of material on nationalisation in general which needs to be considered since the railways' policies are often closely linked with those of other nationalised undertakings. Equally important is the history of demand management and reference to Dow, J. C. R. *The management of the British economy 1945-1960* (1965), or to the two volumes edited by Worswick, G. D. N. and Ady, P. H. *The British Economy 1945-1950* (1952) and *The British Economy in the Nineteen-Fifties* (1962) provide essential backgrounds. Of the many books on the nationalised industries, perhaps Hanson, A. H. (ed) *Nationalisation: A book of readings* (1963), or Robson, W. A. *Nationalised Industry and Public Ownership* (1960) will serve a similar purpose.

On the railways in particular, although sometimes intermingled with other forms of transport, there are several useful analyses. Aldcroft, *British Railways in Transition*, covers a longer period than does Gwilliam, K., *Transport and Public Policy* (1964), which in turn is more theoretical—as are Foster, C. D. *The Transport Problem* (1963), and Sargent, J. R. *British Transport Policy* (1958). For an understanding of recent economic discussions the readings edited by Munby, D., *Transport* (Penguin modern economics, 1968)—and for that matter those edited by Turvey, R. in the same series, *Public Enterprise* (1968) —especially part one—are helpful.

Among the long list of publications which have provided a continuing examination of the railways (many listed in the bibliographies in Aldcroft and Munby) particular reference might be made to Munby, D. L. 'Economic Problems of British Railways'. *Bull Oxford Inst of Statistics*, 24 (1962). The whole issue is devoted to transport. And for more recent material, Munby, D. L. 'Mrs Castle's Transport Policy' *Journal of Transport Economics and Policy* 2 no 2 (1968). An important monograph is Deakin, B. M. and Seward, T. *Productivity in Transport* (1969). A knowledge of statistics is useful for its understanding, but not essential.

Among the many discussions of internal organisation one might select Hughes, J. 'Structures and their adaptation', in Shanks, M. *The Lessons of public Enterprise* (1963), and Fiennes provides a personal view of the problems involved. Bagwell's history of the NUR concludes in the early 1960s, ending with the impact of the Guillebaud report. The troubled years which followed—Beeching, redundancy, incomes policy—are taken up by McLeod, C. *All Change. Railway Industrial Relations in the sixties* (1970).

INDEX